INVESTIGATIONS OF MICROTEACHING

INVESTIGATIONS OF MICROTEACHING

Edited by Donald McIntyre,
Gordon MacLeod and Roy Griffiths

CROOM HELM LONDON

43913

© 1977 Donald McIntyre, Gordon MacLeod and Roy Griffiths
Croom Helm Ltd, 2-10 St John's Road, London SW11

British Library Cataloguing in Publication Data

Investigations of microteaching.
1.   Microteaching 2. Group work in education
I.   McIntyre, Donald, b. 1937 II. MacLeod, Gordon
III. Griffiths, Roy
370'. 733   LB1032

ISBN 0-85664-537-0

Printed in Great Britain by offset lithography by
Billing & Sons Ltd, Guildford, London and Worcester

43913

CONTENTS

43913

INTRODUCTION

The effectiveness of professional education courses in helping students to become skilled classroom teachers has been questioned for many years. Successive generations of teachers have tended to report that they had to learn to teach 'on the job', and that their pre-service training seemed to be of little or no help. By the 1960s many of those involved in the training of teachers had themselves come to share this dissatisfaction with programmes of the established types. What evidence there was on the effectiveness of these programmes was largely limited to their effect on students' attitudes, and generally showed that the effects of professional education on attitudes were nullified by the first few months of employment in teaching. Perhaps more significantly, analysis of the training programmes and procedures suggested several reasons for believing that they might not be very effective. To quote one book of the period, for example:

> Much of the instruction given (on teaching methods) is in the form of a series of practical hints and suggestions which, being pragmatically justified, are not conceptually related to one another . . . The problem is that theoretical courses are not about teaching and that methods courses, which *are* about teaching, have no theoretical foundations (Morrison and McIntyre, 1969, p. 59);

and, after describing the arbitrary and unsystematic arrangements normally made for students to observe and practise teaching, the same authors concluded:

> Although research evidence is lacking, there seems good reason to believe that the procedures outlined above are crude and inefficient means by which to train students in the practical skills of teaching . . . In particular, the complexity of the activity in a classroom at any one time, and the many aspects of teaching, are such that a student beginning to learn how to teach cannot give his attention to more than a small part of it; and, whether observing or teaching, he is likely to be overwhelmed by this complexity, to retain only very vague general impressions and consequently to learn little (pp. 61-2).

9

Despite the obvious weaknesses of conventional practices, there was little development of alternative procedures. Among those alternatives which were suggested, one of the most promising appeared to be *microteaching,* an approach developed at Stanford University from 1963 onwards (Allen and Ryan, 1969). The Stanford team first attempted to simulate teaching situations by having students 'teach' groups of their peers; but, finding that students tended to react negatively to this, they arranged for them to teach short lessons to small groups of school pupils, the goal being to provide experience of 'real teaching', but in simplified conditions. Perhaps the most original idea was that of using these simplified conditions to help students practise specific skills of teaching, with both the student and his supervisor focusing their attention on any one occasion on the predefined skill. A further innovation was the use of videotape recordings so that students might directly observe their own teaching instead of having to depend on the reports of others.

The flexibility of these new microteaching procedures was recognised at Stanford, and many different variants of microteaching were used there during the 1960s. None the less, something approaching a standard procedure began to emerge of the following kind:

1. A particular skill is defined to student-teachers in terms of a pattern of teaching behaviour and the objectives which such behaviour is aimed at achieving; some attempt is made to justify the value of the objectives and the suggested efficacy of the skill.
2. Videotapes are shown of teachers using the skill, in microteaching or in normal classroom teaching, together with a commentary drawing attention to specific instances of the teacher's use of the skill.
3. The student-teacher plans a short lesson in which he can use the skill and teaches it to one group of pupils.
4. A videotape of the lesson is replayed to the student, who observes and analyses it with the help of a supervisor; the supervisor attempts to make reinforcing comments about instances of effective use of the skill and draws the student's attention to other situations which arose where the skill could have been exercised.
5. In the light of the videotape feedback and the supervisor's comments, the student replans the lesson in order to use the skill more effectively.

6. The revised lesson is retaught to a different but comparable group of pupils.
7. A videotape of the 'reteach' lesson is replayed and analysed with the help of the supervisor.
8. The 'teach-reteach' cycle may be repeated.

Microteaching appears to have several potential advantages over conventional methods of teacher-training: (i) it provides a learning-environment for student-teachers which is less complex than the normal school classroom and therefore one in which there is greater opportunity for the deliberate practice of teaching skills; (ii) it provides a context in which the student-teacher's primary responsibility is to learn, not that of coping with the various needs and demands of his pupils; (iii) it allows the student systematically to analyse his own teaching and to make his own evaluations of it; (iv) it allows for repeated practice until a skill is mastered in one context before it is necessary to transfer the use of that skill to other contexts; (v) the systematic definition and practice of teaching skills allows close links to be established between students' theoretical studies and their practice teaching.

That microteaching does indeed have such advantages seems to have been quickly accepted in the United States, for by the late 1960s a large proportion of teacher education institutions there claimed to be making use of it. British colleges and universities were much slower to introduce it and it was left to two new universities, Stirling and the New University of Ulster, to take the initiative. Education courses at Stirling, in the programmes of concurrent academic and professional studies leading to BA degrees with secondary school teaching qualifications, were first taught in 1968; and Professor Elizabeth Perrott, the first Head of the Education Department, planned that microteaching should form a component part of these courses from the beginning. Furthermore, she obtained funds from the Leverhulme Trust for a five-year research project,* starting in 1969, to evaluate the contribution which microteaching could make to the preservice professional education of secondary school teachers. This book is a report of some of the research carried out during the project.

During the first year of the project, decisions had to be taken about the general research strategy. It would have been possible, over a five-year period, to conduct a major experiment in which randomly selected

*The project was later extended for a sixth year, supported by funds from the University.

groups of students were given different kinds of microteaching experience, while a control group followed a more conventional programme.
At various stages, the teaching behaviour and other characteristics of
the various groups of students could have been sampled and compared;
and in particular, their teaching behaviour could have been compared
after they had graduated and become professional teachers. Such an experiment might in some sense have allowed us to conclude whether or
not microteaching experience makes any difference to students' even-
tual behaviour as teachers and, if so, what kinds of difference it makes.

This strategy was rejected for a number of reasons. One practical
problem was that, in the early years of the University, student numbers
were small, and sample sizes would therefore almost certainly have been
so small that differences between the several groups would not be statistically apparent. More fundamentally, it was clear that microteaching
could be used at different stages, to different extents, in innumerably
different ways, and to train students in any of the large number of
teaching 'skills'. Since we had little evidence available to help us choose
among all the possibilities which were open, there seemed every danger
that we might choose inferior ways of using microteaching and/or that
we might focus on variables of little importance, so that our final conclusions, even if clear, might be trivial. More generally, there was the
danger of investing too much of our resources in one high-risk enter-
prise. Finally, in order that students should be exposed to different
kinds of microteaching experience, or none, it would have been necessary for the microteaching programme to be entirely independent of
other aspects of the education courses, so as not to contaminate the
different experimental treatments; yet it seemed likely that the isola-
tion of microteaching from students' other theoretical and practical
studies might seriously undermine any value which it might have.

We have made explicit these reasons for rejecting this strategy since
we have found that it is widely assumed that the purpose of this project should be to reach a verdict about the overall value of microteaching. We believe that such an expectation reflects a mistaken conception of what can usefully be achieved through educational research
in general, but also that it implies a highly oversimplified view of microteaching and the phenomena associated with it. It is very clear to us in
retrospect that microteaching is like many other general methods of
teaching in that no simple verdicts on its value are possible.

The research strategy which was adopted was one of collaboration
between the research and teaching staff in a process of curriculum development. In general we attempted to plan the use of microteaching in

ways which, so far as we were able to judge, would optimise its value in the professional education of student-teachers. Within the resulting frameworks, relatively small-scale investigations of various kinds were conducted. And on the basis of the results of these investigations and also of more impressionistic judgements about the strengths and weaknesses of the various procedures used, successive modifications were made.

This kind of strategy is not without its problems. There were some inevitable tensions between researchers and teaching staff: the interests of researchers were to explore the effects of different procedures as fully as possible, to ask questions of a relatively abstract and generalisable kind, to allocate students to different treatments on a random basis, and to attend to the results of their previous investigations in planning further research and teaching programmes; on the other hand, the interests of teaching staff were to limit the proportion of their time which they had to give to microteaching, to ask questions relating to their own immediate problems in a particular context, to prepare each and all of their students for teaching in the ways which seemed to them most appropriate for these students, and to plan their work on the basis of their impressions of previous courses. The project has accordingly been marked by a succession of (generally amicable) compromises between these two sets of interests.

A related problem is that of the roles which should be adopted by researchers in this kind of research strategy. Ideally, there should be a clear division between the role of curriculum developer — to plan courses as intelligently as possible and implement them as effectively as possible, and that of researcher — to ask questions about the courses and their effects, and to attempt to answer these questions. However, members of the teaching staff quite understandably tended to take the attitude that 'if you want to find out the effects of doing X, we are prepared to modify our courses so that you can do X, but you'll have to do X yourself'. In these circumstances, and with only one full-time research fellow during most of the project, it was often necessary for the researchers to take on the curriculum developer role. As a result, at least as much of the researchers' time has been spent on the planning of courses, the development of materials, and the instruction and supervision of students as on research. Of greater concern here, however, are the dangers inherent in taking on this dual role: one's effectiveness as a curriculum developer would probably be impaired by a lack of commitment to the course one is developing, but such commitment could easily lead to a distortion of one's perceptions and one's judgements as a researcher. Being aware of this danger, we have consistently attempted to avoid any such distortion of our research findings, for example by analysing students' teaching behaviour without any knowledge as to whether they belonged to experimental or control groups. In consequence, we do not believe that our research findings have been contaminated by this dual role which we have had to play; but the reader must judge for himself whether this is likely to have been the case.

The curriculum development aspects of the project's work are not reported in any detail in this book, but to facilitate understanding of the research investigations and interpretation of the results we indicate here the general curricular framework within which the research has been conducted.

The BA degree courses at Stirling University are organised in two parts. In part I, which consists of the first three semesters, students take courses in from three to six different subjects. In part II, which for most students involves three semesters for a general degree or five for an honours degree, students concentrate on one or two main subjects. Students aiming to become qualified teachers study the subject they intend to teach throughout the three- or four-year period, and they take education courses in their third, fourth, fifth and sixth semesters (and the seventh for honours students), together with an additional semester completely devoted to education. There are school practice periods during the vacations between the third and fourth semesters (largely restricted to observational studies) and between the fifth and sixth semesters, and for six weeks during the final semester.

During the first year of the project, the education courses in the third, fourth and fifth semesters, which had initially been of a fairly conventional kind, were redesigned so that microteaching became an integral part of them. This reconstruction of the curriculum was based on the assumptions

(a)   that it was possible to specify many of the basic skills and strategies required for competent classroom teaching;

(b)   that the primary objectives of the education curriculum should be that students should master these basic skills and strategies;

(c)   that this could only be done by planning tasks specifically designed so that students could deliberately practise using these skills and strategies;

(d)   that theoretical components of the curriculum should be closely related to these practical tasks and should primarily be aimed at helping students to understand the principles upon which the skills and strategies might be justified.

The semester 3 course was built around the microteaching practice of five skills of communication and instruction; in relation to each skill, there were lectures on relevant aspects of the psychology of communication or learning, lectures to define the skill and exemplify its use, and seminars to discuss the use of the skill in the teaching of particular subjects. One strand of the semester 4 and semester 5 courses was concerned with the teaching of students' specialist subjects; because of the opposition of some subject specialists to the assumptions underlying the course, this strand was not closely related to the practical work. In semester 4 there were two other strands, in one of which the study and practice of programmed instruction was used to provide a model for lesson planning; in the other, the study of affective aspects of classroom interaction was linked to the microteaching practice of various skills, mostly defined in terms of Flanders' Interaction Analysis Categories. In semester 5, attention was focused on ways in which teachers might take account of the characteristics of individual pupils and their levels of cognitive development; to practise the relevant kinds of decision-making and use of feedback, each small group of student-teachers was given the same school class to teach for one lesson per week throughout the semester. This practical work, in which students were also expected to monitor their use of the various skills practised in the previous two semesters, was seen as an appropriate preparation for their first school teaching practice during the following vacation period.

This revised curriculum was introduced in 1970. During the remaining five years of the project it was amended in various ways, mainly with the intention of more effectively implementing the principles on which it was initially planned. Among these changes have been: the interchanging of the units on cognitive and affective aspects of classroom interaction, with the introduction in semester 3 of some study of ideologies of teaching; the replacement of the programmed instruction unit by one directly concerned with lesson planning skills; and a much greater integration of work on the teaching of specific subjects with the other components of the curriculum. Since the curriculum has thus been far from static, any single detailed description of it would be invalid for much of the period during which the research was conducted; on the other hand, an analysis of the continuous but often erratic process of its development would be a major study on its own. Details of particular curricular contexts are provided where relevant in the reports of specific investigations.

The research reported in this book is diverse both in its methodology and in the issues with which it deals. Furthermore, since at most times during the project several different lines of enquiry were being pursued contemporaneously, there is not a clear overall chronological pattern. Some elements of chronological order are, however, reflected in our organisation of the papers into a number of loosely defined themes. We attempt here briefly to indicate the nature of these themes and to put each of the papers into context.

A necessary, though certainly not sufficient, condition for the success of any new teaching method in tertiary education is that students should perceive it to be of some value to them. Considerable attention was therefore given during the first two years of the project to the monitoring of students' reactions to their experience of microteaching; the findings of these studies are summarised in the paper by McIntyre and Duthie.

Another early concern was with the development of procedures for assessing students' use of the skills they were practising in microteaching. Valid and reliable assessment of students' use of the skills seemed necessary not only as a prerequisite for research into the effectiveness of microteaching but also as a component of microteaching itself: unless students and their supervisors could make valid judgements in these terms, systematic practice of the skills seemed impossible. Rating scales for the skills practised at Stanford were available, but (both from the Stanford evidence (Stanford Teacher Education Program, 1968) and from our own trials) these were demonstrably not sufficiently reliable to be used in diagnosing the strengths and weaknesses of individual students. The paper by McIntyre, McKnight and White describes some of the instruments which were developed to meet the need for such diagnostic assessment. It was recognised, however, that there was also a need for such assessment in school teaching practice, especially for students who had learned to analyse their teaching in these terms, and a procedure which incorporated instruments of the kind used in microteaching was devised for this purpose. White, who during a year spent at Stirling had been primarily responsible for the development of this procedure, was then principal of a college of education in Rhodesia, and on his return there he organised an experimental trial of the procedure; the developed instruments and the experiment are reported in the paper by White and McIntyre. This procedure was not, however, used at Stirling, and no arrangements were made for assessment procedures used on school practice to be related to those used in microteaching. The third of the papers in this section reports a study of the relationships between assessments of students' use of several teaching skills in the microteaching context and the global assessments of these students' school practice teaching made by their supervisors and supervisory teachers.

The studies reported in the next section are concerned more with students' cognitions than with their teaching behaviour. The paper by Millar and McIntyre describes a system which was developed to analyse students' evaluative comments on teaching they had observed, in terms of the focus, structure and validity of the comments. This system was used by Millar to assess the effects of two semester-courses involving microteaching on the kinds of evaluative comments on the teaching of others which students made. Underlying these studies was Millar's insight that microteaching was likely to be effective only in so far as it influenced students' thinking about teaching, and that an understanding of the influence of microteaching upon students' teaching behaviour depended upon an understanding of its effects upon the criteria they used in evaluating their own or other people's teaching.

The studies reported in the fourth section are focused on several different facets of microteaching; all of them, however, were experimental studies to determine the effects of variations in microteaching procedures on students' acquisition of teaching skills. Among the procedural variables examined in these various experiments were: whether students are shown positive or negative models of a teaching skill; whether students are given practice in the analysis of teaching in terms of the use of the specified skill; whether students are given microteaching practice in the specified skill; whether, at the feedback stage, students discuss their lessons with supervisors, with peers, or with both; whether the supervisor initiates points for discussion or encourages the student to take the initiative; and whether the discussion of the lesson focuses on its strengths or on ways in which it might have been improved. Butts' study is distinctive both in that it was not carried out at Stirling but in the context of the one-year postgraduate training course at Jordanhill College of Education, and also in that it was concerned with the effects of microteaching as a whole upon students' use of skills in their teaching of normal school classes.

The fifth section, containing four papers by MacLeod, is concerned with the ways in which students perceive and react to their own microteaching behaviour, and with the relationships between microteaching procedures, students' perceptions, and students' teaching behaviour. In the first paper, MacLeod describes the development of a system for analysing students' comments about their own teaching. In the three subsequent papers, he reports on the kinds of comments which students make, and on how these tend to change with increasing experience of microteaching; on how variations among students in the comments they make are related to variations among the lessons they have taught, and among lessons which they subsequently teach; and on the effects of videotape and skill-related feedback on the comments which are made.

The sixth section of this collection is concerned with the views on microteaching of members of the teaching staff at Stirling who have participated in its use over a number of years. We have not attempted to conduct research into the reactions of teaching staff, partly because of the small numbers involved, and partly because any questionnaire technique could do little justice to the rich diversity of their views. Instead, we invited the four subject specialists in the department who have had most experience in the use of microteaching to contribute directly to this book. Neither we nor they claim that their opinions are in any way representative; but we suggest that, since there can be few specialists in their respective fields in Britain with comparable experience of microteaching, their opinions should be accepted as significant evidence. We asked them for their 'perceptions of microteaching', especially 'from the perspective of its usefulness in the professional education of science/ English/modern languages/history teachers', and we suggested that questions upon which they might comment included: 'How effective has our use of microteaching at Stirling been in training your students? If not effective, why not, and how might it be made more effective? Is it possible to identify specific skills which are valuable in teaching your subject and which can be practised in microteaching, and if so, can you suggest some of these skills? At what stages of preservice (or inservice) training is microteaching likely to be most valuable in your subject? What features of microteaching, if any, do you think are particularly valuable in your subject?'

In the final section we reproduce a paper in which an attempt has been made to take account of some of the findings reported in this volume with the goal of conceptualising more clearly what is happening in microteaching and therefore of how teacher-trainers might most fruitfully view its use. This paper should not be seen as a final report which synthesises the various findings of the project but as a contribution to thinking about one facet of the issues which have been investigated.

The research reported in this book does not provide any conclusive answers either to questions about the value of microteaching or to questions about how or for what purposes it can most effectively be used. We make no apologies for this, since we believe that the function of educational research is not, and cannot be, to answer such questions of policy. In principle, educational research, like other empirical research, can answer *theoretical* questions: it can show the extent to which hypothetical explanations are valid. Unfortunately, most educational thinking and virtually all thinking about the professional education of teachers, is still at a pre-theoretical stage; that is, there are no coherent theories which pretend to explain how student-teachers' teaching behaviour, or their thinking about teaching, tends to change as a consequence of events of a specified kind in specified kinds of conditions.

In these circumstances, we believe that there are three general ways in which educational research can be useful. First, it can contribute to a body of evidence about relationships between variables which, although collected in response to a variety of rather crude and pragmatic questions, is none the less fairly precise and accurate; and the availability of which is probably a necessary basis for constructive theoretical thinking. Second, it can raise new questions and generate new constructs, which is again likely to facilitate theory construction. Third, it can be of immediate practical value both in providing a general conceptual and informational framework for decision-making and in challenging assumptions which, if acted upon, could have unfortunate consequences or could lead to an expensive and inconsequential waste of resources. We hope and believe that the research reported here will be of value in all three of these ways, in relation not only to microteaching but to teacher education in general.

References

Allen, D.W. and Ryan, K.A. (1969). *Microteaching,* Addison-Wesley, Reading, Mass.

Morrison, A. and McIntyre, D. (1969). *Teachers and Teaching,* Penguin, Harmondsworth.

Stanford Teacher Education Program (1968). *Microteaching: a Description,* Stanford University, California.

One of the major stimuli for reform of teacher education procedures has been the evidence of negative reactions from student-teachers to the courses provided for them. Perhaps because of this, there has been some tendency to evaluate innovations primarily in terms of their acceptability to students. It hardly needs to be said that this is an inadequate criterion on which to judge the value of innovations in professional education, since students are ill-placed to assess the demands which will be made of them or the skills which will be of greatest value to them on entering the profession. On the other hand, it is a necessary criterion, for unless students understand the tasks they are asked to undertake, feel able and motivated to undertake these tasks, and afterwards believe that completing these tasks has been a useful experience, they are unlikely to assimilate much of value.

The acceptability of microteaching to students could not confidently be assumed. The strongest and most consistent complaint against more traditional programmes had been about their lack of 'relevance', and the components of such programmes most highly valued by students were school practices; this might not have augured well for the deliberately artificial contexts for teaching by which microteaching is characterised. Nor was there any reason to assume the acceptability to students either of the analytic conceptualisation of teaching implicit in the approach or of the self-observation procedures used.

The development of a curricular innovation generally depends, however, less on obtaining clearcut answers to such major questions than on the resolution of large numbers of minor issues. Thus decisions about the inclusion or exclusion of many potential components of microteaching, or about the particular ways in which they should be implemented, initially had to be somewhat arbitrary, pending modification on the basis of monitored experience. Attending to students' reactions to the various aspects of microteaching was one important part of this monitoring.

The paper by McIntyre and Duthie collates the relatively systematic evidence on students' views on microteaching which was collected during the formative years of its use at Stirling, from 1969 to 1971. Their use of questionnaires, most of the items of which were highly structured, had the advantages of facilitating a high response rate and of providing simple, unambiguous and easily summarised evidence. On the other hand, the use of such questionnaires has the disadvantage of limiting students' expression of views largely to those issues which the researchers believe to be significant, and of obliging students to respond to these issues in the researchers' terms. These disadvantages were reduced, however, by the strategy of designing the questionnaires given to one year-group of students in the light of the reactions of the previous year-group as reflected either in their questionnaire responses or in comments from them in more informal contexts.

As always, generalisation from the findings reported in this paper should be extremely cautious and should take equal account of comparable findings elsewhere. Students react to their own individual experiences and neither the individual student nor anyone else can tell to what extent his reactions have been influenced by the particular institution in which he is studying, the amount of time devoted to a particular phase of the programme, the particular model videotapes used or the particular supervisor with whom he has worked. The most that we as editors can say is that our experience with later year-groups at Stirling has not led us to question the validity of the findings reported in this paper as indicative of the general reactions of Stirling students.

1 STUDENTS' REACTIONS TO MICROTEACHING

Donald McIntyre and Jack Duthie

This paper is based on the questionnaire responses of students who have had experience of microteaching during the first two and a half years for which it has been used at Stirling University. During this time four year-groups of students, involving eighteen, then, forty and one hundred and thirty students respectively, have taught a total of some 2,000 microteaching lessons. After each semester's microteaching programme, the students involved have been invited to complete questionnaires to express their reactions and attitudes to various aspects of the programme. Response rates varied between 90 and 100 per cent for the first three year-groups, but fell to 71 per cent for the fourth.

The microteaching programme for the first two year-groups was in two four-week periods in the second and third semesters of the education programme, before students had any experience of teaching practice in secondary schools but after they had spent two weeks in primary schools as observers and teachers' aides. During these four-week periods, microteaching replaced lectures and seminars in other education courses. No organised attempt was made to relate microteaching to these other courses.

The course was then reorganised so that students in subsequent years have had microteaching practice in their first education semester. More fundamentally, the whole first semester course was planned around microteaching, the theoretical work for the semester being a study of the psychological rationale for the skills being practised. Curriculum seminars have also been included in this course to help students perceive the relevance of each skill to their own particular teaching subjects. (Microteaching plays some part, in a similar way, in a second semester course, but the data to be reported here relate only to the first semester course.)

As certain questions were resolved, and as we proceeded to explore new possibilities and to face new problems with each successive semester, the questionnaires given to students were modified accordingly. One consequence of this is that in many respects it is not possible to compare the reactions of all the different groups of students; another is that there are data available on the responses of one or more groups of students to a large number of questions. In order that these

43913

data can be presented in a reasonably coherent way, this article is organised in terms of several broad themes, evidence from different groups of students being reported where it is relevant to the discussion of each theme.

Some Questions of Timing

In planning a microteaching programme one has to make a number of decisions about the timing of lessons, decisions which are of some importance from an administrative perspective. It was with such matters, therefore, that a number of questions in the earlier questionnaires were concerned.

Length of lessons

A fairly clear consensus emerged from student responses on this question, asked of the first two year-groups, with different skills being perceived as requiring different lengths of lesson. Modal responses were as follows:

Reinforcement of Pupil Participation:	5 minutes appropriate
Varying the Stimulus:	5 minutes too short
Set Induction:	20 minutes appropriate
Exposition:	both 12 minutes and
	20 minutes appropriate
Use of Examples:	20 minutes appropriate
Stimulating Pupil Questions:	20 minutes appropriate
Closure:	20 minutes too short
Probing:	12 minutes too short

As can be seen, students discriminate to a considerable degree among skills, but their preference tends generally to be for relatively long microteaching lessons.

Interval between lesson and reteaching of lesson

The procedure developed at Stanford was for each lesson to be retaught thirty minutes to an hour after it had been first taught, with the videotape playback and tutorial discussion intervening. For administrative reasons, however, this is not always convenient, and from the beginning at Stirling there were some 'split cycles' with the lesson being retaught on the following day. Twelve of the students in the first year-group had one or more 'split cycles'; six of them thought this a disadvantage, six did not.

ƐƖ

The second year-group were asked what they considered the optimal time for replanning lessons (after their tutorial discussions). Reinforcement and Varying the Stimulus, the two 'five-minute skills', were said by most students to require only a few minutes for replanning. For other skills the majority expressed their optimal replanning time as 'at least . . . ', the modal response being 'at least one hour'. Since a replanning period of this length virtually implied a split cycle, and since this was administratively convenient, it became standard policy, except for the two five-minute skills, for lessons to be retaught on a different day.

Students in the third year-group were each given two standard times in the week for microteaching. Of twenty-one students for whom the interval between teach and reteach was one or two days, seventeen thought the interval 'about right'. On the other hand, eight of the thirteen respondents for whom the interval was three days or more thought that this was too long.

Timetabling of Microteaching

Twelve out of seventeen students in the first year-group said that they would prefer microteaching to be spread out over the semester rather than in one four-week block which interrupted other courses.

Skills of Teaching

A major purpose of microteaching is that students should be provided with a simplified environment in which they can concentrate their attention upon specified skills of teaching. Several questions were related to the value of this analytic approach and the effectiveness with which the microteaching context allowed it to be pursued.

Concentration on Skills

Students in the first two year-groups were asked: 'In the microteaching situation, did you find you were able to concentrate your attention on the exercise of the skills? If not, can you say why not?' Three-quarters of them reported that, in some lessons at least, they had not been able to concentrate on the skill. The obstacles to focusing attention upon a defined skill which were most commonly reported by these students were presented as possible sources of difficulty to students in the third and fourth year-groups.

Of the 128 respondents from these later groups, seventy reported some such difficulty, although many of them said that this was only in one or two of their lessons. The frequency with which each of the suggested sources of difficulty was checked was as follows:

'I did not have a sufficiently clear idea of the skill'   :   15
'I could not distinguish the skill from other aspects
of my teaching'   :   31
'I was not convinced of the value of focusing
attention upon the skills'   :   22
'I had to give too much attention to the subject-
matter'   :   23
'I tended to be distracted by the feeling that I was
being observed'   :   7
'I tended to get "carried away" in my discussions
with the pupils'   :   20

In addition, several students commented that they had felt that to concentrate on the use of a skill was simply to make use of the pupils
whereas they had felt an obligation to help pupils to learn something.
Another frequent comment was that, while it was difficult to focus
one's attention upon a particular skill while teaching a lesson, it was
both possible and useful to do so in planning the lesson and in observing
it afterwards.

Value of Skills Approach

Only the second year-group were asked about the general value of
analysing teaching in terms of skills: all of them found this to be at
least 'helpful', six of the ten rating it 'very helpful'. Responding to
suggested alternative procedures, only three of the ten thought it would
be valuable to define skills in different ways for different subjects, but
five of them thought that microteaching would be more useful if each
individual were free to decide which aspects of his teaching he should
focus his attention upon.

The later year-groups were asked how important they thought each
of the skills they had been asked to practise was in teaching. All five
skills (Varying the Stimulus, Questioning for Feedback, Clarity of Explanation, Use of Examples, and Higher Order Questioning and Probing)
were rated as 'very important' by the majority in both year-groups. As
well as thinking it valuable to identify and practise particular skills of
teaching, 86 per cent of these students also reported that the first
semester course, which dealt with teaching skills, dealt with aspects of
education 'among those in which I am most interested'.

Content of Lessons

Students have generally been left free to choose the content of the lessons they teach in microteaching, although they have been told that their subject tutors would be glad to advise them on this.

When asked if they had found that the content of their lessons had allowed them scope for practising the skills, students in the first year-group were almost unanimously confident that this was the case. However, seven out of ten in the second year-group thought that their microteaching would have been more valuable if they had been given more help in the choice of appropriate topics for their lessons. It was partly for this purpose that, when the course was reorganised, weekly curriculum seminars were introduced; but this was not a success since the majority of students found these seminars 'not very useful' for this purpose. Some commented that it was sufficient to think about skills at this stage without also having to think about the subject. It would seem that what many students want is not a discussion of the sort of subject-matter for which each of the skills is likely to be most relevant, but suggestions of specific topics which would be appropriate.

Tutor and Peer Feedback

Most previous American research (cf. McKnight, 1971) appears to suggest that, at least in the short term, the acquisition of teaching skills through microteaching is not influenced by whether one has a tutor with whom to observe and discuss one's lessons.

It is therefore important, especially in view of the heavy demands which microteaching makes on staff time, to consider students' attitudes to the provision of tutors. Can students work equally well on their own? Or might any functions which tutors fulfil be equally well fulfilled by other students?

The majority of students who have worked with tutors have consistently reported that they found tutors' comments and suggestions 'very helpful', and all other evidence confirms this straightforward judgement of the tutor's value in the eyes of students. In one four-week block of microteaching, students in the second year-group each practised two skills with a tutor and two skills on their own; all ten of them reported a preference for working with a tutor. When students in the third year-group were asked what advice they would give their tutors, most had no advice to offer; of the suggestions which were made, none was made by more than one student.

Most students in the first two year-groups said that they preferred to have the same tutor on each occasion, but only ten out of twenty-seven said they would like this to be their subject tutor. Those in the third year-group, who did work with the same tutors throughout the

semester, gave systematically differing evaluations (although generally
high) of the help they had received from tutors: in general, the help
given by psychology lecturers and postgraduate students engaged on
research into microteaching was more valued than that given by subject
specialists.

It was not possible to provide tutors on every occasion for all 130
students in the fourth year-group. For three of the skills which they
practised, therefore, students were allocated at random to one of three
working conditions: working individually with a tutor; working in
groups of three with a tutor; and working in groups of three without a
tutor. Students were invited to form their own groups, but those who
did not were allocated to groups at random.

Asked at the end of the semester about the advantages and disadvantages of working with tutors or peers, the majority of students from
all three conditions suggested that the major advantage of having a
tutor was in the authoritative guidance which he could give as a result of
his experience and his superior understanding of the various skills.
Those who had worked with peers suggested a number of advantages in
this, including the greater informality and frankness of discussion, the
variety of perspectives, the tendency to argue through a problem until
it was better understood, and the appreciation of each other's problems
(some of which might be too elementary to attract a tutor's attention).
The great majority of those who had worked with both tutors and peers
rated the comments and suggestions of both as either 'helpful' or 'very
helpful', and they made many more mentions of the advantages associated with both sources of help than of the disadvantages. Those who
had worked in groups without tutors, however, did not rate their peers'
comments quite so highly and they raised several disadvantages in
having to depend upon peers for help. The most commonly mentioned
of these were peers' lack of expertise or understanding of the skills, the
lack of commitment or effort of some of them, and the tendency for
group discussions to drift without a clear direction.

Students who had worked individually with tutors were almost un-
animous in preferring the help of tutors to that of peers; those who
had worked in groups with tutors were evenly divided in their preferences and tended to consider working with both tutors and peers most
satisfactory; and among those who had worked in groups without
tutors, 42 per cent reported a preference for tutors and 31 per cent a
preference for peers.

The Components of Microteaching

In addition to supervision there are a number of different component parts of the microteaching procedure used at Stirling. The psychological theory discussed in lectures is intended to provide a rationale for the skill, which is then explicitly defined in a lecture leading into the microteaching practice. In addition to the verbal definition, one or more concrete 'models' of the skill are shown on videotape. Curriculum seminars in subject groups are intended to show the relevance of the skill to the teaching of a student's own subject. Videotape playback of a student's teaching gives him feedback on his performance, and systematic observation schedules for each skill are intended to help him focus his attention on relevant aspects of his teaching and make a relatively objective diagnostic assessment of it. Finally, reteaching the same lesson to a different group of pupils is intended to allow the student to capitalise upon the strengths and to overcome the weaknesses which he has observed in his first teaching of the lesson.

How effective and valuable do students find each of these components to be? Since the third and fourth year-groups followed very similar courses in their first education semesters, and since the relevant questions which they were asked were the same, the responses of the two groups have been combined in table 1.

Students clearly feel that they gain most from the basic components of microteaching: the videotaped models, the playbacks of their own lessons, and the reteaching of their lessons. The major weaknesses are in the inadequate establishment of the relations between the skills and the psychological theory, and in the lack of value which most students find in curriculum seminars. In response to other questions, the majority of students suggested that the psychological theory should be dealt with more fully and, asked how the balance of the course should be changed, one of the most commonly expressed views was that less time should be given to curriculum seminars and more to relating psychological theory to skills.

Effects of the Microteaching-Centred Course upon Students

How does experience of microteaching influence students' conceptions of teaching and of themselves in relation to teaching? It was hoped and intended that the microteaching-centred course would lead students towards perceiving teaching as an intellectually demanding job which requires considerable skill in interpersonal relations and, in particular, involves the use of a range of distinctive professional skills; and also as a job which involves considerable application of the social sciences, par-

Table 1 Percentage Distribution of Students' Evaluations of
Components of Microteaching-Centred Course (n = 128)

Component	Criterion	Percentage Distribution			
		Very	Fairly	Not very	Not at all
Psychological Theory Introductory lectures	How clearly was it related to teaching skills?	10	37	46	7
	How clear an idea was given of the sort of behaviour to be practised?	13	68	20	0
Videotapes of model lessons	How helpful were they in clarifying conception of skills?	37	44	17	2
Curriculum seminars	How useful in showing relevance of skills to teaching of subject?	8	31	38	23
Observation schedules	How useful in helping focus attention on relevant aspects of behaviour?	27	44	24	6
Videotape playbacks	How valuable in addition to tutors' or peers' comments?	80	16	3	1
Reteachof of same lesson	How valuable in practising skills?	52	30	14	3

ticularly psychology. It was further hoped that, because of an increased awareness of these aspects of teaching, it would appear a more interesting job to students. At the same time, there was some fear lest, as a result of the analytic and prescriptive approach, students might come to underestimate the need for creativity and originality in teaching.

Finally, an important purpose of microteaching is to give students a gradual introduction to teaching, thus avoiding the distress sometimes associated with students' first experience of classroom teaching. If this purpose were being achieved one would expect some tendency for students, while moving towards a more realistic conception of themselves in relation to teaching, also to become more confident in themselves as teachers.

Questions seeking students' assessments of how their attitudes had changed in these respects were asked of both the third and fourth year-groups, and the distributions of responses for the two groups combined are given in table 2. In most respects it would appear that our hopes were justified and our fears unjustified. The one unrealised expectation is that relating to students' assessments of the suitability of their own personalities for teaching. In this case, however, it is necessary to distinguish among different groups of students. At one extreme were those who worked individually with tutors, of whom 33 per cent felt their personalities more suitable for teaching, as opposed to 12 per cent less suitable, as a result of the course. At the other extreme, only 10 per cent of those who worked in groups without tutors came to believe that their personalities were more suitable for teaching than they had thought, while 33 per cent came to believe their personalities less suitable.

Table 2 Percentage Distribution of Reported Effects of Microteaching-Centred Course on Students' Conceptions of Teaching (n = 128)

		Percentage Distribution		
		More than I thought	As I thought	Less than I thought
	Interesting	41	57	2
	Intellectually demanding	52	43	5
	To require skill in interpersonal relations	52	46	2
The job	To involve use of distinctive professional skills	75	21	4
of teaching	To involve application of psychological theory	49	42	9
appears	To require creativity and originality	26	69	5
	A job to which my own personality is suited	19	62	19
	Attractive as a career	64	25	11

Conclusions

The evidence which has been reported in this paper appears to show that the majority of these Stirling students found most aspects of microteaching interesting and rewarding. Furthermore, they tended to express fairly clear preferences on most issues, preferences which do not seem to run counter to other evidence or arguments about how microteaching can be made most effective, and which can therefore, in principle, provide a basis for planning microteaching programmes to optimise their attractiveness to students.

This satisfying conclusion must, however, be qualified in two ways. The first of these relates to economic criteria. Microteaching can be very expensive in the manpower, equipment and organisation which it involves, and for it to be an economically viable training technique, these various resource requirements must be minimised. Yet on every issue, students' reactions suggest that the more expensive alternative is preferable. It has already been noted that students tend to prefer longer lessons and that they feel the need for supervisors at the feedback stage. Another example is that when students in the fourth year-group were asked to suggest how the first semester course might be improved, much the most common suggestion was that they should have more microteaching. Thus economic considerations and students' reactions lead to contradictory conclusions.

The second qualification stems from the fact that all the evidence reported in this paper has concerned the reactions of students before they had experience of teaching in schools. On the other hand, when students in the first two year-groups were asked, after their first secondary school teaching practice, how valuable they thought microteaching had been to them, their response was generally lukewarm; the most frequent comment was that the relevance of microteaching to normal classroom work was limited by the absence of discipline problems in microteaching. The importance of this finding should not be exaggerated: it is to be expected that when students move on to more complex tasks they will become conscious of the limited nature of those which they undertook earlier. It does indicate; however, that a microteaching programme which is satisfactory to students does not necessarily guarantee that the relationships between microteaching and school practice are equally satisfactory to them.

Reference

McKnight, P.C. (1971). 'Microteaching in Teacher Training: A Review of Research', *Research in Education*, vol. 6, pp. 24-38.

PART 2 THE ASSESSMENT OF TEACHING SKILLS

Perhaps the most fundamental idea of microteaching is that students should focus their attention upon specific aspects of teaching and should plan, practise and analyse these aspects of their teaching in terms of clearly conceptualised criteria. Thus at any one time a student is generally concerned with one 'teaching skill', which may be defined as a set of related types of teaching behaviour which in specified types of classroom situations tends to facilitate the achievement of specified types of objectives.

The specification of skills in microteaching thus has two purposes. The first of these is to direct students' attention to particular limited aspects of their teaching in order that they may reflect carefully on the function and justification of those aspects of their intended or observed behaviour. The second is to make explicit the criteria in terms of which students are asked to plan and evaluate these aspects of their teaching, in order to minimise the use of vague and idiosyncratic criteria and to facilitate the use of criteria based on the best available knowledge about teaching.

Unfortunately, the best available knowledge about teaching is at present such that few skills can be specified with any great confidence. There are sufficient grounds, on the basis of empirical research on classroom teaching, of psychological theory, and of the consensus opinions of experienced teachers, for many criteria to be suggested as probably appropriate in situations of given kinds, but insufficient grounds for such criteria to be authoritatively prescribed. Given these circumstances, one can only treat specified patterns of teaching behaviour as hypothetical skills of teaching.

To enable students to practise specified skills, and to enable them, their supervisors or researchers to assess their use of these skills, it is necessary to provide operational definitions of the relevant patterns of behaviour. Such operational definitions necessarily involve descriptive distinctions between different kinds of behaviour, although these distinctions also have quite explicit evaluative meanings. In so far, however, as there is doubt about the validity of a specified skill, so the relative emphasis must move away from the evaluative meanings of the distinctions and be placed upon the value of the purely descriptive distinctions.

One may contrast three approaches to the practice of teaching:

(i)   The traditional approach, in which there is no planned
       narrowing of focus, in which criteria are commonly neither
       explicitly theory-based nor even explicit, and in which evalu-
       ations are often not based on descriptions of the observed
       teaching.
(ii) The skills approach, in which evaluations are based upon des-
       criptions of teaching in predetermined terms, and in which
       both descriptive distinctions and the associated evaluative cri-
       teria are explicitly theory-based.
(iii) The exploratory analytic approach, in which emphasis is
       placed on the description of teaching in predetermined theory-
       based terms, and in which any evaluations are tentative and
       based on reflection upon the observed teaching as described in
       these terms.

It is the skills approach which has been used in microteaching at
Stirling, but a commitment to students' analytic reflection on their teaching and an awareness of the hypothetical status of the prescribed skills
has meant that there has been a consistent tendency to lean towards the
third rather than the first of these three approaches. It is primarily for
this reason that skills have consistently been operationalised in terms of
simple systematic observation procedures rather than in terms of rating
scales such as those used at Stanford. Although considerable use has
been made of observation systems devised elsewhere, notably Flanders'
FIAC system, several such systems were devised explicitly for microteaching purposes at Stirling. Some of these systems, which have been
used not only for teaching purposes but also as a basis for criterion
measures in the research reported in this book, are described in the first
paper in this section.

The arguments for evaluative judgements of teaching being based on
clear descriptions of the teaching in terms of theory-based criteria are
not relevant only to the microteaching context, but apply equally to
teaching in normal school classrooms. Furthermore, it is particularly
desirable that students who have learned to describe and evaluate their
teaching according to various explicit criteria in the microteaching context should be helped and encouraged to use the same criteria, among
others, in their school teaching practice. A natural extension of the
development of systematic observation systems for microteaching was,
therefore, the development of a procedure incorporating these systems

for use in school practice supervision. The paper by White and McIntyre describes the development and trial of such a procedure.

To specify a set of teaching behaviours as 'a skill' is justifiable only if these behaviours do tend to be interrelated, and if students' use of such behaviours does lead to them being assessed as more competent teachers. Evidence in relation to both these issues is provided in the third paper in this section. Having practised three skills in a semester-course, students were asked at the end of the semester to teach an eighteen-minute microteaching lesson in which they made use of all three skills. These lessons having been analysed in terms of the frequency of the various types of behaviour which defined the three skills, factor analysis was used to explore the relationships between the incidence of these types of behaviour; and multiple regression analysis was used to discover the extent to which students' use of these types of behaviour in the microteaching context was related to the global ratings of their teaching competence made by university supervisors and supervising teachers during the school practice which followed some months later.

2 THE DIAGNOSTIC ASSESSMENT OF STUDENTS' MICROTEACHING BEHAVIOUR

Donald McIntyre, Philip McKnight and Donald White*

If student-teachers are to be asked deliberately to acquire particular skills of teaching, it is necessary that these skills should be clearly specified. Such specification is required both in order that students may understand what it is that they are being asked to do and also in order that they may, with or without the help of a tutor, be able to identify the strengths and weaknesses of their own trial performances.

A broad conceptual understanding of a suggested skill, of the rationale offered for its value, and of the circumstances and purposes to which it is relevant, is likely to be necessary to enable a student to make intelligent efforts to practise its use. But before he can make specific plans, or make specific judgements about whether he has acted in the intended way on a particular occasion, he will generally also need to be able to use more precise criteria through which his abstract ideas can be operationalised. It is just in this process of critically applying general ideas to their practice of teaching that student-teachers appear to experience greatest difficulty; and it is this difficulty experienced in making use of general ideas which appears to underlie much of the dissatisfaction which student-teachers so commonly express about the theoretical elements of their courses.

In the Stanford microteaching programme (Stanford Teacher Education Programme, 1968), each skill is most clearly defined by a number of rating scales, each concerned with a specific aspect of the skill. For example, for the skill of Reinforcement of Pupil Participation, one of the five scales is concerned with the extent to which the 'teacher encourages the students' comments and answers by nonverbal cues such as smiling, nodding his head, writing the student's answer on the blackboard, etc.'. Such scales systematically direct attention to much more precisely defined aspects of teaching than do most other observation or evaluation procedures used in teacher training. After each lesson, ratings on each of the seven-point scales are made by the teacher, his

*The authors wish to express their appreciation of the contributions made to this work by Jean Black, Jack Duthie, Lawrence Ingvarson, Donald Maclennan, Gordon MacLeod, Clive Millar, Elizabeth Perrott and Ann Savage.

supervisor and/or his pupils.

The way in which microteaching has been used at Stirling was initially, so far as possible, an imitation of the highly developed Stanford programme, and in most respects has continued to follow this pattern. One of the few respects, however, in which it was felt possible to improve on Stanford procedures was in relation to the rating scales. These seemed inadequate for a number of reasons:

(i) As with most rating scales, the reliability with which assessments can be made tends to be low (Stanford Teacher Education Programme, 1968). For training purposes, reliable assessments of each student's performance are necessary so that he can identify ways in which he should attempt to modify his behaviour.

(ii) The use of rating scales tends to emphasise *evaluation* of a student's teaching, which is not likely to serve any useful purpose; what is most needed is *description* and *analysis* of a student's interaction with pupils, and a search for alternative teaching behaviours where those observed appear unsatisfactory.

(iii) Generalisations indicating aspects of teaching behaviour to be rated are often inadequate in helping students to apply the definition of the skill to their own behaviour and in helping them to identify specific incidents relevant to the skill.

(iv) Students should learn to make critical judgements of their own teaching behaviour. Such learning seems most likely to occur if tentative judgements can be discussed with supervisors in relation to detailed and objective records of relevant aspects of students' teaching.

For these reasons an attempt has been made to develop for each skill a systematic observation instrument which can be used instead of rating scales to record relevant aspects of teaching behaviour. These instruments, if they were to be useful, had to be *valid* (i.e. each had to allow for the recording of those aspects of teaching behaviour with which the defined skill was concerned), to be potentially highly reliable (i.e. such that different trained observers would generally record the same events and record them in the same ways), and to be sufficiently *simple* for students to be able to use them with fair reliability and to be able to interpret recorded behaviour after only a brief training. We have found it difficult, and in one or two cases so far impossible, to construct instruments which meet all three of these criteria; the instruments described in this paper are in all cases the result of several successive modifications of those which we first designed. While further improvements to these instruments are doubtless possible, they are now, we feel, adequate to exemplify the sort of operational definitions of teaching skills and the diagnostic approach to assessment which we believe can best contribute to students' acquisition of skills.

Described below are the observation procedures which have been developed for six of the skills practised in the Stirling microteaching programme. Although this programme is part of an integrated theoretical/practical course, a major part of which is concerned with the theoretical rationale for each of the defined skills, no attempt is made here to justify these definitions. Each skill will be defined in terms of the general nature of the teaching behaviour prescribed; the observation instruments will be described and suggestions made about how to interpret records obtained with them; and some data will be presented on the reliability with which each instrument can be used after a few hours' training.

The reliability trials for these instruments were carried out at various times in different conditions for different immediate purposes; the evidence is, therefore, represented in different forms for the different instruments. In no case were there sufficient observers or a sufficient number of lessons observed for authoritative statements to be possible about the reliability level which can generally be expected with the instrument. The evidence presented does, however, give a fair indication of the reliability which is likely to be achieved on the basis of a few hours' training.

I. Varying the Stimulus

Definition: The purpose of this skill is to arouse pupils' attention and to focus their attention upon key points in a lesson. The general psychological principle upon which the skill is based is that, whereas uniformity of the perceived environment tends to lead people into mental inactivity, changes in the perceived environment attract attention and stimulate mental activity. As defined below, the skill applies most obviously to class teaching, although the same principles apply to any mode of teaching.

Observation Procedure: For each of the six aspects of classroom behaviour listed below, any instance which occurs within each thirty-second interval is recorded.

Teacher Movements: Movements from one place to another which seem likely to encourage useful shifts of attention (e.g. *record* movement towards blackboard to discuss diagram on it; *do not record* pacing up and down).

Teacher Gestures: Movements of parts of the body to direct attention, to emphasise importance, to express emotions, or to indicate shapes, sizes, movements, etc.

Change in Speech Pattern: Sudden or radical changes in tone, volume or speed of the teacher's speech.

Change of Sensory Focus: Changes in sense-channels which pupils are asked to use, e.g. listening to looking, reading to writing, discussion to manual activity; record such changes as from listening to listening *and* looking; *also* major changes of visual focus, such as from blackboard to film.

Verbal Pupil Participation: Pupil speech of at least one sentence (defined minimally as 'four words including a verb') which results from such teacher activity as a question or an extended expectant silence.

Physical Pupil Participation: Purposeful movement by one or more pupils which results from teacher activity, other than writing or turning their heads.

The record of a seven-minute lesson might look like the following table.

Interval (30 sec. each)	1	2	3	4	5	6	7	8	9	10	11	12	13	14
Teacher Movement	*					*			*					
Teacher Gesture	*	*	*	*	*	*			*	*			*	
Change in Speech Pattern	*	*	*			*	*			*		*	*	
Change of Sensory Focus	*			*			*		*	*				
Verbal Pupil Participation				*				*					*	*	*
Physical Pupil Participation				*										*

Interpretation of Record: Very crudely interpreted, the more of each category of behaviour which is recorded, the more fully the skill is

being exercised; but beyond a certain level, of course, more variation
of any particular type can become counterproductive. Furthermore,
the categories are not comparable in this respect: while an entry in
every interval for Verbal Pupil Participation would often be highly
desirable, the same would not generally be true for Teacher Movement.

As with all the instruments, interpretation of the record is most
fruitful when it is considered in relation to the particular lesson.
Thus for categories in which there are very few entries, one can ask
whether pupils' attention could have been better aroused or focused
if there had been more variation of this particular type; and one can
ask whether the teacher's failure to vary the lesson in this way
results from a deliberate decision or, on the contrary, reflects a
habitual pattern of behaviour.

Reliability: Three observers watched twenty videotaped five-minute
episodes of class teaching. For each of the six categories, Kendall's
Co-efficient of Concordance was calculated, with the results shown
in table 1. This reliability trial was undertaken before the introduction of the rule that only one entry in any one category should be
made during a thirty-second interval. Detailed inspections of the
three sets of records, however, showed that the major source of unreliability was the difficulty which observers had in determining a
unit of behaviour: what one observer coded as one change in speech
pattern another might code as three changes. Since such differences
in interpretation did not seem relevant to the validity of the instrument, the thirty-second rule was introduced to simplify observation
and to increase reliability.

Table I Reliability Data for Varying the Stimulus

	Coefficient of Concordance	Percentage of total no. of entries
Teacher Movement	0.71	15
Teacher Gesture	0.72	21
Change in Speech Pattern	0.80	23
Change in Sensory Focus	0.80	23
Verbal Participation	0.80	8
Physical Participation	*	10

*Ranking was not possible because two-thirds of all entries were for two of the
twenty episodes; observers agreed that there was none of this behaviour in
thirteen of the episodes.

II. Reacting

Definition: The purpose of this skill is to encourage pupils to answer questions, to make suggestions and generally to participate in classroom discussion. In accordance with reinforcement theory, it is suggested that pupils will be encouraged to participate if they are rewarded, in one way or another, for those contributions which they do make.

Observation Procedure: The coding is designed to record teachers' reactions in relation to three types of potential rewards:
  (i)   the reward of success, with such success being made explicit by the teacher;
  (ii) the reward of teacher approval; and
  (iii) the reward of seeing one's contribution being used.
Four categories are used, with further differentiation in three of them by the use of different symbols:

Answer Accepted Verbally: (or partially accepted)

Record + if manner of acceptance clearly conveys approval by wording (e.g. 'that's very good'), warmth of tone, emphasis, or accompanying smile, or for encouragement to elaborate on the contribution.
Record 0 for neutral acceptance (e.g. 'yes' without emphasis)
Record − for acceptance with disparaging or sarcastic tone of voice or accompanying comment.

Answer Rejected Verbally:

Record + for rejection alleviated by approval or encouragement (e.g. 'no, but that was a good try', 'no, have another go').
Record 0 for neutral rejection (e.g. 'no' without emphasis).
Record − for rejection with disapproval conveyed by wording (e.g. 'no, of course not'), emphasis or gesture or for cutting an answer short.

No Verbal Reaction:

Record + for approving non-verbal reaction.
Record 0 for neutral non-verbal reaction or for no reaction.
Record − for disapproving non-verbal reaction.

Use of Pupil Contribution:

Record + if the teacher makes use of pupil's contribution by using it as a premise for a new question or an argument, or by linking it

with the next, or a previous, idea discussed. Rejected answers
should never be coded in this way.

The record of part of a lesson might look like the following table.

Accepted verbally	+	0			+			0
Rejected verbally	0		–	–		–		
No verbal reaction		+					0 – 0	
Contribution used		+			+			+

Interpretation of Record: The most obvious general goals of this skill
are the elimination of reactions which are disapproving and of those
which provide no feedback at all, the maximisation of the use of
pupil contributions, and the acquisition of a habit of praising pupil
contributions and explicitly recognising their validity whenever
appropriate. It is difficult to formulate rules about when it is appropriate to give positive feedback, but the following seem likely to
have some general validity: praise of *every* pupil contribution is
likely to sound insincere and in any case to result in a devaluation
of praise; one cannot say that an incorrect pupil statement is correct,
but in many imperfect pupil contributions some element can be
found which it is meaningful for the teacher to recognise explicitly
as correct; if the teacher is obliged to evaluate a large proportion of
pupil contributions as incorrect, it is probable that his questions are
inappropriate.

It would have been useful if negative entries could have been included in the fourth category to indicate missed opportunities for
using pupil contributions, but in our attempts to make such codings
we found that inter-observer agreement was very poor.

Reliability: As for Varying the Stimulus, three observers coded twenty
five-minute episodes of class teaching. In this case, however, it was
possible to match the specific reactions coded by the three observers
so that instead of rankings of the total entries in each category per
episode being compared, the more demanding measure of percentage
agreement among observers in their coding of specific reactions was
used. 'Percentage agreement' was defined as

$$\frac{3 X_{ABC} + (X_{AB} + X_{BC} + X_{AC})}{X_A + X_B + X_C} \times 100,$$

where X_{ABC} represents the sum of all agreements among all three coders, X_{AB}, X_{BC}, X_{AC}, the sum of other agreements between the respective pairs of coders, and X_A, X_B, and X_C the sums of symbols recorded by each coder. That is, it is the number of agreements expressed as a percentage of the number of entries. The results are given in table 2.

Table 2 Reliability Data for Reacting

Category	Percentage Agreement	Percentage of total No. of entries
Accepted verbally	86	86
Rejected verbally	76	9
No verbal reaction	67	5
Approving	81	9
Neutral	85	87
Disapproving	76	4
Contribution used	64	84

III. Questioning for Feedback*

Definition: The purpose of this skill is that the teacher should obtain
reliable information about specific aspects of pupils' thinking, and
especially about pupils' cognitive and affective reactions to the tasks
which the teacher (explicitly or implicitly) sets for them. Although
there will in any case be many cues from pupils' verbal and non-
verbal behaviour, both the quantity and the quality of the information available to a teacher will generally depend on the questions he
asks.

Observation Procedure: Five aspects of teacher behaviour are observed:
1. *Untested Assumptions about Pupils:* A tally is entered whenever
the teacher appears to act upon a predetermined assumption about
pupils without attempting to test its validity. Major types of untested
assumptions are:
(i) Exposition which pupils can only understand if they have
previous knowledge or comprehension of specific facts or concepts, where such understanding has not been checked and
cannot, in the opinion of the observer, normally be assumed

---

*Most of the work involved in the development of the coding instrument for
Questioning for Feedback, including the assessment of its reliability, was done by
Jean Black and Ann Savage as part of their dissertations for honours education
degrees at the University of Stirling.

for pupils of this age.

(ii)   Attempts by the teacher to build upon ideas presented earlier
       in the lesson without checking pupils' understanding of these
       ideas.

(iii) Use of vocabulary which is distinctively abstract or technical
       in comparison with that used in the remainder of teacher-pupil
       conversation, without checking pupil understanding.

(iv)   Use of material which appears to have been introduced largely
       on the assumption that it will be particularly interesting to
       pupils, without this assumption being tested.

2(a) *Types of questions:* All questions which are not rhetorical or
procedural are classified into four categories:

Recall questions, asking pupils for previously learned information,
or asking them to recount a specified aspect of their previous
experience.

Comprehension questions, asking pupils to demonstrate understanding of concepts, to give explanations, to formulate relationships etc. (including all questions which are 'closed', cognitive,
and demand more than recall).

Attitude questions, directly or indirectly asking pupils to express
their attitude towards, or their degree of interest in, the topic of
the lesson or other specified objects.

Open questions, which invite the pupils to answer (usually at
some length) from the background of their personal experience
and ideas, with the nature of links between pupils' ideas and the
themes of the lesson being left open for the pupils to decide. The
distinguishing characteristic of such questions is that they encourage the pupils to reveal their own conceptual schemata,
rather than being formulated in terms of the concepts which the
teacher is endeavouring to teach.

2(b) *Distribution of Responses:* Questions are also classified in terms
of which of the five pupils in the microteaching class respond. Each
response from a different pupil is coded. If a question is followed,
after more than two seconds of silence, by further teacher talk, 'No
Response' is coded. (If the teacher continues talking after less than
two seconds the question is regarded as rhetorical, or as part of a
following question.)

3. *Inadequate Questions:* Of the many ways in which questions may

be unsatisfactory as a means of seeking feedback, two of the most common are recorded (in addition to the coding of questions in part 2(a)):

Lack of Definition: Questions which are so formulated that pupils may be uncertain or misled about the sort of answer which would be appropriate. (Whether a question lacks definition in this sense or is deliberately 'open' can usually be judged either from the wording of the question or from the teacher's reaction to a response.)

Leading Questions: Questions in which the teacher unintentionally gives a clue as to the correct or approved answer.

4. *Lack of Attention to Pupil Response:* Instances are coded where the teacher proceeds with his discourse after asking a question apparently without taking account in his subsequent behaviour of the nature of a pupil response or of lack of such a response.

The record of a lesson might look like this (some of the notes would only have meaning in the context of the lesson, and should not be taken as examples of the various categories):

1.

Untested assumptions about pupils	++++ II	*Notes:* fifteenth century; value of reading; 'theology'; Reformation

2.

TYPES OF QUESTION	PUPIL RESPONSES					
	A	B	C	D	E	None
Recall	II	I	++++ ++++ II	IIII II	IIII	II
Comprehension		II	++++	++++ III	I	++++ ++++
Attitudes			III	I		III
Open				I		

3.

Lack of definition	++++ I	*Notes:*	'What would you do if you couldn't read?'; 'What do you think?' (3 times); 'Why?'
Leading questions	I	*Notes:*	'You all listen to pop music, don't you?'

4.

Lack of attention to pupil response	++++ I I I	*Notes:*	Interruption of pupil response — four times; ignored suggestions about television, travel; didn't use 'work' response

Interpretation of Record: A disadvantage of this instrument is that it does not preserve the sequence of events, thus making it more difficult to identify in retrospect particular events which have been recorded. It is, therefore, useful to supplement tallies with occasional handwritten notes. Interpretation of the record is otherwise straightforward: practice of the skill is aimed at minimising entries in parts 1, 3 and 4 of the schedule, at asking answerable questions which are distributed over the different question-type categories, and at obtaining a not too uneven spread of responses from the different pupils. Although the most obvious weakness, so far as question-type is concerned, is to concentrate on Recall questions, a more common weakness appears to be a failure to ask Open questions.

Reliability: More data have to be recorded in this instrument than appears to be possible, with any reliability, at one viewing. Since microteaching supervisors, however, observe lessons both while they are being taught (on TV monitors) and also when they are replayed to the student-teachers, this is not an insuperable disadvantage. The reliability data given in table 3 are based on two viewings, with parts 1, 3 and 4 being completed in one viewing and part 2 in the other. Two observers each coded twelve twelve-minute lessons; Spearman rank-order correlations and mean frequencies for each category were calculated.

Table 3 Reliability Data for Questioning for Feedback

Category	Rank-Order Correlation between coders	Mean Frequency per lesson per observer
1. Untested assumptions	.92	3.0
2. Recall questions	.96	10.0
Comprehension questions	.95	14.8
Attitude questions	.95	14.0
Open questions	.85	1.4
Distribution over pupils	.89	—
No response	.96	1.6
3. Lack of definition	.89	1.4
Leading questions	.94	4.0
4. Lack of attention to pupil response	0.88	2.2

IV. Higher Order Questioning and Probing

Definition: The purpose of this skill is that pupils should be led into 'higher order' cognitive activity so that, from a long-term view, they can develop higher order skills such as those involved in problem solving and so that, more immediately, they can extend their understanding of the issues being discussed. The teacher as questioner is seen both as a model (asking the sort of questions it is useful for one to ask oneself) and as a setter of tasks.

Observation Procedure: Questions are recorded in sequence and categorised in two ways:

(1) *In terms of the nature of the task set:* The categorisation used here was particularly influenced by Bloom's (1956) classification of objectives and by Bellack's (1966) classification of classroom language.

Lower Order questions are those for which the teacher's intention appears to be that the pupil should answer in terms of his existing knowledge and ideas.

Corresponding roughly to Bloom's Knowledge category and to Bellack's categories of Fact-Stating, Opining and Defining, this category includes all questions which appear to be asking for recalled information or ideas, simple descriptions or unsubstantiated opinions.

Application questions are those for which the teacher's intention appears to be that the pupil should apply ideas or procedures (previously known or newly acquired) to specific contexts where he has not previously applied them. This corresponds to Bloom's Comprehension and Application categories and includes Bellack's Interpreting category. Questions asking for the interpretation of specific communications, for the use of rules and procedures in new contexts, or for examples of concepts or relationships (except where pupils can recall such examples) fall within this category.

Analysis/Synthesis questions are those for which the teacher's intention appears to be that the pupil should make distinctions, specify relationships, formulate hypotheses, or define or elaborate on concepts not previously made explicit. This category is comparable with Bellack's Explaining and Justifying categories and with Bloom's Analysis and Synthesis categories.

In coding questions according to these three categories it is of course necessary to attend as much to the context in which the question is asked as to the question itself.

(2) *In terms of the function of the question in teacher-pupil interaction:* probing questions, defined as questions addressed to a particular pupil to follow up his initial response. The importance of such questions is seen to be that their starting-point is the *pupil's* attempt to relate his own ideas to a task set by the teacher. Probing questions include the following: questions seeking *justification* of the pupil's initial answer; questions seeking *elaboration* on the pupil's initial answer; questions seeking *clarification* of the pupil's initial answer; *prompts* which reformulate or break down the initial question in reaction to the pupil's attempt to answer it. (Attempts to distinguish different kinds of probing question by the use of different symbols have not proved very reliable; nor have such formal distinctions appeared very valuable in practice.)

q: all questions other than probing questions

→x, qx: questions which are not answered, or the answers to which are rejected by the teacher.

The record of part of a lesson might appear something like this:

Analysis/Synthesis			q								qx	→x
Application					q		q→	qx			q q		
Lower Order	q	q	q			q	q		→	→			

Interpretation of Record:

(i) In general, one wishes to minimise the proportion of lower order questions. Although effective teaching probably requires a fair number of lower order as well as higher order questions, much the more common weakness is to ask almost exclusively lower order questions.

(ii) Apart from lower order questions, teaching by questioning is not likely to be very effective if Application questions are asked to the exclusion of Analysis/Synthesis questions. The danger of this appears particularly great in certain subject areas, such as mathematics (example problems) and English (interpretation questions).

(iii) It is worth while to examine the sequential patterns in which various types of questions are used. Long sequences of questions of any one type seem likely to be less effective than continual movement from one level to another, as in the example shown above. Common strategies which probably tend to be useful are to follow opinion questions (lower order) by questions seeking justification of the opinions expressed (anal./synth.), and to follow knowledge questions by ones requiring synthesis or explanation of the facts given, following this by a request for examples of the concept or relationship which has been identified.

(iv) The record does not tell one when a probing question would have been appropriate; but if there have been only two or three probes in a ten-minute lesson, it is likely that opportunities for valuable probing have been missed. Experience suggests that a reasonable expectation on average is for about one question in four to be followed by a probe.

(v) A large number of unanswered or inadequately answered questions suggests that questions have either been lacking in clarity or have been too difficult. Unanswered Analysis/Synthesis questions are particularly significant in this respect.

(vi) The objective for practising this skill is that students should learn to teach by questioning; a low frequency of questions is, therefore, undesirable but, in the context of practising the skill, unlikely. A less obvious weakness is that of asking too many questions: if the teacher averages more than two or three questions a minute, it is likely either that many of the questions have been trivial or that the teacher has given little attention to the answers (cf. Adams, 1969).

Reliability: Reliability studies for this and the next two skills described
followed the same pattern: three observers each coded ten videotapes of twelve-minute lessons in terms of the skill and rank-order
correlations between each pair of observers were calculated for
lesson-scores on a number of indices. Further checks on observer
agreement were made during the subsequent coding of experimental
lessons. The data for the reliability trials for this skill are given in
table 4.

Table 4 Reliability Data for Higher Order Questioning and Probing

Index	Rank-Order Correlations between Coders		
	p12	p13	p23
Number of Questions	.96	1.00	.94
Anal./Synth. questions as proportion of total	.91	.83	.85
Lower Order questions as proportion of total	.70	.87	.61
Number of Probes	.77	.64	.79
Proportion of questions not adequately answered	.94	.88	.92

Subsequent checks confirmed that inter-observer agreement of this
order can be maintained, with the exception that the above figures
may exaggerate the ease with which Analysis/Synthesis questions
can in general, be distinguished from others.

V. Clarity of Explanation

Definition: The purpose of this skill is that teachers' explanations
should be as lucid as possible. The 'skill' is based less on any coherent
theoretical foundation than on common sense, on the results of exploratory empirical studies of teachers' classroom language (e.g.
Barnes et al., 1969), and of the correlates in teachers' explaining behaviour of pupils' attainment (e.g. Rosenshine, 1968).

Observation Procedure: The following types of behaviour are sequen-
tially coded:
Lack of Continuity: This is defined as occurring when the teacher
introduces a new idea, problem or information without relating this
to what has immediately preceded it, or when the teacher reverts to
a previous topic without showing the relation of what he has been
discussing to this previous topic.

Lack of Fluency: This includes all sentences which are unfinished or which are reformulated to a significant extent in mid-sentence: and all questions for which pupils are not given a reasonable time (three seconds) to answer before the teacher goes on talking, including the fairly common phenomenon where a question is immediately followed by a different question.

Inappropriate Vocabulary: While this is obviously a crucial aspect of explaining, it seems impossible to establish criteria by which an observer might objectively judge what vocabulary is or is not appropriate. All 'technical' terms are coded which the observer judges to be unnecessary for the explanation with which the teacher is concerned; so also are all words used which the observer judges to be unknown by most pupils of the relevant age-group, unless the teacher stops to explain the 'new' word.

Vague Words or Expressions: All expressions are coded which indicate that the teacher is failing to make something explicit, such as 'sort of', 'you know', 'etcetera'. So also are all words which, in the observer's judgement, make the explanation less clear because of their lack of precision, e.g. 'about', 'a lot'.

Explaining Statements or Questions: This includes all statements which give, and all questions which seek, an explanation, i.e. an explicit logical, causative, functional, teleological or historical link between two objects. In most cases, such statements or questions may be distinguished by the fact that they include one or more of the following link-words:

because	therefore	why
in order that	so that	what if
the result of	the purpose of	the function of
the cause of	the consequence of	the implication of
by	though	if . . . then

Visual Techniques for Explaining: All uses of visual techniques are recorded which, in the judgement of the observer, make relationships between objects more clear.

The record of a lesson might look like this:

Lack of Continuity   *
Lack of Fluency   *   *
Inappropriate Vocabulary   *   *   *
Vague Words or Expressions   *   *   *
Explaining Statements, Questions   *   *   *   *   *
Visual Techniques for Explaining   *

Interpretation of Record: In general, it is hypothesised that the fewer
entries there are for the first four categories, and the more there are
for the last two, the more effective an explanation is likely to be;
but even if these hypotheses are valid, the generalisations cannot be
applied uncritically to all teaching contexts. It is our experience that
that one of the most useful functions of records on this schedule can be
to provide a starting-point for discussion about the appropriateness
of the use of technical vocabulary, of assumed shared assumptions
('you know'), or of discontinuities in theme in the context of specific lessons.

Reliability: Rank-order correlations between total scores for ten twelve-
minute lessons for each category according to the three observers are
given in table 5.

Table 5 Reliability Data for Clarity of Explanation

Category	Rank-Order Correlations between Coders		
	p12	p13	p23
Lack of Continuity	.68	.50	.47
Lack of Fluency	.68	.54	.49
Inappropriate Vocabulary	.88	*	*
Vague Words or Expressions	.28	.13	.28
Explaining Statements, Questions	.85	.65	.71
Visual Techniques for Explaining	Frequencies insufficient for ranking		

*Observer 3 did not code sufficient instances for ranking to be meaningful

Especially for 'Vague Words and Expressions', and in the relatively
low level of agreement between observer 3 and the others, these
results show an unsatisfactory level of reliability. After discussion of
their differences on these ten lessons, however, the observers used
the schedule to code experimental lessons, observers 1 and 2 coding
one set of eight lessons, observers 2 and 3 another set of eight. Dis-

cussion of differences had apparently helped, since the rank-order
correlations for 'Vague Words and Expressions' rose from .28 to .80
and from .28 to .60 respectively; and for 'Inappropriate Vocabulary'
the two correlations were .85 and .65. Considering all the results, it
appears that with sufficient training reasonable reliability may be
possible for all categories except 'Lack of Continuity' and 'Visual
Techniques'; for both of these, frequencies tend to be too low.

VI. Use of Examples

Definition: The purpose of this skill is that teachers should use
examples, and seek examples from pupils, in such a way as to help
pupils to comprehend new concepts by modifying and extending
their previously acquired conceptual schemata. Research into conceptual development and concept attainment suggests the importance of both the choice of examples and also the ways in which
they are presented in relation to the concepts they exemplify. (Both
the choice of concepts to be introduced to a particular set of pupils,
and the choice of examples to be used in facilitating this introduction, are important pedagogical issues on which student-teachers
should and can be given guidance. These are not, however, issues
in relation to which it seems possible to define generalisable teaching
skills, nor are they the kind of tasks which can generally be very well
practised in a microteaching context. This skill is not, therefore,
concerned with the psychological appropriateness of the choice of
examples, but rather with the logical relationships between examples
and concepts, with the sequencing of their presentation, and with
patterns of interaction between teacher and pupils.)

Observation Procedure: The symbols used in coding the use of examples
are:
  r: The explicit statement of a rule or generalisation which the
     teacher wants pupil to understand.
  e: An example given by the teacher, exemplifying such a rule. (An
     example is defined as a *statement,* not an *object.* For example,
     a picture or a poem cannot itself be an example: an indication
     of some characteristic of a picture could be an example.)
  q: A teacher request for a pupil to give an example of a rule he is
     attempting to teach; different consecutive responses to the
     same request are coded as different requests.
  ⓔorⓠ: After the example has been stated, the way in which it exem-
     plifies the general rule is made explicit, either by the teacher or

by a pupil.

qx: A request which does not result in a pupil giving a valid example of the rule.

Symbols are entered across the page as relevant behaviours occur; but when the teacher moves on to consider a different rule, this is indicated by moving to a new line. When a rule which has been 'established' is then used as an example for a higher-order rule, this should be indicated by an (e) at the beginning of the new line.

The record of a lesson might look like this:

I		e	e	r	ⓔ	e	qx	q	q	r
II		(e)	r	e	q	qx	q	ⓠ	
III		e	ⓔ	ⓠ	r	e	r		

Interpretation of Record:

(i)   It is generally desirable that a high proportion of the examples given for each rule should be given by pupils. Pupil examples sought before statement of the rule probably indicate that the teacher is encouraging pupils to develop the concept from their own previous ideas. Pupil examples sought after the final statement of rule indicate that the teacher is attempting to ensure that pupils have understood the concept.

(ii) If examples are to be useful, it is necessary that pupils should perceive their relationship to the stated rule. It, therefore, seems appropriate that the teacher should make this relationship explicit for at least some of the examples of each rule.

(iii) No valid generalisations seem possible about the relative value of inductive strategies (examples then rule) or deductive strategies (rule then examples). It may, however, be fruitful to note whether the teacher has tended to use one type of strategy rather than the other, and to consider whether this seems appropriate for this particular topic.

(iv) Research evidence (Rosenshine, 1968) does indicate, however, that explanations tend to be more effective if the first statement of a rule (whether or not it is preceded by examples) is followed by examples and then by a second statement of the rule.

Reliability: Rank-order correlations between three observers for a number of indices, calculated for ten twelve-minute lessons, are given in table 6.

Table 6 Reliability Data for Use of Examples

Index	Rank-order Correlation		
	p12	p13	p23
Number of examples	.58	.59	.87
Number of examples given by pupils	.34	.33	.76
Number of examples explicitly related to rules	.81	.59	.48
Number of rules without rule-example-rule sequence	.56	.50	.80

During experimental lessons which were subsequently observed, further checks were made. In general, the correlations were of the same order as those given in table 6, except that observer 1 now appeared to be using the same criterion as the others for pupils' examples (p = .74).

The inter-observer agreement for this instrument is thus rather low. Examination of different observers' records indicated that the major problem was that of determining what rules a teacher was trying to establish. (Only after this decision has been made can one decide what is an example.) It does not seem possible to infer teachers' intentions in this respect from their observed behaviour. An obvious way of overcoming this problem is to ask student-teachers to give observers their lesson-plans beforehand, with particular emphasis upon the concepts or generalisations which they aim to teach. This depends on students' *ability* to specify their objectives, an ability which for most students is dependent on systematic instruction and practice.

Conclusion

The six observation procedures have been presented here in similar terms to those in which they are presented to students at Stirling. Their effective use is dependent on students having had one or two hours' practice with them, and also on students and tutors having the commitment and self-discipline to base their consideration of microteaching lessons on the records provided by the instruments rather than concentrating on their own intuitive personal insights.

In order to attain the levels of reliability reported in this paper, several hours' practice and discussion is generally necessary, together with the formulation of specific ground-rules derived from the general definitions provided. Details of the ground-rules have not been included, since it is not our intention in publishing an account of these instruments to suggest that they should be used as research instruments elsewhere. As research instruments, their primary value is that they allow the researcher reliably to assess students' microteaching behaviour in terms of precisely the same criteria as those which the students themselves have been asked to try to meet; that is, they are valid for the specific training context.

References

Adams, T.H. (1969). *The Development of a Method for the Analysis of Questions asked by Teachers in Classroom Discourse,* Rutgers State University, New Brunswick, New Jersey.

Barnes, D., Britton,J. and Rosen,H. (1969). *Language, the Learner and the School,* Penguin, Harmondsworth.

Bellack, A.A., Kliebard, H.M., Hyman, R.T. and Smith, F.L. (1966). *The Language of the Classroom,* Teachers College Press, Columbia University, New York.

Bloom, B. (ed.) (1956). *Taxonomy of Educational Objectives, Handbook I: Cognitive Domain,* Longman, London.

Rosenshine, B. (1968). 'Objectively measured behavioral predictors of effectiveness in explaining.' Paper presented at the annual meeting of the American Educational Research Association, Chicago.

Stanford Teacher Education Programme (1968). *Microteaching: a Description,* Stanford University, 1968.

3 THE ANALYTIC ASSESSMENT OF STUDENTS' SCHOOL PRACTICE TEACHING

Donald White and Donald McIntyre

Introduction

According to a survey conducted by Stones and Morris (1972) of school practice assessment procedures in England, the normal pattern is for students to be awarded 'teaching marks', based either on single ratings of their teaching competence or, much less commonly, on a profile in terms of ratings on a number of scales. These tend to be supplemented by unstructured written reports made by visiting supervisors and by supervising teachers. Few, if any, of the 122 institutions covered by the survey appeared to use any systematic procedures for the description, as opposed to the grading of students' teaching.

The major emphasis of assessment procedures is thus on the grading of students, despite the considerable body of evidence demonstrating the low reliability and even lower predictive validity (e.g. Wiseman and Start, 1965) of such grades. On the other hand, teacher education institutions do not seem to have made organised attempts to use the type of criterion-referenced assessments which would be necessary to enable them to evaluate the effectiveness of their curricula in preparing students for teaching. Nor is there much sign of attempts to ensure that students are provided with valid and useful feedback on their teaching, although there has been evidence for many years (e.g. Robertson, 1957) of wide differences among supervisors in the criteria they use. The lack of such efforts is exacerbated by the emphasis on grading: students are inevitably inclined to focus attention on the grades in terms of which they are summed up rather than on the ad hoc comments of their supervisors, and it is difficult for them to accept supervisors as sympathetic observers with whom they can frankly discuss their problems: as Cope (1969) concludes, the supervisor 'becomes virtually an examiner — an examiner, moreover, operating in conditions which are known to make objective and valid judgement virtually impossible'.

One aim in the development of microteaching procedures has been to overcome some of the difficulties associated with the school classroom as a learning environment for student-teachers, such as lack of control over contextual factors, and the difficulty of giving sustained attention to particular aspects of teaching. In particular, emphasis has been placed in microteaching on descriptive feedback and supervisory discussion in relation to those aspects of teaching on which students have been asked to concentrate their attention. The value of micro-teaching, however, is likely to depend heavily on the extent to which students are encouraged to see what they have learned from it as relevant to their teaching in the context of school classrooms. The provision of microteaching, therefore, far from being a solution to problems of school practice supervision, rather emphasises the need for more systematic and analytic assessment by school practice supervisors.

It is largely through commenting on students' lessons which they have observed that tutors conventionally attempt to contribute to students' learning during school practice. While very little is known about the effects of different kinds of supervisory observation and comment, it may *a priori* be hypothesised that supervision will be more helpful to students if the following criteria are met.

(i)   that the observation of lessons should be largely independent of individual tutors' idiosyncracies;

(ii) that most of the comments made by a supervisor about a lesson should be related to what the student-teacher was attempting to do in that lesson;

(iii) that, over the course of a number of observed lessons, account should be taken of a wide range of facets of each student's teaching;

(iv) that most comments made on lessons should be in terms of concepts which students, through their college courses, have learned to understand and to apply to their teaching;

(v)   that tutors should support and illustrate their interpretations and evaluations of students' observed teaching (many of which must necessarily be subjective and debatable) by referring to detailed and relatively objective descriptions of relevant aspects of the students' teaching.

The purposes of this paper are to describe a system for the observation of school practice teaching which was designed in order that these criteria might more easily be met, and to report some evidence on the use of this system.

A System for the Observation of School Practice Teaching

The system described in outline here, and more fully by White (1972), offers a framework for the supervision and assessment of school practice teaching in teacher education programmes in which teaching skills have been studied in analytic terms. The system reflects the particular choice and definition of teaching skills used in the Stirling microteaching programme, but it could relatively easily be adapted to take account of any different set of skills selected for inclusion in another programme. In other respects, the system is intended to be sufficiently flexible for its usefulness not to be affected by the particular arrangements made for school practice.

In any attempt such as this to provide a generalisable procedure for structuring the observation of practice teaching, it is necessary to make a number of distinctions among the kinds of observations and assessments which can be made. There are four such distinctions which are of importance in this system:

(a)   A distinction is made between a teacher's *plans* for a lesson and his *implementation* of these plans. For example, a teacher's introduction of pupils to a new concept might be unsatisfactory either because the teacher had not, in his planning, clarified the defining characteristics of the concept which he wanted pupils to master or because, despite adequate planning, he did not explain or exemplify the concept clearly.

(b)   A distinction is made between *recurring* characteristics of teaching behaviour and characteristics which tend to be *specific* to particular lessons. For example, the giving of explanations and the asking of questions by teachers tend to recur in most lessons; but the content of each lesson is, in general, different, as in many respects are the ways in which lessons are introduced and developed.

(c)   A distinction is made among recurring characteristics of teaching in terms of whether or not they can be described through *low-inference* judgements. Can the relevant characteristics be defined in terms of units of behaviour which an informed observer can recognise and categorise through the direct application of explicit definitions? It is possible, for example, to recognise and to categorise teachers' questions through such low-inference judgements. On the other hand, judgements about the warmth of a teacher's relationship with his pupils depend on a high level of inference from a large number of specific cues; and it does not seem possible to define 'warmth' adequately in terms of more operationally definable aspects of behaviour, such as the number of times a teacher smiles.

(d)   A distinction is made between the *occurrence* of units of be-

haviour of a given general type and the *appropriateness* of the
particular behaviour in its distinctive context. For example,
while the frequency of questions making higher order cognitive demands may be noted (and a relatively high frequency
of such questions generally valued), the appropriateness of
any particular higher order question can only be judged in
relation to its specific content and context.

The instruments used for describing and assessing students' teaching
reflect these distinctions. Two types of instrument are used. The first
type is concerned with recording *low-inference* judgements about the
occurrence of various *recurring* aspects of teaching behaviour. There
are four instruments of this systematic observation type, all of which
are related to skills practised in the Stirling microteaching programme.
The construction of the instruments was influenced by the work of
Bellack *et al.* (1966), and a rough correspondence can be seen between
three of the instruments and the three main types of teacher moves
described by Bellack, *structuring, soliciting* and *reacting.* Thus two of
the instruments, labelled Questioning and Reinforcement, are concerned respectively with soliciting and reacting moves; and a third instrument, Structure of the Discourse, is concerned primarily, though
not exclusively, with the teacher's structuring moves. The fourth instrument, Varying the Stimulus, is concerned with several ways in which a
teacher may introduce variety into a lesson, and is not associated with
any particular type of move.

The Reinforcement and Varying the Stimulus instruments are virtually identical with those used in microteaching at Stirling and have
been described in the paper by McIntyre, McKnight and White in this
volume. The other two instruments, however, are rather more complex
than those used in the microteaching context.

In the Questioning instrument, the following types of information
are recorded:

Each question is categorised according to whether it is an initiating
question (q); or a redirected question (r) — the same as the previous
question, put to a different pupil; or a probe ($\rightarrow$) — a follow-up question to a pupil who has answered a question, asking him to carry his
answer further, for example by clarifying or justifying it;

each question is categorised according to whether it is an open
question — one to which a wide range of answers are acceptable; or a
pseudo-open question — one which, while appearing open, is shown

not to be so by the teacher's reaction to the answer (denoted by ringing the recording already made); or a closed question;

each closed question is categorised according to the type of task it sets: lower order, which includes tasks of factual recall, sensory description and opining; middle order, which includes tasks of application, exemplification and interpretation, and higher order, which includes tasks of explanation and justification;

each question is categorised according to whether or not it is affective (denoted by underlining the relevant recording) in that it seeks an answer reflecting the pupil's own emotions, value-systems or preferences;

finally, a record is made of questions to which no answers are received or the answers to which are rejected (denoted by an x after the recorded question).

A sequence of a teacher's questioning as recorded by this instrument might be as follows:

Open								$\underline{q}$	$\textcircled{q}$	
Higher Order			$\rightarrow$qx							
Middle Order				qx	rx	r				
Lower Order	$\underline{q}$	q	r						q$\rightarrow$	$\rightarrow$q

Use of the Structure of the Discourse instrument is dependent upon the student-teacher's provision of a clear statement of his plans for the lesson, and especially of all generalisations, or rules, which he considers to be important components of the substance of the planned lesson. The major function of the instrument is to record significant features of the way in which these rules are introduced and discussed in the lesson. In particular, all instances of each of four kinds of operation are abstracted from the classroom talk. These are:

Statements of rules,
Explanations or justifications of rules, showing for example the functional or causal relationships upon which the rule is based.
Applications of rules in specific contexts and the giving of specific

    examples of rules.
Interpretations of rules, by restating them in different words, expressing them in different symbols, or representing them diagramatically.

A record is made of whether these contributions to classroom talk came from the teacher (t) or from a pupil (p), and of which contributions are related to the same rules. Any of the recorded elements of the discourse which are judged to be unclear as a result of over-complex grammatical constructions, vagueness, or unexplained technical terms are recorded by ringing the relevant symbols. In addition, a fifth line on the instrument is used for recording discontinuities in the discourse: any self-interruption by the teacher, for example by following a question by another question in less than two seconds, is denoted by a 't'; and a clear shift in the substance or the development of the discourse is denoted by an oblique stroke.

    A segment of lesson discourse as recorded by this instrument might be as follows:

Explanation				(t)				
Appl./Exempl.	t	t		p		p	p	t t
Interpretation			t		p			
Statement of Rule		(t)				t		
Discontinuities		t		t		t		/
		Rule 1			**Rule 2**		**Rule 3**	

The records of teaching behaviour provided by these four instruments do not reflect any judgements about the appropriateness of the specific behaviours which have been recorded, although built into the instruments there are of course many judgements about the general desirability of certain types of teaching behaviour. It is intended, however, that these records, together with students' lesson plans, should be helpful to supervisors and students in facilitating discussion and judgements about the appropriateness of the recorded behaviour.

    The second type of instrument used in this system is concerned with characteristics of teaching whch tend to be specific to particular lessons and with those about which only high-inference judgements are possible. The instruments of this type are rating scales, the use of which implies judgements about both the occurrence and the appropriateness of the behaviour rated. Ten aspects of teaching are each rated on a five-point scale, the first three of these being taken from Ryans' (1960) study of teacher characteristics:

1. Warm and understanding *versus* Cold and aloof
2. Businesslike and systematic *versus* Slipshod and poorly organised
3. Stimulating and imaginative *versus* Dull and stereotyped
4. Clear mastery of subject-matter *versus* Inadequate understanding of subject-matter
5. Affective set, the success of the teacher's attempts to develop and maintain interest.
6. Cognitive set, the success of the teacher's attempts to make clear the relationships between the new work and previous knowledge
7. Cognitive thread of discourse, the success of the teacher's attempts to show connections among the key points of the lesson
8. Suitability of language
9. Fluency
10. Closure, the success of the teacher's attempts to consolidate and make explicit what had been learned.

These two kinds of instrument are concerned with a wide range of aspects of teaching. One of the major problems in the supervision of school practice is that of reconciling the small number of lessons which it is usually possible for a supervisor to observe with the desirability of considering many different facets of a student-teacher's behaviour. Clearly it is necessary for the best possible use to be made of those lessons which are observed. In this system it is assumed that a supervisor will observe each student teaching a minimum of three lessons of thirty-five to forty minutes, and that the student will be actively teaching and attempting to communicate with pupils during the larger part of these lessons. Given these conditions, it should usually be possible for the supervisor to use each of the four systematic observation instruments to record at least two appropriate samples of a student's teaching, and still be able to devote at least half his time to less structured observation of the lessons.

The first requirement for a lesson-sampling approach is a clear plan, produced by the student-teacher, showing the intended sequence and the purposes of lesson activities. On arrival, the supervisor scans the lesson plan and decides which instruments he will use, and the stages at which he will use them. The Structure of the Discourse instrument requires a ten-minute spell of recording, but appropriately chosen five-minute periods provide meaningful samples for each of the other three instruments. When he is not using any of these instruments, the supervisor can focus his attention on whatever appears to him to be particularly significant for that lesson, and for that student. Although he should normally discuss the strengths and weaknesses of each lesson with the student immediately after the lesson, he is asked to refrain from completing the rating scales until he has observed at least three lessons; and it is only then that he may have used each of the observation instruments sufficiently to consider profiles of the student's teaching performance.

Experimental Evaluation of the System

Preliminary assessments of the reliability with which each instrument could be used were made at Stirling and satisfactory levels of agreement were attained in most cases. The main trial of the system as a whole was then conducted at Bulawayo Teachers' College, of which the first author was then principal. The trial was directed towards answering two questions:

1. What degree of agreement would be found between two supervisors in their description of school practice lessons, given that they agreed in advance on sections of each lesson for which they would use the same instruments?
2. Would pairs of supervisors using the system in this way agree with one another on the points to which they would draw students' attention more closely than would pairs of supervisors following conventional procedures?

Design of Experiment

The trial was conducted in the context of a four-week school practice for students nearing the end of the second year of a three-year course. These students had not had microteaching experience and their supervisors had no previous experience of systematic observation procedures. The experiment involved a sample of sixty students practising in high schools and in the upper classes of junior schools within a reasonable distance from the College. They were assigned to schools in the usual way and then formed into groups of three, on a subject basis in the high schools and on a proximity basis in the junior schools. This gave:

4 groups for high school mathematics
2 groups for high school geography
2 groups for high school history
2 groups for high school art
2 groups for high school English
8 groups for junior schools.

Tutors were then allocated, one pair to each group of three students, on the basis of such conventional criteria for the supervision of school practice as that one of a student's supervisors should be his tutor for the subject he was training to teach. Half of the groups in each of the given subject and school type strata were allocated to an experimental treatment, and half to a control treatment. The constraint was applied that no supervisor should be involved in both the experimental and the control treatments, and since some pairs of supervisors had to work with more than one student group, the allocation of groups to treatments was therefore not entirely random.

The experimental treatment consisted of the use of the system which has been described, while the control treatment involved using the procedures for school practice conventional at the College, which consisted of unstructured observation, post-lesson discussions with students, the completion of a narrative form of report and the awarding of a single grade.

Fourteen tutors (i.e. seven pairs) were involved in the experimental treatment. They received twenty hours of training, spread over one week, in the use of all aspects of the system. Tutors involved in the control treatment met to discuss conventional procedures for teaching practice observation and supervision, but after one two-hour session they felt there was nothing more they could usefully discuss.

The students were informed that the purpose of the experiment was to test a method of lesson observation, and they were reassured that no individual's grading would be adversely affected by the procedure. They were asked to present their lesson plans to visiting supervisors in a specified way, including information on aims or objectives, the sequence of intended teacher and pupil activities, pupil grouping, key points of content, audio-visual aids and proposed arrangements for rounding off the lesson.

Supervisors in both experimental and control groups were required to visit their students in pairs. After considering students' lesson plans, pairs of supervisors following the experimental treatment were to agree about which observation instruments to use and at which stages of the lesson to use them; but the two supervisors, whether following the experimental or control treatments, were not to consult each other either in observing the lesson or in interpreting their observations. All supervisors were to write their reports in the conventional narrative form, with one of the two supervisors giving the student a copy of his report and discussing the lesson with the student. Each supervisor was asked to indicate up to five of the strengths or weaknesses identified in his report which would be the most important points on which he would base post-lesson discussion with the student.

Analysis of Data

The degree of agreement between supervisors in their use of systematic observation instruments was assessed by attempting to match their sequential records of the teaching for which a given instrument had been used and by then counting the number of specific items which they categorised in the same way. For each type of decision that had to be made, the following formula was used:

$$\text{Percentage agreement} = \frac{2 \times (\text{Number of agreements})}{\text{Entries by supervisor A} + \text{Entries by Supervisor B}} \times 100$$

A detailed scheme was developed in order to categorise the main strengths and weaknesses of each lesson identified by supervisors. The categories in this scheme were grouped according to the facets of teaching with which they were concerned, there being a number of specific categories and one general category in each group. The six groups of categories were:

Motivating (10 specific categories)
Explaining (14 specific categories)
Soliciting (12 specific categories)
Reacting (8 specific categories)
Pre-lesson Preparation (14 specific categories)
General Qualities of Teacher (10 specific categories)

The specific categories may be exemplified by those in the Reacting group, which were, in their positive form:

(1)   encourages further participation by the reinforcing nature of

his reactions to acceptable pupil contributions;

(2) encourages further participation by the sympathetic and encouraging nature of his reactions to pupil contributions which have to be rejected;

(3) attends to individual difficulties revealed by pupil contributions, showing awareness of individual differences and awareness of children's needs;

(4) generally shows sympathy, patience, tolerance and consideration for all pupils;

(5) reacts appropriately to restlessness and other signs of inattention or boredom;

(6) reacts appropriately to signs of incomprehension or bewilderment;

(7) acknowledges or responds verbally to most pupil contributions;

(8) shows senstivity to feedback received from the pupils and adapts his subsequent behaviour in the light of it.

The general categories were used for points which were either very general or vague or which, while clearly being within the general facet, did not correspond to any of the specific categories. All points which did not fall within any of the specific or general categories were coded as 'miscellaneous'.

The points made by each supervisor in relation to each lesson were independently categorised by the first of the authors and by the supervisor himself. Agreements between supervisors about the strengths and weaknesses of the observed lessons were defined as those which were placed in the same categories by the supervisors themselves and which were also categorised this way in the independent analysis. (In the event, in almost every case where both supervisors made points which they coded as belonging to the same category, the points were coded in the same way in the independent analysis.)

Results

The percentage agreements among supervisors in the use of the systematic observation instruments are given in table 1.

A total of 792 strengths or weaknesses were identified by control group supervisors and there was 62 per cent agreement between them and the researcher in categorising these. Supervisors in the experimental group identified 672 strengths or weaknesses and the agreement between them and the researcher in categorising them was 55 per cent.

Table 1 Percentage Agreement between Supervisors in the Use of
Systematic Observation Instruments

Instrument	Decision	Percentage Agreement
Questioning	Initiating/redirecting/probing	66
	Lower/middle/higher order	66
	Open	50
	Pseudo-open	89
	Affective	56
	No accepted answer	53
Structure of	Interpreting/applying/explaining/stating	63
Discourse	Teacher or pupil	74
	Not clear	15
	Self-interruptions	50
Varying the	Teacher movement	51
Stimulus	Teacher gesture	66
	Change in speech pattern	59
	Change in sense mode	51
	Pupils participate physically	78
	Pupils participate verbally	82
Reinforcement	Accepted/rejected/no reaction	74
	Positive/neutral/negative	69
	Cognitive feedback used	48

Table 2 shows the distribution of the supervisors' points (as classified
by the researcher) over the different facets of teaching, the numbers of
strengths and of weaknesses, and the number of agreements between
supervisors.

Table 2 Strengths and Weaknesses Identified by Supervisors in Control
and Experimental Groups

Group of Categories	Control Group				Experimental Group			
	Strengths	Weaknesses	Total	Agreements	Strengths	Weaknesses	Total	Agreements
Motivating	101	45	146	7	80	44	124	8
Explaining	75	92	167	8	76	56	132	3
Soliciting	36	46	82	0	57	50	107	6
Reacting	20	34	54	0	35	20	55	6
Preparation	107	113	220	12	146	64	210	28
Gen. Qualities	70	14	84	8	20	0	20	0
Miscellaneous	14	25	39	0	7	17	24	1
Total	423	369	792	35	421	251	672	52
Percentage Agreement				8.8				15.8

An x^2 test of the difference between the total number of agreements
obtained by pairs in the control group and by those in the experimental
group showed this difference to be significant at the 1 per cent level.
Other marked and significant differences are that supervisors in the experimental group made fewer comments on 'general qualities' of students (e.g. their rapport with classes or their emotional stability) and
that they commented less on students' weaknesses.

Discussion

The most striking aspect of these results is the very low measure of
agreement obtained by pairs of supervisors in both the control and the
experimental groups. Reading some of the narrative reports of pairs
alongside one another, it is difficult to believe that the writers had in
fact observed the same lesson. After selecting not more than five points
from their lesson reports, pairs of supervisors agreed on only 12 per
cent of them. This finding must of course be interpreted in relation to
the large number of categories used in the analysis, there being an expected agreement by chance of considerably less than 1 per cent. None
the less, it is remarkable that the supervisors could not, on average,
agree on even one of the five most important points which they would
mention to students.

While the supervisors using the system outlined in this paper did
achieve almost twice as much agreement as those using conventional
procedures, it is *their* lack of agreement which is particularly interesting.
They agreed quite well in their systematic descriptions of the teaching,
and yet they agreed very little in their qualitative evaluations of it. Thus
although the system seems practically feasible and although the
evidence suggests that it could facilitate attainment of the criteria listed
in the introduction, its use is far from sufficient to prevent the advice a
student receives from being largely dependent on the idiosyncracies of
his supervisor.

References

Bellack, A.A. (1966) *et al. The Language of the Classroom,* Teachers' College
    Press, Columbia University.
Cope, E. (1969). 'Students and School Practice', *Educ. for Teaching,* vol. 80,
    pp. 25-35.
Robertson, J.D.C. (1957). 'An analysis of the views of supervisors on the attri-
    butes of successful student teachers', *Brit. J. Educ. Psychol.,* vol. 27, pp. 115-
    26.

Ryans, D.E. (1960). *Characteristics of Teachers, Their Description,Comparison and Appraisal*, American Council on Education, Washington, D.C.

Stones, E. and Morris, S. (1972). 'The Assessment of Practical Teaching', *Educational Research*, vol. 14, no. 2.

White, D.R. (1972). 'The Stirling Lesson-Sampling Instruments: The Preparation, Testing and Trial Use of a Battery of Lesson-Sampling Instruments', unpublished M.Sc thesis, University of Stirling.

Wiseman, S. and Start, K.B. (1965). 'A follow-up of teachers five years after completing their training', *Brit. J. Educ. Psychol.*, vol. 35, pp. 342-61.

4 MICROTEACHING BEHAVIOUR AND ASSESSMENTS OF PRACTICE TEACHING IN SCHOOLS

Gordon MacLeod, Roy Griffiths and Donald McIntyre

Introduction

Brown (1975) has summarised six studies in which performance in microteaching has been related to subsequent assessments of performance on school practice. In general, a substantial correlation has been shown between the scores arising from microteaching, when assessed by the Stanford Teacher Competence Appraisal Guide (Aubertine, 1964; Allen and Fortune, 1966; Kallenbach and Gall, 1969), or by grades from supervisors (Brown, 1973; Spelman, 1975), and the scores assigned to teaching practice performance by supervisors. Whilst these studies, by their correlational nature, cannot show that it is microteaching which is responsible for this relationship, they do also fail to indicate which factors in microteaching performance relate to subsequent 'success' on teaching practice. The aims of this study were, therefore, to correlate specific performance measures on microteaching with global ratings on teaching performance carried out eight months later, and to interrelate these specific performance measures to determine whether empirical support could be provided for the concept of 'skills'.

Design of Study

The microteaching performance data of this study were derived from subjects' performances on an eighteen-minute criterion lesson, carried out at the end of a semester's programme of microteaching in which students were introduced to three microteaching skills — Variation, Clarity of Explanation, and Questioning. For this criterion lesson, subjects were asked to attempt to practise all three skills, and systematic coding of performance was carried out by three observers. (For full details of the semester programme, the criterion lesson and the data coding see chapter 9.)

On completion of the semester course which included microteaching, those fifty-eight students continuing with education undertook a further further semester course of education before going on secondary-school teaching practice for four weeks. During this second semester, all students attended an individual tutorial with one of the three experi-

71

menters, in which the videotape of the criterion lesson was viewed, and systematic feedback was provided on the student's performance of the three skills. Also during this semester, students undertook further university-based practice of teaching with fourth-year non-certificate pupils.

At the end of this second semester, and approximately eight months after teaching their criterion lesson, students embarked on their secondary teaching practice. For this practice, grades (on a five-point scale) were assigned, both by university supervisors and by supervising teachers. The genesis of these teaching practice grades is not clear in that some tutors claim to take account of the school grades in arriving at their own grades, in that the method by which the schools arrive at their grades varies from school to school, and in that some of the university grades represent the consensus view of more than one tutor.

Analysis of Data and Results

To assess the relationships between these two sets of grades, and the microteaching practice of eight months earlier, a correlational analysis was carried out, with its outcomes being shown in table 1.

To determine more clearly the relationship between microteaching performance and university supervisors' grades, a multiple stepwise regression analysis was carried out in which the eight significant single correlates of grade were included as independent variables. The outcomes of this analysis are shown in table 2.

Discussion of Results

It should be noted that three of the components of the skill of Clarity of Explanation (indicated in table 1) occurred infrequently, and care should be taken in interpreting these.

Perhaps the most striking feature of the results of table 1 is the dissimilarity between the pattern of the several significant correlates of university grade, and the solitary significant correlate of school grade. Although university and school grades are significantly correlated ($r = .32$, $p < .05$), this indicates a shared variance of only 10 per cent, and this latter figure, together with the difference between the patterns of correlates of table 1, does show the disparity between the two sets of grades. This disparity is further exemplified by the multiple correlations of all skill components with the two sets of grades. For university supervisors' grades, multiple R is .80 (64 per cent of the variance), whilst for school grades, multiple R is .55 (30 per cent of the variance), thus again suggesting the use of differential criteria, and that

Table 1 Correlations of Skill Components with Teaching Practice Grades

Skill Component	University Grade	School Grade
Variation		
Teacher movement	.23	.14
Teacher gesture	.51***	.41**
Speech pattern change	.36**	.22
Sensory focus change	.24	.11
Verbal pupil participation	.13	.16
Physical pupil participation	.30*	.00
Questioning		
Higher-order questions	.03	.02
Middle-order questions	.13	.01
Follow-up questions	.04	.06
Total number of questions	.50***	.15
Lower-order questions	.46***	.16
Non-follow-up questions	.53***	.16
Clarity of Explanation		
Rule-e.g.-rule +	.25	.13
Explaining links	-.06	.17
Planned repetition +	.18	.10
Use of audio-visual aids	-.01	¬.18
Lack of fluency	-.39**	.11
Lack of continuity	-.16	.08
Vagueness	-.27*	.12
Inappropriate vocabulary +	.01	-.12

+ = low frequency of occurrence   *** (p < .001)
                                              ** (p < .01)
                                               * (p < .05)

Table 2 Multiple Stepwise Regression of Eight Selected Independent Variables on University Grade

Independent Variable	R	$(R^2 \times 100)$ %
Non-follow-up questions	.53	28%
Teacher gesture	.65	42%
Lack of fluency	.74	54%
Physical pupil participation	.75	56%
Lower-order questions	.76	57%
Total number of questions	.76	59%
Change of speech pattern	.77	59%
Vagueness	.77	59%

university supervisors are making use of microteaching skills criteria.

The correlates of university grade seem to imply a regard by univer-

sity supervisors for a high frequency of questioning, for the use of
gesture and variation in speech pattern, for the physical involvement of
pupils, and for fluency and lack of vagueness.

A clearer picture of the criteria used by supervisors can be seen in
table 2. Here, three of the skill components account for over 50 per
cent of the variance in grades, whilst the other five components add
little to the variance accounted for. If the microteaching behaviour of
students is a typical example of their teaching behaviour, then these
data seem to imply that a lesson which is fluent, animated and with
many questions is one which will receive a high grade. Alternatively, it
may be that these three variables are representative of the more
general concepts of skills, and that it is a lesson marked by variation, by
avoidance of unclear explanation, but by a high frequency of any
level of questions which received a high grade.

To explore further the relationships between the single skill components and the predefined sets of components or skills, factor analysis
was used. The initial principal components analysis yielded seven components (henceforth identified as factors so as to avoid confusion with
skill components) with eigenvalues greater than unity, which cumula-
tively accounted for 74 per cent of the variance. The application of the
screentest to the complete principal components solution (Cattell,
1966) suggested no obvious alternative cut-off point, and so it was decided to examine several alternative Varimax solutions, with the number of factors ranging from three (the number of nominal skills) to
seven (Kaiser's criterion), and to accept that solution which fitted best
with our conceptualisation of the skills. Although all solutions seemed
to identify 'skill' factors, it was the five-factor solution with Varimax
rotation (accounting for 61 per cent of the variance) which seemed to
fit the criterion of conceptual clarity best, and this is presented in table
3 with only loadings of greater than .40 being shown.

The interpretation of the factors in table 3 seems relatively simple.
Factor I can be identified as a 'frequency of questioning' factor, with
the high loadings reflecting the high correlations of Follow-up, Lower-
Order and Non-Follow-up Questions with Total Number of Questions
(.52, .89 and .99 respectively).

The second factor is one which clearly identifies the skill of Variation, with five of the six components loading on it, together with a
loading of .44 from Use of Audio-Visual Aids, a loading which is unsurprising given the probable link between a coding of Use of AVA for
Clarity of Explanation and a coding of Change of Sensory Focus for
Variation.

Table 3 Five-Factor Varimax Analysis of Microteaching Skills Performance

		I	II	III	IV	V
T. Movement		–	.71	–	–	–
T. Gesture		–	.70	–	–	–
Speech Pattern Change		–	.63	–	–	–
Sens. Focus Change		–	.74	–	–	–
Verbal P. Participation		–	–	–	–	.67
Physical P. Participation		–	.41	–	–	–
Higher-Order Q's		–	–	–	–	.74
Middle-Order Q's		–	–	–	–	–
Follow-up Q's		.50	–	–	–	.50
Tot. No. Q's		.97	–	–	–	–
Lower-Order Q's		.92	–	–	–	–
Non-follow-up Q's		.96	–	–	–	–
Rule-e.g.-rule		–	–	.75	–	–
Explaining Links		–	–	.73	–	–
Planned Repetition	+ve.	–	–	.87	–	–
Use of Audio-visual aids		–	.44	.44	–	–
Lack of Fluency		–	–	–	.80	–
Lack of Continuity		–	–	–	.68	–
Vagueness	–ve.	–	–	–	.80	–
Inappropriate Vocabulary		–	–	–	–	–

Factor III is one which clearly identifies the four positive components of Clarity of Explanation, while this is complemented by factor IV's identification of three of the four negative components of Clarity of Explanation.

The fifth factor is one which groups together Higher Order Questioning, Follow-Up Questioning and Verbal Pupil Participation, a pattern which again seems conceptually clear and consistent.

The only two skill components which do not load above .40 on any of the five factors are Middle-Order Questions and Inappropriate Vocabulary. Of the five factor solutions examined, it is only the seven-factor one which does show these variables loading at above .40 on any factor. Teacher's use of Inappropriate Vocabulary is found to be opposed to Verbal Pupil Participation (−.75 and +.43 respectively), whilst Middle-Order Questions loads along with Higher-Order Questions and Follow-up Questions (.42, .46 and .49) in opposition to Teacher Movement, Change of Sensory Focus, and Physical Pupil Participation (-.70, -.61 and -.54), suggesting a bipolar factor opposing higher-order questioning behaviour to a set of mainly physical variation behaviours.

In summary, the five-factor solution seems to provide substantial evidence as to the conceptualisation of the listed components as 'skills'. Variation in particular seems to emerge as a consistent skill; Clarity of Explanation splits into its positive and negative parts, perhaps suggesting a differentiation between the two parts of this skill. Questioning, like Clarity of Explanation, is also split into two sections, but this seems more a consequence of the original category system, for unlike the other two skills, the components of Questioning are not independent, but have correlation built in. Overall, therefore, the factor patterns seem to provide fairly satisfactory evidence as to the interrelatedness of the components used to define the skills.

References

Allen, D.W. and Fortune, J.C. (1966). 'An analysis of microteaching: new procedure in teacher education', *Microteaching: a Description*, School of Education, Stanford University.

Aubertine, H.E. (1964). An Experiment in the Set Induction Process and its Application in Teaching, unpublished doctoral thesis, Stanford University.

Brown, G.A. (1973). The effects of training upon performance in teaching situations, unpublished D. Phil thesis, New University of Ulster.

Brown, G.A. (1975). 'Microteaching: Research and Developments', in Chanan, G. and Delamont, S. (eds.), *Frontiers of Classroom Research*, NFER Publishing Company, Slough.

Cattell, R.B. (1966). *Handbook of Multivariate Experimental Psychology*, Rand, McNally, Chicago.

Kallenbach, W.W. and Gall, M.D. (1969). 'Microteaching versus conventional methods in training elementary intern teachers', *Journal of Educational Research*, 63, pp. 136-41.

Spelman, B. (1975). Contrasting Models of Teacher Effectiveness, unpublished D. Phil thesis, New University of Ulster.

PART 3 STUDENTS' EVALUATIONS OF OBSERVED TEACHING

The observation of teaching is a key element in most approaches to teacher preparation. In particular, students on school practice commonly spend more time in the observation of teaching than in any other activity. Yet remarkably little attention appears to have been given to clarifying the purposes of such observation, far less to training students how to set about it or to assessing its effects.

Researchers have found considerable difficulties even in reliably describing predetermined aspects of classroom activity. One should not, therefore, be surprised if the impressions formed by naive student-teachers, without any specification of, or training for, their tasks as observers tend to be vague, crude and idiosyncratic. Yet if students' observations are to contribute to the development of their professional competence or understanding, they must do more than describe; unless it is intended that they should simply imitate the teaching they observe, their professional growth must depend on the ways in which they interpret, explain and form judgements about that teaching. Like other observers, of course, they tend to be quite ready to engage in such interpretative and evaluative activity.

It is, indeed, in the quality of students' evaluations of teaching that one is likely to find the best indication of how much they are gaining from their observations. On one hand, making evaluative judgements appears to be a pervasive feature of observer activity; but, on the other, the process of evaluation incorporates all those other processes — of description, interpretation and explanation — upon which the value of observation is likely to depend, and the quality of an evaluation must depend on the quality of these various other processes.

One of the general goals of the Stirling microteaching programme has been that students should learn to reflect analytically upon their own teaching and that of others. Broadly, analytic reflection implied an attempted objectivity and precision in description, self-critical interpretation and explanation of the observed behaviour of teacher and pupils, and the use of explicit and justified criteria in making evaluations. A thorough elucidation of what was intended by this general goal was, however, a major task; and it is with the undertaking of this task that this section is concerned.

77

In the first of the two papers, an analysis is made of the specific goals which a teacher preparation programme might seek to attain in relation to the characteristics of students' observations of teaching; and as a procedure for operationalising such specific goals, a system is developed for the content analysis of students' unstructured evaluations of observed teaching in terms of their focus, their structure and their validity. In the second paper, this system is used in a quasi-experimental investigation to examine the effects of a microteaching-based course on students' evaluations of teaching.

5 THE ANALYSIS OF STUDENTS' EVALUATIONS OF OBSERVED TEACHING

Clive Millar and Donald McIntyre

What criteria are relevant in assessing the way in which someone has evaluated teaching which he has observed? Since the processes of description and interpretation are implicit in those of evaluation, a satisfactory answer to this question would allow one, in a given context, to clarify the tasks which student-teachers should be asked to undertake when observing teaching, help one to prepare students for such tasks, and enable one to judge the quality of their observations.

In this paper, an attempt is made to answer this question, first by deriving criteria from theoretical models of the logic of evaluation, of classroom teaching, and of the process of acquiring the professional understanding necessary for effective classroom teaching; and second, by developing procedures whereby these criteria can reliably be related to discernible variations among evaluations of observed teaching made by student-teachers.

There appear to have been relatively few previous studies of observers' behaviour in evaluating teaching. Wright, Nuthall and Lawrence (1969) were concerned, as is the present study, with the quality of student-teachers' evaluations. Although their hypothesis that cognitive or affective emphasis would be related to whether students had observed a live lesson or only listened to an audiotape of it was not confirmed, more detailed analysis of their data did lead them to conclude that the students were relatively insensitive to cognitive aspects of the lesson.

Cicirelli (1969), unlike Wright and his colleagues, made no attempt to structure observers' evaluations. From examination of supervisors' reports of observed lessons he derived twenty-three categories of statements and content analysed a sample of reports in terms of these categories. Relating the categorised contents of the reports to supervisors' scores on a test of creativity, he found that, as hypothesised, more creative supervisors tended to attend to more aspects of the observed teaching, to use broader, less specific constructs in assessing teacher performance, and to attend more to teacher-pupil relationships. In relation to the present study, Cicirelli's work is significant in his effective use of observers' unstructured evaluations, in his use of the criterion 'range of categories used', and in his distinction between broad and narrow categories.

While there have been a number of studies of the 'validity' of observers' evaluations of teaching, most of these have been limited to comparisons of the ratings made on predetermined scales by different sets of observers, or to comparisons between such ratings and frequency counts based on systematic observation procedures. An important exception to this rule is the study by Unruh (1968), in which a content analysis of 1,768 free-response judgements on observed lessons was carried out in order to ascertain which of the resulting seventeen categories of judgements gave valid cues in discriminating between good and bad lessons, the criterion being measured achievement of pupils. The results showed that judgements concerned with cognitive rather than affective aspects of teaching were more valid discriminators, particularly judgements on skill in presenting the subject, knowledge of material, and planning and organisation of lessons. Unruh also found that an audio-visual presentation of the lessons permitted much more valid judgements than did audio-recordings, written transcripts or other types of presentation.

General Design of the Present Study

As it was initially conceived, the research problem was seen as being concerned with the characteristics of 'spontaneous' evaluations of observed teaching. This intention to use free-response procedures was confirmed by the finding that it was those previous studies in which such procedures had been used, particularly those of Cicirelli and Unruh, which had been most productive.

The research problem was more precisely defined as follows:

to describe objectively in quantitative terms, and in relation
to explicit criteria of good or valuable judgements,
characteristics of the following aspects of students'
'spontaneous' evaluations of observed teaching:
(a)   the aspects of teaching attended to and the range of aspects
       attended to;
(b)   the structure of evaluative statements;
(c)   the validity of judgements.

In order to develop and test procedures for quantifying characteristics of evaluations, it was necessary to sample the evaluative behaviour of student-teachers. Videotape recordings of lessons were chosen as the form of stimulus because this enabled all observers to evaluate the same lessons, without preventing these lessons from being 'realistic', and because videotapes had been shown by Unruh (1968) to allow judgements of higher validity than other forms of recorded teaching. In order that various different lessons might be evaluated without making unreasonable demands on students' time, four ten-minute microteaching lessons were selected for observation. The four lessons, chosen from a large sample, were chosen because of the marked differences between them in content, teaching strategy and patterns of social interaction. The instructions to students observing the lessons, developed through a series of pilot studies, were as follows:

EXERCISE IN LESSON EVALUATION

1. Please write down on the sheets attached your evaluation of each of the four videotaped lessons you will be shown.
2. You will be given seven minutes to evaluate each lesson.
3. You may make notes while watching the lessons if you think that this will be helpful.
4. In making your evaluation use a different numbered space for each point you make. Do not combine in one space points that are not clearly related.
5. See that each statement you make is clear and explicit. (It may be helpful to assume that your evaluations will be read by someone who has had no professional training for teaching.)
6. Use a separate page for each lesson.
7. Avoid comparisons between lessons.

The attached sheets consisted of blank pages, ruled horizontally with numbered sections each capable of containing a statement of about thirty or forty words. Thus much the most important constraint imposed on the task was the requirement that evaluations be made in the form of a number of separate statements, a requirement which seemed necessary in order to provide units of measurement. The instruction to avoid comparisons was included since it had been found in the pilot studies that a few students judged the lessons primarily in terms of differences between them, with the result that those aspects of the first lesson which caught their attention tended to determine the focus of their evaluations of all the lessons.

The pilot studies had shown that seven minutes allowed enough time for most students to record their views on each lesson. This meant that the entire test-situation would take about seventy minutes and could be completed in one session.

This procedure produced on average five evaluative statements per student per lesson, a total of twenty statements per student.

Aspects of Teaching Attended to

Objectives of Training

Students can learn from their observation of teaching only about those aspects of teaching to which they attend. On the assumption that there are many aspects of teaching about which useful learning can result from observation, one objective of training for observation must therefore be to sensitise students to a wider range of aspects of teaching. The complexity of classroom activity is generally so great that observation must necessarily be highly selective, but this selectivity can vary both in degree and in the extent to which it is deliberate. Whereas the naive observer's attention may unwittingly be concentrated on one limited aspect of what is happening, the trained observer could be expected to attend to a greater variety of aspects of classroom activity because of the wider range of analytical categories at his disposal.

In certain contexts, one might wish students not only to extend the range of their attention, but also to change the focus of their attention. For example, if Wright, Nuthall and Lawrence (1969) are correct in suggesting that students tend to be relatively insensitive to cognitive aspects of teaching, an appropriate objective might be for students to shift the focus of their attention towards cognitive aspects of teachers' behaviour.

Changes in the focus of students' attention might also be appropriate as, in the course of a teacher education programme, their theoretical studies concentrate upon different aspects of teaching. For example, a major concern of the first two semester-courses in the Stirling five-semester programme is with classroom interaction and with the 'tactical' skills required for effective classroom teaching; it would therefore be appropriate that, at this stage of the programme, students' evaluations of observed teaching should show increased emphasis upon these aspects of teaching. It would also be appropriate, at this stage, for students' evaluations to reflect attention to relatively specific aspects of teaching, while at other stages of the programme much broader perspectives on the observed teaching might be appropriate.

Categorisation of aspects of teaching

In order to classify the aspects of teaching attended to in students' evaluations, it was first necessary to develop a generalised description of teaching in terms of a predetermined set of categories. This categorisation should differentiate classroom activity, and particularly the teacher's activity, into a number of clearly distinguished aspects or phases, most of which should be thought to be 'significant' in the sense that they would be aspects of teaching likely to have effects upon pupils. The set of categories of teacher activity should be comprehensive, and it should allow distinctions between phases of teaching in terms of the degree of specificity with which they are identified. The number of categories should be sufficiently large to allow systematic differences in the range and focus of students' attention to become apparent, but small enough for reliable assessment of such differences to be possible; study of previous investigations (Unruh, 1968; Cicirelli, 1969) suggested that about twenty categories would be suitable.

There have been few attempts to provide a general conceptual framework for describing teachers' classroom behaviour, most workers concerned with analysing teachers' behaviour having limited themselves to providing more or less detailed analyses of particular aspects of teaching. One conceptual framework, however, which did provide a starting-point was the account by Bellack and his co-workers (1966) of classroom verbal interaction. Viewing verbal interaction as a 'language game', they found it possible to classify teachers' and pupils' verbal activity in terms of four kinds of 'pedagogical move':

Structuring: moves which set the context for subsequent behaviour
Soliciting: moves designed to elicit a response
Responding: moves fulfilling the expectations of soliciting moves
Reacting: moves occasioned by previous moves, but not directly elicited by them, serving to modify and/or rate what has been said previously.

Bellack found that teachers made only 12 per cent of responding moves but over 80 per cent of each of the other three types. Since our observations suggested that Scottish secondary school teachers tended, if anything, to do even less responding it was decided to subsume the 'responding' category under 'reacting'.

A second modification which seemed necessary for our purposes was the introduction of a further category: 'motivating'. There were two reasons for this. One was that Bellack's study dealt only with verbal interaction, and while those non-verbal activities relating to the logical or substantive development of the lesson could probably be classified in terms of his categories, those concerned with motivation (e.g. 'the warm social climate' he engendered, 'the varied activity of the lesson') could not be. Secondly, it seemed valuable to follow previous studies in distinguishing between evaluations focusing on cognitive or affective aspects of teaching, and this would be facilitated by introducing the 'motivating' category, concerned only with affective aspects of behaviour, and restricting the 'structuring' category relabelled 'explaining', to cognitive aspects. 'Soliciting' was also defined as being concerned solely with cognitive aspects of teaching, but since evaluations of 'reacting' moves might be in terms of either their cognitive or their affective qualities, these evaluations were to be sub-classified in terms of their cognitive-affective emphasis.

The tentative basis of the system for classifying aspects of teaching was thus a division into four phases: *motivating, explaining, soliciting* and *reacting.* It was hypothesised that all evaluations concerned with teachers' interaction with their pupils could be placed in one of these categories. Additional categories thought to be necessary were for evaluations of teachers' personal characteristics (e.g. 'shy', 'aggressive', 'attractive', 'knowledgeable'); for those concerned with the teacher's planning and preparation, labelled *content and organisation* (e.g. choice of content, understanding of content, choice of objectives, general strategy for achieving objectives); and for evaluations focusing on *pupil behaviour.*

To assess the adequacy of this set of broad categories, and to define them with greater precision, it was necessary to try them out on a sample of student evaluations. More fundamentally, it seeemed necessary to classify teaching into a larger number of more narrowly defined categories if variations were to be detected in the range of students' attention or in the specificity with which they identified phases. On the one hand, theoretical considerations gave little guidance on a more detailed analysis; on the other, in order that the classification procedure should be sensitive to aspects of teaching dealt with in a particular course, it seemed best to generate the categories from evaluations made by students who had completed that course.

At the same time, therefore, as the broad categories were being developed on a theoretical basis, more specific categories were generated through the content analysis of evaluations made by a sample of students who had completed the first year of the Stirling course. The list of categories generated in this way was used to code a further sample of evaluative statements by trained students and difficulties of classification were solved either by redefining phases, combining categories or creating new ones.

An important constraint upon the generation of specific categories was that each of them should be a sub-category of one of the four tentatively defined general phases of teachers' interaction with pupils, although modifications to the definitions of these general categories were possible. This classification of specific phases of teaching within four master categories made possible both a distinction between attention to general and specific phases of teaching and a degree of elasticity in the instrument dependent on such a distinction.

The major category 'motivating', for example, had the following six subdivisions:

General statements
Use of variation
Use of materials, audio-visual aids, examples
Encouraging pupil participation
Social climate
Other specific statements.

An evaluative statement to do with motivation could thus be classified as general, specific in one of four defined ways, or specific but undefined. This inclusion of 'general' and 'other specific' categories within each of the four major categories ensured both that all evaluations could be categorised and also that the distinction between general and specific evaluations was consistently maintained.

It would also, of course, have been possible to define sub-categories of 'teachers' personal characteristics', 'content and organisation' and 'pupil behaviour', but this would have produced an unwieldy number of categories and, in the particular context within which the instrument was to be used, our primary concern was with teachers' skills in classroom interaction. The o.ly subdivision made of any of these categories, therefore, was a distinction between cognitive and affective aspects of pupil behaviour. In a different context it might be appropriate, for example, to introduce a number of sub-categories of 'content and organisation' and to ignore the sub-categories of the four phases of interaction.

In formulating the final version of the categorisation system, checks for omissions were made against the list of teaching skills formally dealt with in the Stirling course, against available rating schedules such as the

Stanford Teacher Appraisal Guide, and against the sets of seventeen categories identified by Unruh (1968) and twenty-three categories identified by Cicirelli (1969) in their content analyses of evaluations of teaching.

Since most students' evaluative statements were not obviously concerned with one and only one of the defined categories, it was necessary both to accept that each statement might be coded in several categories and also to establish some rules for coding procedure. As with the definition of categories, these rules were influenced by the emphasis in the first two semester courses at Stirling on teachers' behaviour in interacting with pupils. Thus all statements about a lesson, apart from those dealing solely with content and organisation, were regarded as falling within at least one of the four major categories of teacher behaviour, even if only pupil behaviour was explicitly mentioned. Another rule was that parsimony was to be applied in relation to these four major categories: 'Only code in more than one major phase or in more than one sub-category of a phase if the evaluator is clearly attending to more than one aspect of teaching'. This parsimony principle was not, however, applied so strictly to categories outside the four major phases; unrelated decisions were to be made about which phase, if any, a statement dealt with, about whether it dealt with content and organisation, about whether it dealt with the teacher's personal characteristics and about whether it referred to pupil behaviour.

Detailed definitions of the categories, together with coding instructions, are given by Millar (1972).

The Structure of Evaluative Statements

Objectives of Training

It was suggested in the previous section that a necessary condition for learning to occur in relation to any particular aspect of teaching is that the observer should attend to that aspect of the teacher's activity. But before one can suggest what other characteristics of observer activity might be conducive to useful learning, it is necessary to specify objectives which are hypothesised to be attainable, and worth attaining, through the observation of teaching.

Assuming that uncritical imitation of the observed teaching is not one of these objectives, one may list some possible objectives as follows:

(1) Comprehension of various kinds of problems with which teachers may be faced.

(2) Comprehension of various procedures, techniques or strategies which a teacher might appropriately use in specifiable circumstances.

(3) Comprehension of various factors which may lead teachers and/or pupils to behave in certain predictable ways.

(4) Ability to apply appropriate criteria in judging the value or appropriateness of different aspects of teaching behaviour.

(5) Ability to analyse teachers' and pupils' behaviour, particularly in terms of the influence each has on the other.

(6) Ability to formulate possible courses of action which teachers might take in particular situations, and to decide, in the light of explicit criteria, which of these is preferable.

(7) In relation to each of the last three of the above objectives, a predisposition or, in Krathwohl's (1964) terms, a 'generalised set' to respond to observed teaching situations by using these abilities. (This objective is not, like the previous six, concerned with the cognitive competence of students, but rather with their affective orientations, with *what they do* rather than *what they can do*.)

These objectives (or more precisely, sets of objectives), while not exhausting the possible kinds of learning which might result from the observation of teaching, probably include those with which teacher trainers are most commonly concerned, although few would expect much progress towards these objectives *solely* from the observation of teaching. (However, since explicit statements about the function of observation in teacher-training are rare, it is hazardous to generalise about the objectives which others seek to attain through it, and it must be admitted that the above list may reflect only the distinctive perspective of one teacher-training institution.)

The attainment of some of the objectives listed above does not necessarily involve student evaluation of observed teaching; but the extent to which students are engaging in activities conducive to the achievement of these objectives is likely to be reflected in the evaluations which they make. For one thing, achievement of these objectives would seem to be dependent on the adequacy of students' comprehension of what they observe, which should be reflected in the 'validity' of their evaluations (considered in the next section). But, secondly, the achievement of these objectives, especially objectives (4) to (7), depends on the nature of the tasks which students set themselves in relation to the observed teaching. It is from the 'structure' of their evaluative statements that the best indication can be expected of what these tasks are.

Defining Structural Aspects of Evaluative Statements

The procedure adopted in order to define relevant structural characteristics of evaluative statements was to attempt to relate criteria derived from a simple model of the logical components of any evaluative judgement, and from the objectives outlined above, to observed differences among the statements made by a large sample of trained and untrained student teachers.

The model was that of Toulmin (1958) in the form used by Meux (1963; Meux and Smith, 1964) in his analysis of the logic of evaluation as it occurs in verbal interaction in the classroom. Evaluation in its ideal form was seen to consist of four elements: the *object* to be evaluated; the *claim* – the evaluation of the object in terms such as 'good', 'false', 'desirable', etc.; the *warrant* or criterion by which the evaluation is supported or justified; and the *connecting facts* which show the connection between object and warrant and give the warrant relevance.

When this model is applied to evaluative statements on observed lessons, the object may in some cases be the lesson as a whole, in which case both it and the claim tend to be implicit, with the warrant usually being a description of some aspect of the lesson (e.g. 'The teacher used a lot of visual aids'). In other cases, the object may itself be an aspect of the lesson, sometimes without a warrant (e.g. 'The teacher asked good questions') and sometimes with a warrant given but the claim implicit (e.g. 'The teacher had a *friendly* approach to the children').

Aspects of the model that were used in classifying structural characteristics of statements were: (i) the kind of warrant given, if any; (ii) whether or not a warrant was given; (iii) whether or not connecting facts were given; and (iv) the nature of the claim.

(i) *Type of warrant:* Meux divided warrants into four kinds: application of rules, comparison with criteria, appeal to personal factors, and examination of consequences.

As applied to the evaluation of teaching, distinctions among the first three did not appear to be either of great importance or, in many cases, possible. Use of 'examination of consequences' warrants, however, seemed to reflect just the sort of activity which would facilitate progress towards objective (5) above. The first category for classifying structural aspects of statements was therefore *consequentialism*, the distinction between warrants which dealt with consequences and those which did not. For example, the statement 'His higher order questions bewildered the class' has a consequential warrant, whereas the statement 'He asked lots of higher order questions' does not.

In most cases this distinction was not difficult to make. Borderline cases were those in which the warrant might be said to be implicitly consequential, as in 'The teacher spoke in an interesting way', and those in which inevitable and obvious implications of actions were stated, e.g. 'The teacher's voice hardly rose above a whisper and it was difficult to hear what he said'. Cases of both these types were categorised as nonconsequential.

Although in most consequential warrants studied the cause was teacher behaviour and the consequence pupil behaviour, there were exceptions, and it seemed potentially useful to distinguish between consequences in these terms.

A second basis for classifying evaluative statements was suggested by the fact that the cause-effect links in some of the statements studied were not consequential but *purposive* (e.g. 'He asked questions to gauge the level of the class'). This characteristic of evaluations seemed worth distinguishing because it indicated an approach which not only involved the analytic emphasis of objective (5) but also the more productive, strategic sort of thinking with which objective (6) was concerned. Statements could be both consequential and purposive: 'He played a record to interest the class in the topic, but they found it too embarrassing'.

Although most of the statements coded consequential or purposive consisted of generalisations based upon and confined to relationships observed in a given lesson there were cases where generalisations took a universalistic form. Instead of saying 'X caused Y' a student would say 'Things like X cause things like Y', and instead of saying 'He did X to achieve Y' would say 'The purpose of X is to achieve Y', in both cases generalising beyond observed phenomena. It was decided therefore to sub-categorise consequential and purposive statements as *theoretical* or universalistic as opposed to *observed* or lesson-bound. Although it did not seem possible to determine any clear objectives in terms of this distinction, it did seem to be a classification which might indicate ways in which students' observing behaviour could profitably be modified: one might hypothesise that students are likely to gain most from their observation when they attempt both to identify events which exemplify theoretical generalisations and also to detect the consequences of observed behaviour.

(ii) *Warrant given:* Warrants which were not 'purposive' or 'consequential' could be in terms of rules, personal preferences or external criteria. In those cases where an aspect of the lesson was identified as the object, a warrant might either not be given or be given in terms of a descriptive adjective or adjectival phrase with evaluative connotations (e.g. 'sensitive', 'precise', 'at an appropriate conceptual level', 'confused'). It was judged that students who provided such warrants rather than making unwarranted claims were manifesting behaviour conducive to the achievement of objective (4), learning to apply appropriate criteria to various aspects of teaching behaviour. Such evaluative statements were therefore categorised as *specifically qualified,* in contrast to those statements in which the only adjectives relating to the identified aspect of teaching were in purely evaluative or quantitative terms (such as 'good', 'bad', 'effective', 'successful', 'too little', 'too much').

(iii) *Facts supporting the warrant:* Whenever a warrant took the form of a generalisation some *substantiation* in the form of reference to observed facts was appropriate. For example, the warrant that 'The children found the questions too difficult' might be substantiated by the statement 'Only one pupil answered', an observed fact that backs the assertion. Most claims in the sample of evaluative statements were justified by warrants in the form of generalisations, but few of these were substantiated. It seemed that the habit of backing assertions about teaching with factual references was generally desirable and a necessary component of several of the listed objectives.

(iv) *Nature of the claim:* All evaluations were categorised in terms of three kinds of claim: unqualified *approval;* unqualified *criticism;* and *qualified* approval or disapproval. These categories would allow one to detect any tendency for students to become either hypercritical or open-minded to the extent of being totally uncritical. More positively, one might expect an increased proportion of qualified claims as students become more sensitive to the complexity of classroom teaching.

Categories not derived from the model: In making evaluative statements, students frequently suggested alternative procedures, what they would have done or what should have been done in the observed circumstances. Since activity of this sort appeared to be highly relevant to the ability to formulate courses of action and to choose among them (objective (6)), statements of this type were categorised as *alternativistic.*

One further basis of categorisation was formulated solely on the basis of observed differences among evaluative statements. It became clear that among statements which lacked all the characteristics identified above there was none the less considerable variety in the level of their organisation of ideas and in their general sophistication. A category of *complexity* was therefore defined to include all statements in which distinguishable generalisations were clearly linked to one another. It was postulated that an increase in the 'complexity' of evaluations would be a desirable outcome of training.

Detailed definitions of the structural criteria, together with coding instructions, are given by Millar (1972).

The Validity of Evaluations

Objectives of Training

Any contribution which the observation of teaching might make to the achievement of the objectives outlined at the beginning of the previous section must depend upon the quality of students' perception and interpretation of the teaching they observe. In so far as their perception is distorted or inaccurate, or their interpretation misled, any conclusions which they draw about teaching in general or about what they might attempt in their own teaching are likely to be of little value to them. It follows that an important requirement of evaluations of observed teaching is that they should be valid, not only in the sense that the assertions they contain should square with observed facts but also in the sense that the judgements made should correspond to some criteria of appropriateness and justifiability. The obviously considerable element of subjectivity involved in any assessment of specific judgements about teaching does not make this requirement of validity any less important, although it does make its operationalisation more difficult.

Defining Criteria for Validity

The validity of observers' spontaneous judgements could only be
assessed by comparing them with some 'ideal' set of judgements. To ask
what such judgements might be is to ask, in narrowed context, the
perennial question: 'What are the characteristics of effective teaching?',
for valid judgements are clearly those concerned with aspects of
teaching that influence its success or failure, not those incidental to its
outcomes.

One approach to this problem would be to follow that of Unruh
(1968) and restrict one's set of valid judgements to conclusions which
could be derived in the context of the specific set of lessons observed,
by correlating measured aspects of pupil attainment and behaviour with
aspects of teaching behaviour. But the rigour of this approach is
counterbalanced by the restricted conception of effective teaching
which it would imply. Apart from the problem of demonstrating relationships between characteristics of teaching and pupil attainment,
there are many aspects of teaching which one might hypothesise to
have important long-term effects but which would be unlikely to influence pupil behaviour significantly in the context of one short lesson.

A second approach is to assume that 'good judgements' are those
that attend to characteristics of teaching which are believed to be
generally related to effective learning and which are manifested in the
behaviour of the teacher being observed. While this approach is both
less complex and less restricted than the former, it necessarily involves
elements of subjectivity both in the choice of criteria and in the judgements as to which of these criteria are relevant to a particular lesson.

The decision to use this latter approach was influenced by the belief
that the subjective elements in both these processes could be limited.
On the one hand, the use by trained observers of carefully prepared and
tested systematic observation procedures would allow relatively objective judgements as to the relevance of the general criteria to particular
lessons. On the other, the procedure for assessing student evaluations
was being prepared primarily for use in relation to courses in which
definitions of a variety of teaching skills were presented in precise and
generalised terms and justified as far as possible on the basis of psychological theory and research evidence. The fact that a major concern in
the choice of skills had been that as much justification as possible could
be provided for them, together with the fact that the students' training
had been concentrated upon the comprehension and use of these skills,
made it possible *in this context* to choose the general criteria on a fairly
objective basis.

In order to generate criterion judgements, videotapes of the four ten-minute lessons to be evaluated by students were observed and coded in terms of the battery of instruments developed by White (1972) for use with students on teaching practice after they had completed a micro-teaching-based course like that at Stirling. The battery consists of four systematic observation instruments concerned with 'questioning', 'structure of classroom discourse', 'varying the stimulus' and 'reinforcement and the use of cognitive feedback', together with two sets of rating scales concerned with 'classroom personality and subject mastery' and 'lesson structure'. White's data show agreement among trained observers to be around 70 per cent in most instances, and correlations between raters to be around .70 for most of the rating scales.

For each lesson, four trained observers each used one of the observation instruments and, at the end of the lesson, completed all the rating scales. The patterns of teacher and pupil behaviour recorded on the four instruments, together with the mean scores for each teacher on the rating scales, were expressed graphically as a profile for each lesson. By recording high and low points in the profile of each lesson, a total of forty-seven evaluative statements were generated (e.g. 'very little probing', 'much pupil participation', 'stimulating teaching'). It could not be assumed automatically, however, that characteristics which are generally strengths or weaknesses of teaching need to be such in the context of a specific lesson, and each of the forty-seven judgements was checked for appropriateness in terms of inferred lesson goals and observed effects. This screening led to three judgements of 'higher inference' than the others. Two of these concerned teaching behaviour coded as desirable and subjectively assessed as desirable *in one respect*, but as dysfunctional in another respect; in these two cases, it was concluded that statements could be made approvingly or disapprovingly with equal validity provided the consequences were made explicit. The third, a judgement that the extensive use of the blackboard in one lesson was both unnecessary and confusing, led to a reversal of the initial judgement. The remaining forty-six initial judgements survived the screening and were supplemented by the three higher inference judgements.

Of these forty-nine judgements, twenty-two were positive and twenty-seven negative. They were distributed fairly evenly over the four lessons, with a minimum of eleven for each lesson.

Each student's judgements were compared with the criterion judgements to assess the number of agreements and contradictions. 'Validity scores' were then calculated by expressing the total number of a stu-

dent's judgements corresponding with criterion judgements, less the
number contradicting criterion judgements, as a percentage of the total
number of evaluative statements he had made.

Reliability of Coding

To test the reliability with which evaluative statements could be coded
according to the criteria developed, the sets of statements made by
twenty students, selected at random from groups of trained and untrained students, were coded. One group of three coders, after being
given about seven hours' training, coded statements according to the
'focus' criteria; another group of three, after about fifteen hours'
training, used the 'structure of evaluation' criteria. Two coders, without
practice or training, used the validity criteria.

For those categories for which student totals were sufficiently varied,
product-moment correlations between coders were calculated. These
correlations are given in tables 1a and 1b.

Table 1a Correlations between Coders for Each Category (Focus Criteria)

Focus Categories	Total Number of Codings	r12	r13	r23
Motivating	487	.58	.84	.66
Explaining	399	.85	.80	.79
Soliciting	151	.86	.80	.75
Reacting	95	.91	.77	.86
Number of Specific Phases	—	.66	.45	.53
Cognitive	586	.92	.80	.70
Affective	495	.58	.86	.67
Content and Organisation	198	.90	.81	.71
Teacher's Personal Qualities	92	.87	.95	.82
Pupil Behaviour	811	.82	.36	.63
Pupil Behaviour (Cognitive)	421	.78	-.05	.20
Pupil Behaviour (Affective)	390	.84	.77	.72

The results given in tables 1a and 1b suggest that all these categories can
be used with an adequate degree of reliability, although in two or three
cases, most notably pupil behaviour (cognitive), individual coders were
clearly out of step with the other two.

The frequencies of statements categorised in most of the sub-
categories were too low for meaningful correlations to be calculated between coders. For these, estimates of reliability could only be made in
terms of the percentage agreement among coders in their categorisation
of individual statements.

Table 1b Correlations between Coders for each category (Structural Criteria and Validity)

Structural Categories	Total Number of Codings	r_{12}	r_{13}	r_{23}
Alternativism	174	.79	.91	.62
Consequentialism	328	.66	.79	.80
Purposiveness	80	.80	.79	.72
Theoretical	106	.75	.83	.68
Complexity	724	.68	.82	.67
Specific Qualification	480	.75	.58	.28
Substantiation	109	.28	.78	.51
Approving	442	.93	.96	.95
Critical	546	.97	.96	.98
Qualified	91	.80	.73	.64
Validity	—	.85	—	—

There were wide variations in the reliability with which specific phases of teaching were coded. The average percentage agreement for the fourteen identified specific phases was 54 per cent; for the four 'other specific' categories it was 35 per cent; and for the four 'general' categories it was only 3 per cent. It was concluded that in the operational use of the instrument coding of specific phases should be used only as a basis for finding the *number* of specific phases used by a student.

The structural sub-categories also tended to be used with lower reliability than the main categories; the percentage agreement for 'consequentialism (other than pupil behaviour)' was particularly low, and it was therefore decided to abandon this distinction. It may be worthy of note that the least reliable categories were all defined in residual rather than positive terms.

Stability of Observer Behaviour

A number of characteristics of observers' evaluative behaviour have been defined which would seem on theoretical grounds to be important determinants of how much students are likely to gain from their observation of teaching; and it has been shown that individual differences among observers in terms of these characteristics can be assessed with a fair degree of reliability. But if these individual differences were of a random nature, so that an observer's categorised behaviour on one occasion would not allow one to predict his behaviour on other occasions, coding in terms of these characteristics would be of little value. To demonstrate that this is not the case it is necessary to show that these are relatively stable characteristics of behaviour.

On the other hand, however, programmes of professional training are aimed at changing students' behaviour. To discover differences between two occasions in the evaluative behaviour of individual students might indicate either that the training was having various effects or that there were random variations in the categorised aspects of their behaviour. A check on the consistency of evaluative behaviour was therefore made on a sample of twenty-two students who, although intending to become teachers, had not yet started their course of professional training. They were asked to evaluate the same set of four videotaped lessons on two occasions, twelve weeks apart. Correlations between the two sets of scores are given in Table 2.

Table 2 Product-Moment Correlations between Scores of 22 Untrained Observers on Two Occasions

Focus Categories	r
Range of Specific Phases	.70**
Affective	.16
Motivating	.31
Explaining	.37
Soliciting	.14
Reacting	.72**
Content and Organisation	.03
Teacher's Personal Qualities	.49*
Pupil Behaviour	.72**
Pupil Behaviour (Affective)	.15

Structure Categories	
Alternativism	.68**
Consequentialism.	.51*
Purposiveness	.44*
Theoretical	.08
Complexity	.41
Specific Qualification	.34
Substantiation	.43*
Approving	.72**
Qualified	.14

Validity	.00

*p $<$ .05
**p $<$ .01

As can be seen from table 2, a fair degree of consistency is apparent for only about half the categories. It is perhaps not surprising that little consistency is apparent for several of the focus categories, since schemata for describing teaching are unlikely to be developed among untrained observers, so that training might tend to reduce unsystematic or random responses. If this is the case, a consistency trial with experienced teachers could be expected to give more satisfactory results.

More obviously, it might have been predicted that the proportion of 'valid' evaluations made by untrained students would be a matter of chance. In order to check that this was not the case among students who had received some training, the validity scores obtained by nineteen students on two occasions at the beginning and end of their second education semester were correlated, giving a coefficient of .50. Among trained students, therefore, the ability to make valid evaluations appears fairly stable. The structure categories are concerned with patterns of evaluative behaviour which one might expect to be well-established even among observers unaccustomed to evaluating teaching. It is therefore reassuring that there was a fair degree of consistency in what had appeared on theoretical grounds to be the more important categories — alternativism, consequentialism, purposiveness and substantiation. But the data suggest that there may be little value in retaining the 'theoretical' and 'qualified approval or disapproval' categories, and cast some doubt on the value of the 'specific qualification' and 'complexity' categories.

Conclusion

This study has been an attempt to chart a neglected area of professional performance — to design procedures for analysing spontaneous evaluations of observed teaching and for quantifying tendencies that seem desirable as outcomes of professional education. What has resulted is a rather loose conceptual framework for making judgements about kind and quality of evaluations, a basis both for the definition of objectives of professional education and for the evaluation of its outcomes.

Designed as it is to be sensitive to behaviour valued at one stage of the training programme of a specific department, this framework is not likely to be regarded as entirely suitable for similar use in other institutions. What it may do, however, is provide a starting point, conceptually and procedurally, for the development of other course-based instruments.

The most direct ways of applying the procedures which have been devised are in the assessment of progress towards the objectives of a course, in the comparison of different procedures directed towards the same objectives and in the diagnosis of individual students' strengths, weaknesses and biases.

A wider application of these procedures may, however, be in the study of professional ideologies. Evaluations of observed teaching may reflect more closely the attitudes with which teachers approach their own teaching than do responses to the questionnaires and attitude scales in terms of which teachers' ideologies have been studied to date. It would be valuable, therefore, to explore the relationships between 'focus', 'structure' and 'validity' scores and, on the one hand, characteristics of teachers' or student-teachers' own teaching, and on the other, scores on a variety of established instruments including educational attitude scales and tests of creative thinking, problem solving and such personality characteristics as abstractness-concreteness (cf. Harvey et al., 1968).

A further area for research and development lies in the use of these procedures in studying the evaluative styles of supervisors of student-teachers, both as a means of providing feedback to them and as a contribution to the study of professional socialisation. In the absence of analytic procedures, the spontaneous judgements made by supervisors and by the teachers with whom students are placed on teaching practice have to date been largely protected from scrutiny, although they may be the most common and influential form of moulding professional behaviour.

References

Bellack, A.A. et al. (1966). *The Language of the Classroom,* Teachers' College Press, Columbia University.

Cicirelli, V.G. (1969). 'University supervisors' creative ability and their appraisal of student teachers' classroom performance: an exploratory study', *J. Educ. Res.* 62, 375-81.

Harvey, O.J., Prather, M.S., White, B.J. and Hoffmeister, J.K. (1968). 'Teachers' beliefs, classroom atmospheres and student behavior', *Amer. Educ. Res. J.* 5(2), 151-66.

Krathwohl, D.R. et al. (1964). *Taxonomy of Educational Objectives: Handbook II: Affective Domain,* Longmans, London.

Meux, M. (1963). 'Evaluating operations in the classroom' in Bellack, A.A. (ed.), *Theory and Research in Teaching,* Teachers College Press, Columbia, 11-24.

Meux, M. and Smith, B.O. (1964). 'Logical Dimensions of Teaching Behavior', in Biddle, B.J. and Ellena, W.J. (eds.), *Contemporary Research on Teacher Effectiveness,* Holt, Rinehart and Winston, New York, pp. 127-64.

Millar, C.J. (1972). A procedure for analysing evaluations of observed teaching and its application in measuring outcomes of professional education. unpublished MSc thesis, University of Stirling.

Toulmin, S. (1958). *The Uses of Argument,* Cambridge University Press.

Unruh, W.R. (1968). 'The modality and validity of cues to lecture effectiveness', in Gage, N.L. et al., *Explorations of the Teacher's Effectiveness in Explaining: Technical Report No. 4,* Stanford Centre for Research and Development in Teaching.

White, D. (1972). The Stirling Lesson Sampling Instruments: The Preparation and Testing of a Battery of Instruments for Sampling Teaching, unpublished M.Sc. thesis, University of Stirling.

Wright, C.J., Nuthall, G.A., and Lawrence, P.J. (1969). 'A Study of Student-Teachers' Perceptions of Observed Lessons', *Educ. Res. Newsletter,* Dept. of Education, University of Canterbury, 2, 5-26.

6 CHANGES IN THE EVALUATIVE BEHAVIOUR OF STUDENT TEACHERS RESULTING FROM PROFESSIONAL EDUCATION

Clive Millar

Introduction

The purpose of this chapter is to describe how the procedures for analysing students' evaluations of observed teaching explained in chapter 5 have been applied in order to discover, under conditions as close to experimental as possible, ways in which student teachers at the University of Stirling improve in their ability to evaluate teaching as a result of professional education.

In chapter 5 'improvement' in evaluative ability was analysed in terms of three areas — focus of attention, structure of evaluative statements and validity of judgements — and an attempt was made to show the relationship between such aspects of evaluative behaviour and general objectives of professional education for teaching. While the same direction of change in structural aspects of evaluative statements and in validity might be expected as the outcome of any course of professional education, in the case of 'focus' criteria the decision as to what shifts of attention are to be seen as desirable can be made only in relation to the content and emphasis of the programme preceding the evaluations to be analysed. It is necessary, therefore, before defining in specific terms the changes in evaluative behaviour expected of University of Stirling students, to give a brief account of the course to which they were exposed.

The students selected as the main experimental group in this study were those undergoing the first semester of a five-semester course of professional education, their programme focusing by means of micro-teaching and theoretical study on cognitive aspects of communication in the classroom, in particular on the skills of questioning for feedback, clarity of explanation, use of examples, higher-order questioning and probing. It was expected that students would become sensitised to these skills and aware of their strategic use in pursuing educational objectives.

In addition, the evaluative behaviour of a group of students undergoing their second semester of professional education was studied as a possible source of confirmatory information, to gain evidence about duration and pace of change and to see the effects of change in course focus on already trained perceptions. The difference between these first and second semester courses lay in the aspects of classroom interaction emphasised, the second semester being concerned with affective rather than cognitive components of interaction, with classroom climate, motivation and reinforcement, as well as with the skills of reacting appropriately to pupil contributions.

All 'improvements' in evaluative behaviour that could be expected as a result of these courses are summarised, with brief justifications, below.

Definition of Course Objectives

A. *'Focus' Goals for First Semester Students*

As a result of their first semester of professional education (concentrating on cognitive aspects of communication) students will

(1) *pay less attention to affective aspects of teacher behaviour* both because the cognitive domain has been emphasised in course work and microteaching and because it is likely that untrained observers of teaching 'are more likely to be aware of the personal satisfactions and frustrations of the participants than they are of the learning of content that is taking place' (Wright, Nuthall and Lawrence, 1969, p. 6).

(2) *pay increased attention to explaining,* and

(3) *pay increased attention to soliciting* because the technical skills learned during the semester fall within these areas of teacher performance.

(4) *pay less attention to affective aspects of pupil behaviour* for reasons given in (1) above.

(5) *pay increased attention to all pupil behaviour* because procedures for analysing classroom interaction stressed reciprocal effects of teacher and pupil behaviour and criteria of teaching effectiveness were shown to rest on desirable pupil response.

(6) *pay less attention to content and organisation of lesson* It is probable that increased sensitivity to the use of technical skills and greater specificity of focus will tend to reduce the proportion of statements of a global nature.

(7) *pay less attention to teacher's personal qualities* because of the emphasis of the microteaching programme on performance rather than personality, training in the use of systematic observation procedures and training in focusing on specific skills.

(8) *increase the range of phases of teaching attended to*
as a result of sensitisation to previously 'invisible' phases of teaching
and the acquiring of technical terms for describing them.

(9) *show greater discrimination from lesson to lesson in specific
phases of teaching attended to*
Not only should the range of phases of teaching attended to widen
but the phases emphasised by a group of trained observers should
tend to vary more consistently from lesson to lesson than those emphasised by untrained observers, in that trained observers can be expected to have developed norms of appropriate performance in
various salient areas of teaching skill and to be alert to deviations
from and correspondence to these norms.

B. 'Structure' Goals for First Semester Students

As a result of their first semester of professional education students will
increase the proportion of evaluative statements that are

(1) *'consequential'*
because cause-effect analysis permeates the course of professional
education, the effectiveness and appropriateness of skills and
strategies being judged by their consequences for pupil performance.

(2) *'purposive'*
for reasons given in (1) above and possibly because closer identification with the observed teacher and, therefore, an increased tendency
to infer intention might result from practical involvement in microteaching.

(3) *'substantiated'*
because the use of systematic observation procedures in microteaching encourages generalisations about observed teaching that are
backed by objective evidence.

(4) *'alternativistic'*
probably because students who have experienced several teach-
reteach cycles develop a habit of considering alternative strategies
for improving on past performance, possibly through identification
as 'fellow craftsmen' with observed teachers.

(5) *'complex'*
for reasons mentioned in (1) and (2) above and possibly because the
experience of discussing playbacks of microteaching with supervisors
and peers may cause a hesitancy to make statements that appear too
simple or unequivocal.

(6) *'specifically qualified'*

because an increasingly sophisticated technical vocabulary is acquired during professional education.

(7) *'qualified judgements'*

both because judgements of supervisors and peers are likely to have provided models of qualification and approval and because a growing awareness of the complexity of the teaching-learning situation will probably make for increased tentativeness in expressing approval or disapproval.

C. *'Validity' Goals for First Semester Students*

As a result of their first semester of professional education students will increase the proportion of judgements made that coincide with criterion judgements both because of their sensitivity to a wider range of criteria associated with effective teaching and because of their training in objective observation.

D. *'Focus' Goals for Second Semester Students*

'Focus' goals (5) to (9) for first semester students apply equally to second semester students, while the following goals apply only to second semester students:

(1) *pay increased attention to affective aspects of teacher behaviour*

because the affective domain has been stressed in course-work and microteaching.

(2) *pay increased attention to reacting*

because technical skills emphasised fall mainly within this area of teacher performance.

(3) *pay increased attention to affective aspects of pupil behaviour*

for the reason given in (1) above.

E. *'Structure' and 'Validity' Goals for Second Semester Students*

These are identical to those for first semester students.

Experimental Design

In all, three groups of students were examined for changes in their evaluative behaviour.

The main experimental group (group A) was drawn from those students undertaking their first semester of a professional course in education.

The second experimental group (group B) consisted of those students, one year senior to those in group A, undertaking their second semester course in education.

A control group of students who had not undertaken, and were not immediately undertaking, education courses was also used. The very real problem of non-equivalence between control and experimental groups was greatly helped (fortuitously) by an administrative decision to allow entry to the first semester of professional education at two points — at the beginning of a student's second or third semester — though a choice was required before the end of the first semester. This meant that while one group of students (group A) underwent professional education, another, equally committed to a first course of professional education and presumably no different in recruitment or vocational orientation, was available as a control group. In spite of this, without random assignment to groups, equivalence could not be taken for granted and it was decided to include pretests within the design rather than using only a post-test. Thus the design of the study was a 'non-equivalent (pretest, post-test) control group' one (Campbell and Stanley, 1963).

Testing, Scoring and Statistical Treatment

In the first week of term following the mid-year vacation all first and second semester students were asked to evaluate videotaped lessons during normal course time. (For rules of procedure see chapter 5.) It was made clear that this pretest, though carried out for purposes of research, not assessment, was regarded as an important component of their programme and it was hoped that all would participate. There were no refusals. One hundred and twenty-four first semester students completed the pretest (out of a possible 131) and a random one in two sample of their response sheets was selected for coding. Twenty-three second semester students — out of a class of twenty-six — completed the pretest. Controls were more elusive. Pretests could not be scheduled during course time and late afternoon sessions were arranged which were attended by thirty out of a possible fifty students.

Post-tests were scheduled twelve weeks later, towards the end of the semester before the start of examinations. These were again regarded as part of the course programme for first and second semester students and arranged during normal class times. Controls were again requested to attend late afternoon sessions. Of the original sample of sixty-two first semester students fifty completed the post-test and formed the first experimental group (group A). Nineteen of the original twenty-three second semester students attended the post-test session and these formed the second experimental group (group B). Twenty-two controls (out of thirty) completed both pre- and post-tests and formed the control group.

The pretest response sheets of all three groups were combined, arranged in random order and coded according to criteria dealt with in chapter 5 by one coder ignorant of students' names or groupings. The same procedure was followed with post-test response sheets twelve weeks later. For all categories of evaluative behaviour pretest scores of each student were subtracted from post-test scores to give individual gain scores and t-tests were applied to differences in mean gain scores between experimental and control groups in order to test a range of null hypotheses.

Statement of Null Hypotheses

In the case of 'structure' and 'validity' criteria null hypotheses are identical for first and second semester students.

A. 'Structure' of Evaluations

There will be no difference between the gain scores of first and second semester students (groups A and B) and controls on the following criteria:

(1) consequentialism
(2) purposiveness
(3) substantiation
(4) alternativism
(5) complexity
(6) specific qualification
(7) qualification of judgements.

B. 'Validity' of Evaluations

There will be no difference between the gain scores of first and second semester students (groups A and B) and controls, in terms of the proportion of judgements made that coincide with criterion judgements.

C. 'Focus' of Evaluations

There will be no difference between the gain scores of first semester students (group A) and controls on the following criteria:

(1) attention to explaining
(2) attention to soliciting.

There will be no difference between the gain scores of second semester students (group B) and controls on the following criterion:
    (1) attention to reacting.

There will be no difference between the gain scores of both first and second semester students (groups A and B) and controls on the following criteria:
    (1) attention to affective aspects of teaching
    (2) attention to affective aspects of pupil behaviour
    (3) range of phases of teaching attended to
    (4) attention to all aspects of pupil behaviour
    (5) attention to content and organisation of lessons
    (6) attention to teacher's personal qualities
    (7) degree of discrimination from lesson to lesson in specific phases of teaching emphasised.

Results and Interpretation

A. 'Focus' Criteria

Nine changes in emphasis on phases of teaching were expected for group A (first semester students). In table 1a the gain scores of group A and controls on 'focus' criteria relevant to eight of these are compared. Results show that of eight null hypotheses defined for group A six must be rejected, five at the .01 level. These confirmatory results can be summarised as follows:

(1) By the end of their first semester of profession education students show an increase in the amount of attention paid to cognitive, as opposed to affective, aspects of teacher behaviour. ($p < .01$)
(2) They pay more attention to teacher questioning. ($p < .01$)
(3) They show an increase in the amount of attention paid to cognitive, as opposed to affective, aspects of pupil behaviour. ($p < .01$)
(4) They appear to pay more attention to all aspects of pupil behaviour. ($p < .05$) (See discussion below.)
(5) They pay less attention to the teacher's personal qualities. ($p < .01$)
(6) They increase the range of phases of teaching attended to. ($p < .01$)

Change in the amount of attention paid to 'content and organisation of lessons' is in the direction expected, though not significant at the .05 level. Only in the case of teacher's explanations does the direction of change contradict expectations, and this only to a slight extent ($t = .058$, 70 d.f.).

Table 1a Gain Scores of Experimental Groups A and B Compared with Control Group on 'Focus' Criteria

'Focus' Categories		A Experimental Group A (N=50)	t_{AC}	C Control Group (N=22)	t_{BC}	B Experimental Group B (N=19)
1. Affective aspects of teacher behaviour	M S.D.	-15.0 18.3	3.13**	- 0.1 19.2	1.05	5.4 13.7
2. Explaining	M S.D.	2.3 18.2	0.58	5.0 16.2	–	– –
3. Soliciting	M S.D.	8.6 9.6	5.19**	- 4.2 9.8	–	– –
4. Affective aspects of pupil behaviour	M S.D.	-21.0 19.2	3.07**	- 5.1 22.6	1.19	3.1 21.2
5. All pupil behaviour	M S.D.	2.9 20.0	2.61*	- 9.7 15.8	2.98**	4.9 15.4
6. Content and organisation of lesson	M S.D.	- 5.4 12.8	1.00	- 2.2 12.1	1.28	- 7.2 13.1
7. Teacher's personal qualities	M S.D.	- 8.6 8.3	2.93**	- 1.9 10.5	1.17	1.8 9.6
8. Range of phases	M S.D.	2.3 2.6	3.67**	0.1 1.4	0.08	0.1 1.8
9. Reacting	M S.D.	– –	–	- 0.4 5.0	1.88	3.6 8.4

*$p < .05$
**$p < .01$

It appears then, that the first semester programme focusing on cognitive aspects of communication in the classroom is successful in changing ways in which students focus on observed teaching and in achieving a range of 'sensitivity' goals.

The picture is different for second semester students (group B). Only one of eight null hypotheses can be rejected by the results of comparison between group B and control group gain scores also shown in table 1a. Group B's relative increase in attention to 'all pupil behaviour' is significant at the .01 level, though this result is of doubtful validity. Changes in 'focus' on other criteria, though not reaching acceptable levels of significance, are with only one exception (attention to 'teacher's personal qualities') in the direction expected, group B showing some increase in attention paid to affective phases of teaching and affective aspects of pupil behaviour and some decrease in emphasis on 'content and organisation of lessons', while the score for range of phases of teaching attended to remains steady.

The marked drop in the control group's emphasis on pupil behaviour suggested that there might have been an appreciable drift in standards from pre to post-test in coding this category. However, a recoding of both pre- and post-test evaluations of a random sample (N = 15) of students from all groups and a comparison of gain scores derived from original separate codings and additional mixed codings indicated that drift had in fact taken place in the direction opposite to that expected (t = 2.5, 28 d.f.) and that the drop in attention to pupil behaviour was both real and larger than anticipated. This change in control group 'focus' on pupil behaviour, for which no adequate explanation can be given, means that it would be unwise to conclude that either first or second semester students had shown a significant increase in emphasis on pupil behaviour in spite of significant differences in control and experimental group gain-scores.

Changes in focus for group B are clearly far less marked than those for group A. The main reason for this is probably that a considerable amount of change in sensitivity to phases of teaching had taken place among second semester students before the pretest, during their first semester, and although change continued in directions hypothesised it did so more slowly. This is likely to be the case for such categories as 'range of phases of teaching attended to', 'attention to pupil behaviour', 'content and organisation of lesson' and 'teacher's personal qualities', where change in focus was assumed to be continuous over both semesters. In those categories where a reversal of first semester trends was expected among group B students — attention to affective aspects of teacher and pupil behaviour — the lack of such reversals to show significance may probably be accounted for by the suggestion that once a relatively high level of attention to cognitive aspects of teaching has been learned this is not lost as a result of change in course emphasis. What is achieved by the experience of the second semester seems more in the nature of a balance between cognitive and affective emphasis, in contrast to the heavy affective emphasis at the start of training and the strong swing towards a cognitive emphasis by the end of the first semester. It is worth noting that marked differences between group B pretest scores on the one hand and group A and control pretest scores on the other correspond with significant group A gain-scores over the semester, providing confirmation that the first semester produces changes in the following focus categories:

in attention paid to affective phases of teaching;
to affective aspects of pupil behaviour;

to soliciting;
to teacher's personal qualities;
and in range of phases of teaching attended to.

One further change related to sensitivity to phases of teaching was hypothesised: that phases of teaching emphasised by a group of trained observers would vary more consistently from lesson to lesson than those emphasised by untrained observers. If the degree of 'popularity' of phases (judged in terms of mean 'focus' scores of a group of observers) did not vary appreciably from lesson to lesson the group could not be discriminating between lessons in any consistent way, at least as far as focusing behaviour was concerned. On the other hand, clear variation in group emphasis on phases of teaching from lesson to lesson would indicate systematic group shifts in attention in response to differences in observed teaching.

What was required was a procedure for estimating the degree of overall association between the four rankings of mean 'focus' scores produced by each student group in response to the four observed lessons, and this need was met by Kendall's coefficient of concordance. A high coefficient of concordance (W) would mean low discrimination, the same categories receiving most attention from the group as a whole irrespective of the lesson, while a low W would mean high discrimination, different categories being popular in different lessons. Clearly, both group A and group B should have a lower W on post-test performance than the control group, while group B should have a lower W than either group A or the control group on pretest performance.

Table 1b gives coefficients of concordance for pre- and post-test responses for all three groups. The rankings from which W was derived were based on the total number of codings for each student group of

Table 1b Coefficients of Concordance of Group 'Focus' Scores on Four Lessons

		Control Group	Group A	Group B
Pretest	W	.51	.35	.23
	N. Ranks	9	8	11
Post-test	W	.35	.43	.42
	N. Ranks	8	13	10

each specific phase of teaching (not 'general' or 'other specific' categories), phases receiving fewer than 5 per cent of the overall aggregate being excluded. Results are contradictory. As far as pretest performance is concerned the degree of association between phase-rankings on different lessons is, as expected, significantly lower for group B than for controls, and to a lesser extent for group A, implying that trained students do, in fact, vary phase emphasis more systematically. On post-test performance, however, controls have a lower, not a higher W than either group A or group B and in terms of the assumptions on which the interpretation of coefficients of concordance have rested must be assumed to have improved in discrimination while trained groups have not. This is not impossible, but it is far more likely that group discrimination among lessons is simply not being adequately measured by these procedures and they can, therefore, provide no evidence for the rejection of null hypotheses. It cannot be claimed on the basis of both pre-test and post-test performance that trained students differ from un-trained in the degree to which they consistently vary their emphasis on phases of teaching from lesson to lesson.

A. *Structure Criteria*

The mean gain-scores on 'structure' criteria of group A and controls are compared in table 2. It had been expected that for each of these criteria the scores of group A would show a significant increase over the semester. In fact, only in three cases is the difference between group A and control group gain scores significant at above the .05 level; for 'purposiveness', 'complexity' of evaluative statements and 'qualification of judgements'. Results in the remaining four categories are equivocal, first semester students having higher gain-scores than controls for 'consequentialism' and 'substantiation', and lower gain-scores for 'alternativism' and 'specific qualification'.

Also compared in table 2 are the mean gain-scores of group B and controls. It had been expected that second semester students would continue to show an increase in the proportion of evaluative statements containing these seven 'structural' characteristics. In fact, in no case is there a significant difference between group A and control gain-scores, nor is there a clear trend in non-significant changes in the direction expected. The structure scores of second semester students are as likely to decrease relative to control group scores as they are to increase. Group B pre-scores do, however, provide a small degree of confirmation of expected changes in that for all seven 'structure' categories they are higher, though often only slightly, than both group A and control pre-scores.

The fact that the few significant differences obtained are partly at

Table 2 Gain Scores of Experimental Groups A and B Compared with Control Group on 'Structure' Categories

Structure Categories		A Experimental Group A (N=50)	t_{AC}	C Control Group (N=22)	t_{BC}	B Experimental Group B (N=19)
1. Consequentialism	M	- 4.5	0.61	- 7.3	0.10	- 7.8
	S.D.	16.9		20.4		12.0
2. Purposiveness	M	1.6	1.99*	2.7	0.61	- 1.0
	S.D.	8.8		7.2		10.2
3. Complexity	M	- 0.8	2.49*	-14.3	0.73	- 9.5
	S.D.	19.6		24.6		15.3
4. Alternativism	M	- 5.0	1.07	- 2.0	0.01	- 1.2
	S.D.	11.8		7.7		16.3
5. Specific Qualification	M	- 5.2	0.86	- 1.3	0.57	- 3.8
	S.D.	19.4		13.0		15.2
6. Substantiation	M	7.1	1.22	3.9	1.69	- 0.8
	S.D.	11.3		8.1		9.6
7. Qualified Judgement	M	1.9	2.04*	- 2.8	1.14	1.1
	S.D.	8.7		9.6		12.0

*$p < .05$

least the result of 'drops' in control group performance rather than gains in experimental group performance makes even these confirmatory results open to question. In particular, the significant difference in gain-scores between group A and controls in 'complexity' of evaluative statements can be called a 'gain' by the experimental group only if it can be shown that there has in fact been some drift in standards during the twelve-week interval between pre- and post-test coding, leading to stricter application of criteria for the admission of statements to the category of 'complexity' during post-test coding. This would mean that the drop in the control group performance is really a gain in experimental group performance. To check whether some such drift had in fact occurred a random sample of thirty group A, B and control group pre- and post-test response sheets were mixed together and re-coded at one sitting and the gain-scores obtained in this way compared with those obtained as the result of separate codings. On none of the 'structure' variables was a significant difference found, indicating that the drop in control group scores was not an artefact caused by drift.

There are two tendencies that call for an explanation: the tendency for the majority of control group scores to drop while group A scores remain relatively stable, and the overall tendency for post-test 'structure' scores, especially those of group B and control, to be lower than pretest scores. A possible explanation, though a highly speculative one, is that groups differ in their attitudes to the post-test situation. In general students may be less inclined to take the task of evaluating lessons as seriously on the second occasion as they did on the first. They are being required to respond to the same lesson as before and may feel some irritation at repeating a task without any clear idea of the point of it. This attitude may well express itself in greater casualness and less explicitness in the formulation of evaluative statements, which must result in reduced 'structure' scores particularly in the case of 'complexity' of statements. It is probable that controls who had developed no rapport with education department staff and who had given up free time to repeat an exercise with little relevance to their experience, would feel this more strongly than group A students completing their first semester, who are likely to have perceived pre- and post-tests in terms of 'before and after' performances, despite their ignorance of relevant criteria.

It is possible that 'structural' aspects of evaluative statements are very susceptible to change in observers' definitions of and attitudes to test situations and that test-retest interactions may differ in complex ways for different groups while having, in general, a depressing effect on 'structure' scores. It is likely, too, that changes in orientation assumed to be reflected with consistency in structural aspects of evaluative statements take far longer to develop than the twelve weeks covered by the period of the experimental study and that expectations were therefore unrealistic. A third interpretation is that the programme of professional education for teaching at the University of Stirling does not develop the desired analytical orientation towards teaching or that if it does such an orientation finds no expression in ways in which teaching is evaluated measurable by these procedures.

C. *Validity of Evaluations*

Gain-scores for 'validity' of evaluations are compared for group A and controls, and for group B and controls in table 3. In neither case are differences significant, group A showing an increase in the expected direction, while group B actually drops in level of 'validity' relative to the control group. However, the fact that the pretest 'validity' score of group B is very much higher than that of either controls or group A, taken together with the fact that group A does show some increase in score, suggests that the first semester of professional education has at least some effect on 'validity' of evaluations.

Table 3 Gain Scores of Experimental Groups A and B Compared with
Control Group on the Validity criterion

Validity Gain Scores	A Experimental Group A	t_{AC}	C Control Group	t_{BC}	B Experimental Group B
M	4.4	0.89	0.9	1.05	- 4.5
S.D.	14.6		17.3		14.9

Conclusion

The kind of evaluative behaviour most affected by professional education at the University of Stirling is clearly sensitivity to phases of
teaching or 'focusing', the first semester course producing changes in
the amount of attention paid to cognitive and affective aspects of
teacher and pupil behaviour, to pupil behaviour as a whole, to questioning, to personal qualities of teachers and in the range of phases of
teaching attended to. Changes in 'focus' take place far more markedly
in the first than in the second semester, though change in course emphasis in the second semester is clearly reflected in change in focus.
Students appear to begin professional education with a bias towards an
affective focus, swing to a strong cognitive emphasis by the end of the
first semester and achieve something of a balance by the end of the
second.

In contrast, the experience of professional education at these early
stages appears to have little effect on the 'structure' of evaluative statements, though there is some evidence that gradual change may be taking
place. If, as has been argued, certain of these structuring tendencies
indicate a high degree of internalisation of basic orientations this result
is to be expected. The position is similar in the case of the 'validity' of
evaluations. Although it cannot be claimed that professional education
increases the validity of judgements the evidence points in this direction.

Clearly the procedure developed for analysing focus of attention has
been validated to the extent that changes over a semester in 'focus'
scores have taken place in directions hypothesised in the light of course
objectives, whereas procedures for dealing with 'structure' and 'validity'
have received no such validation. Although this may be a reflection on
the usefulness of the criteria used, judgement must be reserved until
such a time as 'structure' and 'validity' instruments have been applied
to the evaluations of students who have undergone a far longer period

of professional education than one semester.

This application of procedures for analysing evaluations of observed teaching in studying outcomes of professional education has been one approach to meeting a current need for a fresh orientation in research on teacher education, expressed by B. Othanel Smith in these terms:

> Perhaps the time has come when those who are engaged on research in teacher education should take more seriously the problems of determining how the theoretical knowledge of pedagogy can be rendered more effective in controlling the behaviour of teachers both in the classroom and in their pre- and post-classroom activities. (Smith, 1971)

This study has been concerned not with values or attitudes assumed to underlie professional action but with a central aspect of professional behaviour itself — the perception, interpretation and evaluation of observed teaching — and has shown that to some extent at least the combination of theoretical study and microteaching at the University of Stirling is effective in influencing this behaviour.

References

Campbell, D.T. and Stanley, J.C. (1963). 'Experimental and quasi-experimental designs for research on teaching.' In Gage, N.L. (ed.), *Handbook of Research on Teaching,* Rand McNally, Chicago, pp. 171-246.
Smith, B.O. (1971). *Research in Teacher Education: A Symposium,* Introduction, Prentice-Hall.
Wright, C.J. Nuthall, G.A. and Lawrence, P.J. (1969). 'A study of student-teachers' perceptions of observed lessons', *Educ. Res. Newsletter,* Dept. of Education, University of Canterbury, 2, 5-26.

PART 4 EXPERIMENTAL STUDIES OF MICROTEACHING PROCEDURES

Much of the research which has been conducted elsewhere into microteaching has been directed towards resolving specific issues which arise in the planning of microteaching programmes: should X be included in the programme, and if so, will form X_1 or form X_2 be more effective? Given the specificity of such questions, it has generally been seen to be appropriate to use experimental designs in their investigation.

The curriculum development context within which this research project was conducted led to a need to answer many such planning questions; and where these questions appeared to have some general significance, it was sometimes possible to conduct experiments in the hope of finding answers. The studies reported in this section are all of this experimental kind, concerned with decisions which any potential user of microteaching has to make.

The first of these studies exemplifies very well the interaction between practical decision-making problems and questions of more general significance. When there was, at one stage, a sharp increase in the number of students taking the Stirling course in education, problems arose about the provision of facilities and staff to maintain the microteaching programme for all students. At the same time, research elsewhere had suggested that the provision of a supervisor at the feedback stage might not contribute to the effectiveness of microteaching. This study was therefore concerned with whether it was possible, in certain hypothesised ways, to reduce the provision per student without reducing the effectiveness of microteaching; and a major variable was whether or not a supervisor was present at the feedback stage.

Since pilot studies had suggested considerable variation in supervisors' behaviour, the second investigation reported in this section was initiated into the effects of different kinds of supervisory strategies. One of the values of this investigation was the contribution it made to clarifying the different possible roles which a supervisor can fulfil.

The third of these experimental studies was undertaken to investigate the simple but remarkably neglected question of whether students' microteaching practice of a skill, as opposed to simply having the skill clearly defined for them, aids their acquisition of the skill. A related question was whether instruction and practice in procedures for analysing one's teaching in terms of the skill is a factor in determining how useful the practice is. The results of this study appear to raise neglected questions about interactions between the procedures of training, the skills in which training is being given, and the subject-specialism of the student-teacher.

The fourth study, by Gilmore, examined the relative effects of positive and negative videotape models on skill acquisition. This is one of the few experimental studies on components of microteaching, at Stirling or elsewhere, which has produced outcomes which are clearly interpretable in terms of the basic question underlying the research design.

The final paper in this section reports an investigation by Butts in the context of a one-year postgraduate course, a more constricting context than that of the Stirling undergraduate course, and one which therefore raises different problems. Butts' experiment was concerned with the effects, as judged both by systematic observation and by tutor ratings, of microteaching training on the classroom questioning behaviour of graduate teachers of history. Of equal interest, however, are the issues which arose in his collaboration with subject specialists in order to formulate the teaching skills they considered important, and to assess reliably the students' use of these skills.

7 MICROTEACHING PRACTICE, COLLABORATION WITH PEERS AND SUPERVISORY FEEDBACK AS DETERMINANTS OF THE EFFECTS OF MICROTEACHING

Donald McIntyre

The questions investigated in this experimental study emanated from a need to solve practical problems which arose in relation to the Stirling microteaching programme. While the programme was being established, student numbers were small and it was therefore relatively easy to provide a programme of the Stanford type for all students. As numbers increased, however, it became increasingly difficult and expensive to maintain this programme in its original form: accommodation, videotape feedback and supervisory feedback requirements increased in direct proportion to student numbers. It was therefore necessary to consider ways in which the programme might be modified so that comparable benefits might be attained with fewer resources.

However, although this investigation grew out of an immediate practical problem at Stirling, the questions asked are of more general relevance. The issues with which it was concerned may be considered under two main headings:

(a) Microteaching Practice and Collaboration with Peers

As used at Stanford and at Stirling, microteaching involves several different phases: the skill is defined and a rationale suggested for it; models of the skill are demonstrated; students practise analysing teaching in terms of skill-relevant criteria; they plan microteaching lessons in the context of which the skill will be relevant; they teach these lessons; they observe recordings of the lessons, analyse them in terms of how effectively the skill has been used, and consider possible changes; and they repeat the cycle of planning, teaching, observing and analysing. Of all these phases, perhaps the least investigated (and most expensive) is that of the *teaching* of microteaching lessons by each student. Yet it is far from obvious that this phase does contribute to students' acquisition of skills. Indeed, it appears to be the phase which is least likely to contribute to students' understanding of the skill, since it is the phase in which the conditions appear least conducive to reflective observation and thinking. It is only if acquisition of a skill depends

117

not on understanding, nor on practice in planning, but on practice in using the skill while interacting with pupils, that this phase will be valuable.

It is only possible for a student to participate in every phase of microteaching except that of teaching the microteaching lesson if someone else teaches a lesson which he has planned and which he can then observe and analyse. An approximation to this pattern can be achieved for some students if students work in collaborative groups in planning, observing and analysing lessons, with only one of each group teaching the lesson planned by the group. The value of the teaching phase of microteaching may then be assessed by comparing the group member who teaches the lesson with other members of the group in their acquisition of the skill.

Such collaborative working may have advantages for all members of the group in that each can test his understanding and application of the skill against the views of his peers, can learn from their suggestions, and may find them emotionally supportive; but these possible advantages cannot be assumed.

(b) *Supervisory Feedback*

The evidence from previous investigations of the effects of supervisory feedback, or of supervisors' comments on videotape feedback, on microteaching performance (e.g. Acheson, 1964; McDonald and Allen, 1967; Claus, 1969) is difficult to synthesise. There is some evidence from these studies that if the training procedure includes the demonstration of cued videotape models and also the provision of videotape feedback, then the involvement of a supervisor at the feedback phase does not lead to any greater improvement in performance. Some reviewers (e.g. Borg et al., 1970) have concluded that supervisory feedback is an unnecessary element in microteaching; but others (e.g. McKnight, 1971) have not seen the evidence as warranting this conclusion, and have pointed to the need for an examination of the various functions which a supervisor's involvement might serve.

In a pilot-study at Stirling, ten student-teachers practised four teaching skills, teaching four microteaching lessons for each skill. Five of the students had supervisors for the first two skills only, while the other five had supervisors for only the third and fourth skills. There was some tendency for performance to improve more from the first to the fourth lessons when students were working with supervisors, but there were striking individual differences in this respect. For some students, having a supervisor seemed to make a considerable difference, while others improved as much or as little whether or not they had a supervisor; and one student improved markedly in both skills for which he had no supervisor, but showed no improvement in the skills for which he did have a supervisor. All ten students, however, expressed an unqualified preference for working with supervisors. Thus although there may be little general relationship between the presence or absence of a supervisor and students' performance of skills in the microteaching context, the presence of a supervisor may be necessary, at least in the Scottish context, for student morale. This tentative finding suggests the need to take account of a variety of criteria in assessing the contribution of supervisory feedback, or indeed of other potential components of microteaching. In this study, three types of criteria are used, concerned respectively with students' teaching behaviour, their evaluations of observed teaching, and their attitudinal responses to their microteaching experiences.

Design of the Experiment

The experiment was conducted in the context of the first semester course in the Stirling University undergraduate education programme. In the spring semester of 1971, 130 students were registered for the course. During the semester, five skills were studied and practised, these being 'Varying the Stimulus', 'Questioning for Feedback', 'Clarity of Explanation', 'Use of Examples' and 'Higher Order Questioning and Probing', but the experiment was concerned only with the last three of these skills. The programme for each skill involved three hours of lectures on psychological theory and research relevant to the skill; a lecture in which the skill was defined in terms of teaching objectives and teaching behaviours, exemplified through one or more videotapes modelling the use of the skill; a one-hour session in which students practised using the schedules provided for observing and recording relevant teacher behaviour; one-hour sessions in which the use of the skill in students' own teaching subjects was discussed; and the practice of the skill in microteaching, with a single teach-reteach cycle and with videotape feedback.

The experiment was designed primarily to assess the effects of:

(i)   practising a skill *compared with* collaborating with a peer who practises the skill;

(ii) the involvement of a supervisor in student groups' observation, analysis and discussion of lessons *compared with* groups working without a supervisor.

An additional comparison, in which several factors were confounded, was *between* students working in groups with only one member of the group practising any one skill *and* the 'standard' pattern of students working individually, practising each skill themselves, and having supervisors at the feedback phase. It was decided that it would not be fair to ask any students to practise all the skills without the support of either a supervisor or peers.

Accordingly a sample of twelve students was selected at random to work individually with supervisors. The remaining students were invited to group themselves into groups of three, the minority who did not do so being grouped at random with others with the same teaching subject. In each of these groups, each member taught and retaught a lesson for one of the three skills; the other two participated in the planning of the lesson, observed and analysed the lesson in terms of the defined skill, discussed with the teacher changes which might make his use of the skill more effective in the reteach lesson, and analysed and discussed the second teaching of the lesson. Twelve of these groups of three were chosen at random to work with supervisors; the remainder worked on their own. All students on the course were required, as part of their assessed course-work, to write reports on the teaching they had planned and observed. The available supervisors were allocated at random to the individuals and groups which were to be supervised, and worked with the same individuals or groups throughout the course of the experiment.

Teaching Behaviour

To assess students' acquisition of the patterns of teaching behaviour prescribed in the three skills, a sample of students were asked at the end of the semester to teach microteaching lessons making particular use of these skills. Since these lessons were for research rather than training purposes and were to be taught in the week before the semester examinations, the students participating were informed that a good performance in the experimental lesson would be taken into account in determining their education grade for the semester. The sample of forty-eight students asked to teach these lessons was made up as follows:

the twelve students who had practised all three skills and had worked individually with supervisors;
eighteen students who had worked in groups with supervisors, in three sets of six according to the skill they had taught lessons to

practise;
eighteen students who had worked in groups without supervisors, in three sets of six according to the skill they had taught lessons to practise.

The experimental lessons were taught on four successive mornings. For practical reasons, it was not possible to bring forty-eight different groups of five pupils to the University, with the result that all forty-eight students could not be asked to teach the same lesson. Three different 'prescribed' lessons were therefore chosen, each based on an article in a Sunday newspaper; they concerned 'Changes in Scout Uniform', 'Reasons for Climbing Mountains', and 'Drivers' Physical Fitness as a Factor in Road Safety'. The sample having been stratified in terms of the three main groups, lesson topics were allocated at random to members of these groups. Each student was given a copy of the relevant article and asked to use this as his basic material in an attempt to achieve three or four specified objectives. Otherwise students were free to teach the lessons as they wished, except that they were asked to optimise their use of the three skills.

A maximum of eighteen minutes was allowed for each lesson and students were asked to plan to use most of this time. (In the event, all but two used the full time available.) With the constraint that none of the sixteen groups of pupils should be taught the same lesson twice, students were allocated times at random in the four-day programme (although a few modifications were necessary because of students' prior commitments).

Each of the lessons taught was videotaped and later viewed by a team of trained observers. The observation instruments used to analyse the lessons were slightly modified versions of the schedules which the students had used in their practice of the skills, the modifications having been introduced to increase reliability. Although these instruments were designed primarily for diagnostic purposes, it is possible to abstract from each,four or five countable behaviours which can be reliably recorded and which give crude but fairly valid measures of how well the skill, as it was defined to the students, had been exercised.*
The observers worked in two groups of three, each group analysing half the lessons, with one member in each group using the observation instrument in the use of which he had been particularly trained; a

*The observation instruments, and evidence on the reliability with which they can be used by trained observers, are fully described by McIntyre, McKnight and White (paper in this volume).

fourth observer, the author, observed all the lessons, using the same
instrument as each other observer for some lessons, in order to provide
an extra check on reliability.

Evaluations of Observed Teaching

One of the general objectives of the course was that students should
become 'better' at analysing and evaluating teaching which they observed. The procedures used for eliciting students' evaluations of
teaching and the ways in which these evaluations were analysed are
those described by Millar and McIntyre in paper 5 of this volume; evaluative statements are categorised in terms of their 'structure', their
'focus' and their 'validity'.

In relation to the structure of students' evaluative statements, statements were categorised in terms of whether or not they had each of the
following characteristics: alternativism; consequentialism; purposiveness; complexity; specific qualifier; substantiation; and qualified rating.
The criteria used were the proportion of statements made by a student
which had these respective characteristics.

Eight focus criteria were also used in this investigation. Since the
course was primarily concerned with skills of explaining and questioning, and since students tended at the start of the course to give
much emphasis to affective aspects of teaching, to the content of
lessons, and to teachers' personal qualities, an objective was that the
proportion of statements in the explaining and questioning categories
would increase at the expense of the affective, motivating, reacting,
content and organisation, and personal qualities categories. A further
objective was that as a result of the course students would be more
specific in the aspects of teaching on which they commented, and an
eighth criterion was therefore the number of specific phases of teaching
mentioned.

The evaluative statements made by the students were with regard to
four twelve-minute microteaching lessons (taught by members of
previous classes) which they viewed in the final week of the semester.
The final criterion on which these evaluations were assessed, that of
validity, was the proportion of the statements made by each student
about these lessons which were in agreement with the conclusions
reached by a team of four observers using a battery of systematic observation instruments and a number of rating scales.

Comparisons between students who had worked under different
conditions were based on analysis of the evaluations made by the
twelve students who had worked individually with tutors, sixteen stu-

dents randomly selected from those who had worked in groups with tutors, and twenty-seven students randomly selected from those who had worked in groups without tutors.

Student Opinions and Reactions

A third set of criteria were the opinions and reactions expressed by students in response to a questionnaire at the end of the semester. Three types of information sought in this questionnaire were relevant:

(i)   Students' preferences for working with supervisors *or* with peers in microteaching; and their comments on the nature and quality of the help given by supervisors and/or peers.

(ii) Assessments of the relative value of teaching microteaching lessons compared with that of working with someone else doing the teaching.

(iii) Students' personal reactions to the course and its effect upon their attitudes towards teaching.

There was a 71 per cent response rate to the questionnaire — 75 per cent for those working individually with supervisors, 78 per cent for those working in groups with tutors, and 67 per cent for those working in groups without tutors. This was considered a fairly satisfactory response rate from a group of students already heavily burdened by research demands.

Results

(a) *Teaching Behaviour*

Three of the forty-eight selected students were unable to teach their lessons at the scheduled times, and in one other case there was a breakdown of the video-recording equipment. Videotapes of the remaining forty-four students were analysed and the results are shown in table 1.

For each of the thirteen criterion variables, a two-way analysis of variance was carried out among the six sub-sets of students who had practised the skills in groups, to determine the effects (i) of having or not having a supervisor with the group, and (ii) of practising a skill in microteaching as opposed to only planning and analysing the teaching. In only two cases were there between-group differences significant at the 5 per cent level. For variable 8, 'number of rules discussed without any rule-example-rule sequence', there was a significant interaction effect; as can be seen from table 1, neither of the extreme groups had

Table 1 Means and Standard Deviations of Experimental Groups on Criterion Measures for Use of Three Skills

Group		Individuals with Tutors	In Groups with Tutors				In Groups without Tutors			
Skills Practised		All Skills	C of E	U of E	H O Q,P	Total	C of E	U of E	H O Q,P	Total
n		10	5	6	5	16	6	6	6	18
Clarity of Explanation										
Number of self-interruptions	Mean	10.4	14.6	12.7	14.6	13.9	13.5	12.0	16.8	14.1
	S.D.	2.8	6.1	4.5	6.3	5.7	5.8	5.2	5.9	6.0
Number of uses of inappropriate vocabulary	Mean	1.2	3.0	3.8	2.4	3.1	2.8	2.2	3.7	2.9
	S.D.	1.0	2.3	4.0	1.7	3.0	1.4	1.5	4.0	2.7
Number of vague words or expressions	Mean	9.0	9.4	4.7	12.6	8.6	14.0	11.2	8.2	11.1
	S.D.	5.4	10.1	3.1	14.1	10.4	6.4	5.9	4.4	6.1
Number of explaining statements or questions	Mean	11.8	12.6	10.8	8.6	10.7	11.8	12.8	13.2	12.6
	S.D.	5.0	2.9	3.5	2.6	3.5	3.5	2.1	2.3	2.7
Use of Examples										
Number of examples given	Mean	27.4	26.4	19.0	25.0	23.2	22.0	21.8	25.3	23.1
	S.D.	7.7	10.8	8.8	5.9	9.3	8.8	5.5	3.1	6.5
Number of examples given by pupils	Mean	20.6	14.4	10.7	14.2	12.9	11.2	11.3	17.3	13.3
	S.D.	8.2	12.1	7.7	5.7	9.3	5.3	6.5	8.2	7.3
Number of examples explicitly related to exemplified rules	Mean	5.1	3.2	5.2	8.4	5.6	7.3	5.9	4.8	6.0
	S.D.	5.1	1.5	3.2	6.1	4.5	4.7	3.5	3.5	4.4
Number of rules discussed without use of any rule-example-rule sequence	Mean	5.2	6.8	4.2	5.6	5.4	5.0	6.0	3.2	4.7
	S.D.	1.7	1.9	1.1	1.6	1.9	1.3	2.4	1.5	2.2
Higher Order Questioning and Probing										
Number of questions asked	Mean	41.8	29.6	35.5	33.2	32.9	27.5	27.8	42.5	32.6
	S.D.	13.9	15.0	6.3	9.9	11.0	7.8	8.3	8.6	10.8
Proportion of questions coded as 'analysis/synthesis'	Mean	18.7	22.0	12.0	10.8	14.8	16.8	13.5	17.5	15.9
	S.D.	9.4	15.0	6.7	3.7	10.7	7.9	8.8	8.7	8.6
Proportion of questions not coded as 'lower order'	Mean	51.5	44.0	38.2	41.6	41.1	46.2	35.3	39.0	40.2
	S.D.	11.0	7.3	14.6	13.3	12.6	16.0	13.6	9.3	14.0
Number of probes	Mean	7.9	4.8	5.8	5.6	5.4	3.8	3.3	8.5	5.2

practised the skill of Use of Examples. For variable 13, 'proportion of questions not answered', those who had practised the Questioning skill performed significantly better than the others.

Because of the general lack of differences among those who had worked in groups, the means for all those who had worked in groups were compared with the means for those who had worked individually. Significant differences between the means were found for the following variables:

Variable 2: Number of uses of inappropriate vocabulary: t = 2.02, 42 d.f.
Variable 6: Number of examples given by pupils: t = 2.45, 42 d.f.
Variable 9: Number of questions asked: t = 2.11, 42 d.f.
Variable 11:Proportion of questions not lower order: t = 2.30, 42 d.f.
Variable 12:Number of probes: t = 2.02, 42 d.f.

In all five of these cases, the differences are in favour of those who had worked individually with supervisors. Furthermore, of the thirteen differences between means, eleven are in the direction which favours those working individually, an outcome which has only a 2.2 per cent probability of occurring by chance.

(b) *Evaluation of Teaching*

Means and standard deviations for each of the three categories of students on the sixteen criterion variables are given in table 2. For only three variables were there any significant differences: students who had worked without supervisors tended to make fewer suggestions of alternatives; and those who had worked individually tended to give more attention than others to teachers' motivational behaviour, and less to teachers' explanations.

(c) *Student Responses to Questionnaire*

Responses to some of the more structured questions are presented in table 3.

(i) *Working with Tutors and/or Peers:* When forced to choose between working with tutors or with peers, most of those who had worked individually with tutors judged this to be the preferable condition. There was far less unanimity, however, among those who had had experience of working with peers; and those who had worked with both tutors and peers were evenly divided on the issue.

Table 2 Means and Standard Deviations of Experimental Groups on
Criterion Measures for Evaluations of Teaching

			Percentage of Evaluative Statements having given Characteristics		
			Individual with Tutor	In Groups with Tutors (n=16)	In Groups without Tutors (n=27)
Structure					
1	Alternative behaviour	Mean	14.7	14.3	8.5
	suggested	S.D.	10.2	11.2	6.9
2	Causal, consequential,	Mean	19.9	21.4	19.8
	explanatory connection	S.D.	16.9	13.5	12.1
	made				
3	Teacher's purpose	Mean	7.6	6.5	6.9
	inferred	S.D.	5.9	5.2	7.5
4	Two or more aspects of	Mean	59.5	57.3	54.0
	teacher or pupil	S.D.	17.3	15.4	20.6
	behaviour related				
5	Specific evaluative adjec-	Mean	45.7	37.7	40.1
	tive used to qualify	S.D.	11.1	10.1	15.9
	behaviour described				
6	Generalisation about	Mean	14.9	16.9	15.1
	teacher behaviour sub-	S.D.	9.8	7.7	10.3
	stantiated by specific				
	exemplification				
7	Judgement qualified	Mean	11.0	10.4	10.7
	(behaviour not simply	S.D.	6.9	7.3	9.8
	approved or disapproved)				
Focus					
8	Affective aspects of	Mean	34.8	27.9	28.4
	teacher behaviour	S.D.	10.8	6.7	11.2
9	Motivational behaviour	Mean	32.0	24.9	25.0
	of teacher	S.D.	10.1	6.8	10.6
10	Teachers' explanations	Mean	33.6	43.5	44.8
		S.D.	8.3	8.2	11.5
11	Teachers' questioning	Mean	20.3	21.3	19.1
		S.D.	10.2	5.4	8.2
12	Teachers' reactions to	Mean	14.9	10.6	11.2
	pupil responses	S.D.	8.1	5.0	7.9
13	Content and organisation	Mean	16.7	11.6	14.0
	of lesson	S.D.	5.4	7.1	7.8
14	Teachers' personal	Mean	6.3	7.1	5.4
	qualities	S.D.	5.2	5.5	6.4
15	Specific phases	Mean	11.6	12.3	11.3
	mentioned (number)	S.D.	2.1	1.8	1.9
16	Valid evaluations	Mean	38.1	33.4	32.9
		S.D.	15.4	10.7	9.8

Table 3 Students' Opinions on the Relative Advantages of Working
with Tutors or with Peers (Frequency Distributions)

		Individual with Tutor	In Group with Tutor	In Group without Tutor	Total
Preferences expressed	Tutor preferred	7	11	22	40
for working with	Peers preferred	1	11	16	28
tutor *or* peers	No preference	1	6	14	21
Value of tutors'	Very helpful	3	8		11
comments on	Fairly helpful	4	12		16
teaching	Not very helpful	2	4		6
	Not at all helpful	0	2		2
Value of tutors'	Very helpful	2	9		11
suggestions for	Fairly helpful	4	9		13
changes in lessons	Not very helpful	3	5		8
	Not at all helpful	0	1		1
Value of joint	Very helpful		8	16	24
planning of lessons	Fairly helpful		4	21	25
	Not very helpful		9	15	24
	Not at all helpful		4	3	7
Value of fellow-	Very helpful		13	17	30
students' comments	Fairly helpful		8	26	34
on teaching	Not very helpful		2	8	10
	Not at all helpful		0	3	3
Value of fellow-	Very helpful		7	16	23
students' suggestions	Fairly helpful		13	23	36
for changes in lessons	Not very helpful		5	10	15
	Not at all helpful		0	6	6

Most students appear to have found the comments and advice of both
tutors and peers fairly helpful. There is a slight tendency for those who
worked with both to have found the comments of their peers the more
valuable, and also a tendency for them to report their fellow-students'
comments as more valuable than did those who did not have tutors to
work with.

The students were asked to indicate the advantages and disadvantages
they perceived in working with tutors and in working with peers. The
great majority in all three groups considered it an important advantage
to have the advice and guidance of someone who is an experienced
teacher or who thoroughly understands the skills they are practising.

Relatively few perceive any disadvantages in working with tutors, much the most frequently mentioned disadvantage (by fifteen students) being that the presence of a tutor may inhibit frank discussion. Working with peers has several advantages, according to those who had experience of this condition; of these, the most frequently mentioned were the possibility of frank and relaxed discussion, the usefulness of a variety of perspectives, and the chance to share common problems. Disadvantages were mentioned mainly by those who had worked with peers but without tutors, the most frequent being peers' lack of professional expertise, their lack of effort or commitment, and the danger of discussion being confused and undirected; but such disadvantages were mentioned much less frequently than advantages.

(ii) *Practising Skills or Collaborating with Teacher:* Students who had worked in groups were asked about the relative advantages of teaching or of collaborating with the teacher as a means of (a) learning about the use of a skill, and (b) acquiring the skill.

On the first criterion, 43 per cent of respondents thought that working with the teacher was more useful than actually teaching, while 25 per cent thought it less useful. On the second criterion, doing the teaching oneself was considered more useful by 62 per cent, and less useful by 19 per cent. In relation to both criteria, those who had worked with tutors were significantly more favourable to the non-teaching condition than those who had not.

(iii) *Reactions to the Course and Attitudes towards Teaching:* In reply to the question 'In general, how well satisifed are you with the course?', 56 per cent of respondents who had worked individually with tutors, 33 per cent of those who had worked in groups with tutors, and 23 per cent of those who had worked in groups without tutors chose the response 'very satisfied'. No one reported themselves as 'not at all satisfied', but of nine who were 'not very satisfied', eight had worked without tutors.

To questions about how the course had affected their attitudes, the pattern of responses from students with tutors did not differ according to whether they had worked individually or in groups; but there were marked differences between those who had worked with tutors and those who had not. Thus 53 per cent of those with tutors, but only 35 per cent of those without, reported that the job of teaching appeared more interesting as a result of the course. Similarly the course was said to have made a teaching career more attractive to 78 per cent of those with tutors, but to only 55 per cent of those without. Finally, 33 per cent of those without tutors claimed that, as a result of the course, their own personalities appeared to them less suited to teaching than they had previously thought, but this was said by only one student who had worked with a tutor.

Discussion and Conclusions

One of the questions with which this investigation was concerned was whether there are detectable advantages, when students practise microteaching in groups, in having a supervisor. It was found that the acquisition of skills did not appear to be influenced by the presence or absence of tutors; and students' evaluations of observed teaching seemed to be influenced by working with a tutor in only one of eighteen assessed characteristics, those with tutors tending to suggest more alternative teaching behaviours. Nonetheless, most students considered it advantageous to have a supervisor, mainly so that they might have the benefit of authoritative guidance; and this felt need for a supervisor was clearly reflected in the lower morale of those who had worked without one.

A second question was whether teaching skills could be acquired equally well by working with a fellow-student practising them as by practising them oneself. The majority view of students who attempted both was that one can learn about the use of a skill equally well or even better by working with someone else practising the skill, but that to acquire the skill oneself it was better to practise it through one's own teaching. For only one of thirteen criteria, however, was there any evidence in the teaching behaviour of students that practising the skill oneself is a more effective means of acquiring it.

The third major question was whether working in groups with a tutor, with each student himself practising only one of the three skills, was an equally effective approach to microteaching as the established procedure of working individually with a tutor and practising each skill for oneself. The students who had worked in these two ways did not in general differ significantly in their expressed attitudes and reactions, or in their evaluations of observed teaching; but those working individually showed a significant superiority on teaching behaviour criteria. At one level, this result was useful in that it suggested the undesirability of adopting the method of working in groups as an alternative to the more orthodox procedure. Unfortunately, however, the design of the experiment was such that this finding cannot unambiguously be interpreted in any more generalisable way. The superiority of those who worked individually might have been due to the lack of involvement of peers in their work, or to greater experience of teaching in the microteaching context, or to an interaction between these two factors.

From a curriculum development perspective, the results of this investigation were disappointing, in that they provided no indication of how the Stirling microteaching programme might be made less costly without a loss of effectiveness. From a theoretical perspective, the results, while difficult to interpret, are very thought-provoking.

References

Acheson, K. (1964). 'The Effects of Feedback from Television Recordings and Three Types of Supervisory Treatment on Selected Teacher Behavior', Doctoral Dissertation, Stanford University. Ann Arbor, Michigan: University Microfilms No. 64 – 1352.

Borg, W.R.,Kelley, M.L., Langer, P., and Gall, M. (1970). *The Minicourse: A Microteaching Approach to Teacher Education,* Collier-Macmillan, London.

Claus, K.E. (1969). 'Effects of Modelling and Feedback Variables on Questioning Skills', Technical Report No. 6, Stanford Centre for Research and Development in Teaching.

McDonald, F.J., and Allen, D.W. (1967). 'Training Effects of Feedback and Modelling Procedures on Teacher Performance', Final Report of United States Office of Education Project OE-6-10-078 Stanford University. Also issued as Technical Report No. 3, Stanford Centre for Research and Development in Teaching.

McKnight, P.C. (1971). 'Microteaching in Teacher Training: a Review of Research', *Res. in Educ.,* November.

8 EFFECTS OF SUPERVISORY STRATEGIES IN MICROTEACHING ON STUDENTS' ATTITUDES AND SKILL ACQUISITION

Roy Griffiths, Gordon MacLeod and Donald McIntyre

Introduction

In his comprehensive review of the role of the tutor in microteaching supervision, Griffiths (1972) notes a general lack of specificity in descriptions of that role, a paucity of experimental studies and a lack of well-established findings about effects and effectiveness.

This experimental study was undertaken to assess the effects of four supervisory strategies on students' skill acquisition and on their perceptions of their supervisors.

Design of the Study

Subjects

The subjects in this study were drawn from a group of forty-eight students taking their first semester course in education. Each subject was assigned at random to one of four treatment groups.

Supervisors

Fourteen supervisors, all experienced in microteaching supervision, were provided with written specifications of the four supervisory strategies so that all could carry out each strategy. Any difficulties which arose from the prescription of strategies were resolved in discussion between supervisors and experimenters, and then supervisors were assigned at random to particular subjects, with the subjects' membership of particular experimental groups determining the strategies to be followed in supervision.

Treatments

Combinations of the two dimensions — direct/indirect and strengths/ alternativistic — were used to yield four supervisory strategies: direct strengths (D.S.); direct alternativistic (D.A.); indirect strengths (I.S.) and indirect alternativistic (I.A.). All students participated in a ten-minute teach lesson of the skill of Use of Examples, this being followed by a videotape replay of the lesson and by the appropriate supervisory discussion. Approximately two days later, the reteach of the same skill took place with a different group of pupils, and the videotape records of these lessons which were to provide the dependent variables on performance were retained for analysis.

Description of Strategies

Direct Strengths: A strategy aimed at improving the student's performance on the teaching skill by emphasising tutor-directed attention to, and support of, those episodes in the lesson where the student behaved in skill-appropriate ways.

Indirect Strengths: A strategy aimed at improving the student's performance on the teaching skill by emphasising student-directed attention to those episodes of his lesson where he judged himself to have behaved in skill-appropriate ways, and by providing the tutor with an opportunity to reinforce the student's use of these behaviours.

Direct Alternativistic: A strategy aimed at improving student performance on the teaching skill by emphasising tutor-directed attention to those episodes in the lesson where the student might have behaved in skill-appropriate ways but did not do so. The tutor's role was to provide positive instances of alternative behaviours for improvement rather than to concentrate on any weaknesses of the student's performance.

Indirect Alternativistic: A strategy aimed at improving the student's performance on the teaching skill by providing an opportunity to discuss with the tutor possible alternative procedures for the reteach. This involved student-directed attention to those episodes in the lesson where he judged he could have behaved in skill-appropriate ways but did not do so.

Instrumentation

(a) *Questionnaire*. The questionnaire completed by subjects immediately after supervision of their teach lessons consisted of three sections, the first and third of these being devised by the experimenters, whilst the second was incorporated from a study by McDonald and Allen (1967). Section I of the questionnaire consisted of questions designed to assess students' perceptions of their supervisors' strategies, thereby allowing a monitoring of supervisors' adherence to the prescribed strategies, as well as students' perceptions of the effectiveness of the supervision. Section II consisted of a semantic differential to assess whether

the strategies being followed by supervisors affected student perceptions of the supervisors whilst Section III asked for students' suggestions
as to improvement of the supervision. The questionnaire items are specified in full in the results section below.

(b) *Observation Instrument: Use of Examples.* The microteaching skill
being practised by students was that of Use of Examples, and the
observational instrument used both to operationalise the skill for
students and to assess their performance was the five-category one
described by McIntyre, McKnight and White in this volume and from
which eight performance criteria were drawn. Before coding of the experimental lessons took place, a study of inter-observer agreement in
the use of the observational instrument was carried out by two coders
on ten videotaped microteaching lessons from a previous semester's
microteaching course. Assessment of agreement is shown in table 1.

Table 1 Inter-observer agreement on the eight Use of Examples criteria

Category	r	(between observers)
1. Total number of teacher examples	.99	
2. Total number of pupil examples	.99	
3. Number of teacher examples explicitly linked to a rule or generalisation	.57	(low frequencies)
4. Number of pupil examples explicitly linked to a rule or generalisation	.99	
5. Total number of examples explicitly linked (3. + 4.)	.84	
6. Proportion of rules explicitly stated		Agreement on seven of the ten lessons that 100 per cent of rules were explicitly stated.
7. Number of requested examples not provided by pupils	.95	
8. Proportion of requested examples not provided by pupils	.88	

Procedure

All students were introduced to the skill of Use of Examples by lecture
and model videotape and were provided with a handout describing the
skill and its use, together with a check-list of the five categories of
teaching behaviour believed to be relevant to the skill. All supervisors
were also provided with this check-list and both supervisors and
students were asked to focus on these categories during the critique,
both by attempting to pay attention to all categories listed and by

Table 2 Mean scores on Sections I and II of the questionnaire

	STRATEGY				OUTCOME		
	D.S. N=11	D.A. N=10	I.S. N=12	I.A. N=10	Direct-Indirect	Strengths-Alt.	Interaction
1. In general, viewing and discussing my lesson with the supervisor was an enjoyable experience for me.	2.09	2.00	2.42	2.10	N.S.	N.S.	N.S.
2. The supervisor was tolerant and supportive of any weaknesses in my lesson.	2.36	1.70	2.83	1.60	N.S.	$<.05$	N.S.
3. I feel that the critique will be very useful in improving my performance on the reteach.	2.82	2.30	3.42	1.80	N.S.	$<.02$	N.S.
4. The supervisor's comments were vague.	4.82	4.40	4.00	4.65	N.S.	N.S.	N.S.
5. I feel that the lesson critique helped me gain a clearer idea of what is meant by the skill of Use of Examples.	2.91	3.20	3.50	2.70	N.S.	N.S.	N.S.
6. Much of what the supervisor said was concerned with possible alternative procedures for the reteach.	3.73	1.60	5.25	3.20	$<.001$	$<.001$	N.S.
7. I feel that critiques like this are helpful in making me a more effective teacher.	2.45	1.90	3.58	2.10	N.S.	$<.02$	N.S.
8. The supervisor expected most of the comments on my teaching to come from me.	5.09	4.40	1.67	1.20	.001	N.S.	N.S.
9. The supervisor was objective and fair in his comments during the critique.	1.73	1.90	2.25	1.40	N.S.	N.S.	N.S.
10. Much of what the supervisor said was concerned with strengths in my teaching.	1.91	4.40	2.92	4.00	N.S.	$<.001$	N.S.
11. The supervisor expected most of the suggestions for alternative procedures to come from me.	4.55	4.60	2.33	1.50	$<.001$	N.S.	N.S.

	D.S. N=11	D.A. N=10	I.S. N=12	I.A. N=10	Direct-Indirect	Strengths-Alt.	Interaction
12. I feel that the skill of Use of Examples will become a regular part of my teaching behaviour.	2.18	2.20	2.25	2.40	N.S.	N.S.	N.S.
13. The supervisor spent much of the time discussing teacher behaviours which were relevant to the skill.	4.09	3.20	4.75	4.10	N.S.	N.S.	N.S.
14. The supervisor was 1. skilful ...7. unskilful	2.45	3.00	3.08	2.30	N.S.	N.S.	N.S.
15. The supervisor was 1. considerate ... 7. inconsiderate	2.27	2.30	2.33	1.70	N.S.	N.S.	N.S.
16. The supervisor was 1. warm ...7. cold	5.73	5.20	5.67	5.60	N.S.	N.S.	N.S.
17. The supervisor was 1. likeable ...7. unlikeable	1.82	2.40	1.83	1.90	N.S.	N.S.	N.S.
18. The supervisor was 1. irresponsible .. 7. responsible	6.09	5.90	6.08	5.90	N.S.	N.S.	N.S.
19. The supervisor was 1. interested ... 7. disinterested	2.27	2.40	2.33	1.70	N.S.	N.S.	N.S.
20. The supervisor was 1. authoritarian .. 7. non-authoritarian	5.91	5.20	5.75	5.50	N.S.	N.S.	N.S.
21. The supervisor was 1. critical ...7. constructive	5.27	5.30	4.58	4.30	N.S.	N.S.	N.S.
22. The supervisor was 1. rewarding ...7. punishing	2.45	3.60	2.67	2.60	N.S.	N.S.	N.S.
23. The supervisor was 1. accepting ...7. demanding	3.27	2.60	2.33	2.80	N.S.	N.S.	N.S.
24. The supervisor was 1. intimidating .. 7. encouraging	5.64	5.70	5.58	6.00	N.S.	N.S.	N.S.
25. The supervisor was 1. realistic ...7. unrealistic	3.18	2.58	2.80	2.60	<.05	N.S.	N.S.
26. The supervisor was 1. flustered ...7. calm	5.55	4.80	6.25	6.00	N.S.	N.S.	N.S.
27. The supervisor was 1. caring ...7. uncaring	2.18	2.80	2.33	2.20	N.S.	N.S.	N.S.
28. The supervisor was 1. friendly ...7. unfriendly	1.73	2.10	2.00	1.80	N.S.	N.S.	N.S.

finding at least one example of each. All supervisors were asked to explain to the student before the critique how they would like that critique to run. In the indirect critiques, students were asked to initiate the discussion; in the direct critiques, the supervisor was to initiate discussion. In the strengths critiques, the focus was to be on actual examples of the student's having carried out skill-relevant behaviours with supervisor reinforcement of these; in the alternativistic critiques, the focus was to be on those episodes where the student might have behaved in skill appropriate ways but did not do so, with positive instances of alternative behaviours for improvement being provided. In all cases, students were asked to provide for each supervisor a lesson plan listing the 'rules' or generalisations to be exemplified during the practice of the skill.

During each student's lesson, the supervisor was able to view the video transmission from which both audio- and video-recordings were made. Following the lesson, both supervisor and student viewed the video replay and selected skill-relevant episodes to be discussed. The audio-recording was then replayed and was stopped at the pre-selected points so that discussion of each could proceed according to the specified strategy. At the end of the discussion, the student was asked to complete and return the questionnaire.

Analysis of Data and Results

A. *Questionnaire*

Table 2 shows in summary form the outcomes of the analyses of variance on the twenty-eight items constituting sections I and II of the questionnaire. In section I (the first fourteen items), a six-point rating scale was used, with a rating of 1 indicating 'I agree very much', whilst a rating of 6 indicated 'I disagree very much'. The rating scale and poles of the semantic differential of Section II are indicated in the table.

Table 3 covers section III of the questionnaire in which students were asked to indicate in which ways the supervisory critique could have been improved. In this table analysis is by means of chi-square and covers main effects only. Where expected frequencies in cells fell below five, the chi-square statistic is corrected for continuity (Cochran, 1954). Where frequencies of particular responses were low, categories were combined as indicated.

B. *Observed Reteach Performance*

Table 4 shows in summary form the outcomes of the analyses of variance on the eight performance criteria used in assessing reteach

Table 3 Incidence of suggested improvements to the supervisory critique

	Strengths	Alt.	Direct	Indirect
1. Longer critique	12	12	13	11
Shorter critique (or no response)	11	8	8	11
		$\chi^2 = 0.27$	$\chi^2 = 0.62$	
2. More emphasis on the strengths in my lesson (or no response)	6	16	11	11
Less emphasis on the strengths in my lesson	17	4	10	11
		$\chi^2 = 12.44$ $p < .001$	$\chi^2 = 0.02$	
3. Less reference to skill (or no comment)	10	5	5	10
More reference to skill	13	15	16	12
		$\chi^2 = 1.61$	$\chi^2 = 2.22$	
4. More demanding standards required of my teaching	14	12	15	11
Less demanding standards required of my teaching (or no comment)	9	8	6	11
		$\chi^2 = 0.003$	$\chi^2 = 2.06$	
5. Less emphasis on weaknesses in my lesson (or no comment)	2	5	4	3
More emphasis on weaknesses in my lesson	21	15	17	19
		$\chi^2_c = 1.06$	$\chi^2_c = 0.005$	
6. Less supervisor talk (or no comment)	11	7	15	3
More supervisor talk	12	13	6	19
		$\chi^2 = 0.72$	$\chi^2 = 14.74$ $p < .001$	
7. More reference to subject-matter	11	11	9	13
Less reference to subject-matter (or no comment)	12	9	12	9
		$\chi^2 = 0.22$	$\chi^2 = 1.13$	
8. More time spent discussing alternative procedures for the reteach	19	11	15	15
Less time spent discussing alternative procedures for the reteach (or no comment)	4	9	6	7
		$\chi^2 = 3.87$ $p < .05$	$\chi^2 = 0.05$	

		Strengths	Alt.	Direct	Indirect
9.	More direct guidance from supervisor	13	12	12	13
	Less direct guidance from supervisor (or no comment)	10	8	9	9
		$\chi^2 = 0.05$		$\chi^2 = 0.02$	
10.	More preparation by the supervisor	1	3	3	1
	No comment	22	17	18	21
		$\chi_c^2 = 0.45$		$\chi_c^2 = 0.31$	
11.	Clearer initial definition of the skill to be practised	10	5	8	7
	No comment	13	15	13	15
		$\chi^2 = 1.61$		$\chi^2 = 0.19$	
12.	Fuller understanding of the skill by the supervisor	5	1	1	1
	No comment	18	19	20	21
		$\chi_c^2 = 1.30$		$\chi_c^2 = 0.48$	
13.	More opportunity for me to explain why I taught lesson as I did	6	4	8	2
	No comment	17	16	13	20
		$\chi^2 = 0.22$		$\chi^2 = 5.06$ $p < .02$	
14.	More precise definition of the role of the critique session as an aid to learning the skill	16	7	11	12
	No comment	7	13	10	10
		$\chi^2 = 5.14$ $p < .02$		$\chi^2 = 0.02$	
15.	Better preparation on my part	13	14	15	12
	No comment	10	6	6	10
		$\chi^2 = 0.83$		$\chi^2 = 1.31$	
16.	More opportunity to replay the recording of the lesson at appropriate points	5	4	4	5
	No comment	18	16	17	17
		$\chi_c^2 = 0.06$		$\chi_c^2 = 0.01$	
17.	More support from supervisor	6	6	3	9
	No comment	17	14	18	13
		$\chi^2 = 0.08$		$\chi^2 = 3.18$	

Table 4 Mean scores of groups on the eight performance criteria

	D.S. N=11	D.A. N=11	I.S. N=13	I.A. N=9	Direct -Indirect	Strengths - Alt.	Inter- action
1. Total number of teacher examples	6.64	5.82	4.23	7.67	N.S.	N.S.	N.S.
2. Total number of pupil examples	9.36	10.18	7.31	20.22	N.S.	N.S.	N.S.
3. Number of teacher examples explicitly linked	1.73	0.91	0.62	0.78	N.S.	N.S.	N.S.
4. Number of pupil examples explicitly linked	0.91	1.45	1.08	1.56	N.S.	N.S.	N.S.
5. Number of examples explicitly linked	2.64	2.36	1.69	2.22	N.S.	N.S.	N.S.
6. Proportion of rules explicitly stated	.91	.95	.88	.93	N.S.	N.S.	N.S.
7. Number of requested examples not provided	0.82	2.27	0.54	2.33	N.S.	= .01	N.S.
8. Proportion of requested examples not provided	.11	.16	.12	.21	N.S.	N.S.	N.S.

performance.

Summary of Results

A. *Questionnaire*

In table 2, which covers sections I and II of the questionnaire, eight
items significantly differentiating among the experimental groups at or
beyond the .05 level were found. Four of these items (nos. 6, 8, 10 and
11) were designed to monitor supervisors' adherence to the specified
strategies. In all four cases highly significant differences in the
hypothesised directions were found, although item 6 also served to
differentiate the direct from the indirect group which had initially not
been hypothesised. These results suggest a very clear perceived differentiation among the supervisory strategies by the students.

Three of the remaining four significant items served to differentiate
the strengths from the alternativistic group, with the latter being seen
more as tolerant and supportive of weaknesses in the lessons, and the alternativistic supervisory critiques being seen as more likely to be useful in
improving teaching performance both in the short term (on the reteach)
and in the longer term ('more effective teacher'). The other significant
item shows that indirect tutors are seen as calmer, less flustered than
direct tutors, although it should be noted that both groups were rated
close to the 'calm' pole of the scale.

In table 3, covering section III of the questionnaire, five significant
differences were found. The direct group tends to want less supervisor
talk; the indirect group to want more, whilst a higher proportion (although a minority) of the direct group than of the indirect group wants
more opportunity to explain why they taught the lesson as they did.
The strengths group when compared with the alternativistic group
wants a more precise definition of the role of the supervisory critique,
wants less emphasis on the strengths of the lesson as against the alternativistic group's wish for more emphasis on strengths, and whilst a
majority of both groups would like more time spent discussing alternative procedures for the reteach, significantly more of the strengths
group would welcome this.

B. *Observed Reteach Performance*

On only one of the eight performance criteria is there a significant difference between the groups, with the lessons taught by the strengths
group having significantly fewer requests for examples from the pupils
going unanswered.

Discussion of Results

It seems clear both from the monitoring questions of the first section of the questionnaire and from a sampling of audio-recordings of supervisory sessions that the defined strategies were adhered to by supervisors. Given the one significant difference on reteach performance it seems unlikely that the strategies, as defined here, have much effect on subsequent microteaching performance. None the less, responses to the questionnaire did seem to show something of a preference for the alternativistic strategy, with supervisors following it being seen as more tolerant and supportive, and as likely to have more effect on teacher performance than those following the strengths strategy. These results would lend no support to a simple reinforcement theory view of the role of the supervisor.

The other major feature which seems to emerge from the questionnaire responses is that all groups want more of what they did not receive, and less of what they did receive. That is the students in this study were declaring that more effective supervisory sessions depend on various supervisory strategies and that they could make use of the information which such variety would provide.

References

Cochran, W.G. (1954). 'Some methods for strengthening the common χ^2 tests', *Biometrics*, 10, pp. 417-451.

Griffiths, R. (1972). The role of the tutor in microteaching supervision: a survey of research evidence, University of Stirling (mimeo).

McDonald, F.J. and Allen, D.W. (1967). Training effects of feedback and modelling procedures on teacher performance. Technical Report No. 3, Stanford Centre for Research and Development in Teaching, Stanford University, California.

9 THE EFFECTS OF DIFFERENTIAL TRAINING AND OF TEACHING SUBJECT ON MICRO-TEACHING SKILLS PERFORMANCE

Gordon MacLeod, Roy Griffiths and Donald McIntyre

Introduction

Despite Wagner's (1973) work showing that discrimination training is more effective at producing short-term behavioural change than is microteaching, the role of practice in microteaching has been neglected. One weakness of the Wagner study is the curious conceptualisation of microteaching implying a definition of microteaching (without discrimination training) which is at odds with the received uses of the technique. The author was aware of this difficulty and takes care to point out that

> The results of the present study do not exclude the possibility that practice *in addition* to discrimination training may prove to be effective by serving other functions in the process of behavior change (pp. 304-5).

One aim of this study was to determine the effects of three treatments on microteaching performance. Of these treatments, one represented microteaching with additional discrimination training, one represented microteaching including practice and the third involved only the provision of a clear definition of the skill, but no chance for practice.

The second aim of the study was to explore an hypothesis long held by the authors that the teaching-subject of microteaching participants would serve to differentiate microteaching performance.

Design of the Study

Subjects

The subjects in this study were seventy-seven second-year undergraduates at the University of Stirling, all studying education concurrently with their other academic subjects and participating in their second semester-course of education. Their previous experience of microteaching was during their first education course in which they practised three FIAC-based microteaching skills involving a total of seven ten-minute lessons. The distribution of students in subject-areas was:

History	26
English	26
Modern Languages	13
Science	8
Mathematics	4

Experimental Design

The planned microteaching programme for the semester consisted of teach-reteach cycles of three skills — Variation, Questioning and Clarity of Explanation. The planned experiment called for three training treatments — Major, Intermediate and Minor (defined below). By assigning subjects at random to one of three experimental groups a balanced design was produced in which all three experimental groups participated in all three training treatments over the complete semester course, but for any one skill, each experimental group participated in only one of the training treatments. The design is illustrated in figure 1, in which X, Y and Z represent the three randomly selected groups, and skills 1, 2 and 3 are Variation, Questioning and Clarity of Explanation.

Figure 1 Schematic View of the Experimental Design

			Treatments	
		Major	Intermediate	Minor
	1	X	Y	Z
Skills	2	Y	Z	X
	3	Z	X	Y

The ordering of the skills as 1, 2 and 3 in figure 1 represents the ordering of skill practice during the six weeks in which the experiment was running. A subsequent two weeks was devoted to the preparation and practice of an eighteen-minute criterion lesson taught by all subjects.

Experimental Treatments

The treatments described as Major, Intermediate and Minor consisted of the selection of components indicated in figure 2.

The components listed in figure 2 and used to define the three treat-

Figure 2 Outline of Experimental Treatments

Major	Intermediate	Minor
Skill Definition	Skill Definition	Skill Definition
Modelling	Modelling	—
Practice in use of skill coding instrument	—	—
Microteaching Practice (with Major Treatment Supervision)	Microteaching Practice (with Intermediate Treatment Supervision)	—

ments are described below.

Skill Definition: A one-hour lecture in which the theoretical and practical rationale for each skill was explained and the categories used to define the skill were described and exemplified.

Modelling: A one-hour period in which three model videotapes of skill practice were shown and discussed. Two of the three model tapes were cued visually to focus attention on the salient aspects of skill practice.

Practice in Use of Skill Coding Instrument: A two-hour period in which students were invited to practise the coding of videotaped lessons, and discuss and receive feedback on their codings of these lessons.

Microteaching Practice: A teach-reteach cycle of two ten-minute lessons with five pupils for each lesson. Videotape feedback was provided for both teach and reteach lessons, and tutors were provided for teach only. Participating tutors were all experienced in microteaching supervision, were familiar with the skills being practised, and participated in a two-hour coding-practice session for each skill, similar to the practice given to the 'Major' treatment students. Tutors were assigned randomly to students.

Tutoring of Major Treatment Subjects: The suggestions given to tutors for the supervision of 'Major' treatment students were:

1. Ask student to code his lesson during replay, reminding him of the procedure if necessary.
2. You also should code the lesson.
3. Compare codings and identify sources of major discrepancies.
4. Encourage student to take initiative in decoding, whilst
   (a) reinforcing skill-appropriate behaviour
   (b) helping student to formulate ways of 'improving' his skill-appropriate behaviour in relation to the particular lesson goals and content.

5. Encourage the student to code his own reteach lesson.

Tutoring of Intermediate Treatment Subjects: The suggestions given to tutors supervising 'Intermediate' treatment students were:

1. Ask student to watch the replay with the coding categories in mind. The student should *not* be expected to code the lesson.
2. Code the lesson yourself during the replay.
3. After the replay, briefly explain the coding procedure and show the student your coding of the lesson.
4. Encourage the student to take initiative in decoding, whilst
   (a) reinforcing skill-appropriate behaviour
   (b) helping student to formulate ways of 'improving' his skill-appropriate behaviour in relation to the particular lesson goals and content.
5. Encourage the student to watch his replay with the skill coding categories in mind.

Presentation of Skills to Students

Three tutors undertook the presentation of skills to students. Each tutor was responsible for only one skill, and the extent of his presentation varied according to which training treatment was being undertaken. Thus, no attempt was made to balance for individual tutor effects, although where appropriate, tutors followed a standard approach in presenting each component of the training treatment.

Criterion Lesson

At the end of the microteaching programme outlined above, all students were asked to teach an eighteen-minute video-recorded lesson in which they were asked to practise all three of the skills to which they had been introduced.

Training of Observers and Measures of Inter-Observer Agreement

For the purpose of assessing inter-observer agreement, the three observers worked in three pairs. Each pair practised the coding of one skill, and then separately coded a sample of ten ten-minute microteaching lessons. Thus, each of three coders was involved in the assessment of inter-observer agreement for two of the three skills.

For the skill of *Variation*, a six-category coding instrument was used, and the total number of codings made by each observer on each category was used to calculate the product-moment correlation coefficients shown in table 1.

Table 1 Correlations between Two Observers on Use of Variation
Coding Instrument

Category	r
Teacher Movement	.95
Teacher Gesture	.97
Change in Speech Pattern	.90
Change in Sensory Focus	.98
Verbal Pupil Participation	.92
Physical Pupil Participation	Low frequency, but agreement on six of the lessons that no coding was made, and rank order correlation on other four lessons was .95.

For the skill of Questioning, a six-category instrument was used,
and the total number of codings within each category by each coder
was used to calculate the product-moment coefficients shown in
table 2.

Table 2 Correlations between Two Observers on Use of Questioning
Coding Instrument

Category	r
Total No. of Questions	.99
No. of Higher-Order Questions	.97
No. of Middle-Order Questions	.95
No. of Lower-Order Questions	.98
No. of Follow-up Questions	.76
No. of Non-Follow-up Questions	.97

For the skill of Clarity of Explanation, an eight-category instrument was
used, with the first four categories representing positively valued behaviours and the second four categories representing negatively valued
behaviours. Table 3 shows the results of the assessment of inter-observer
agreement.

Coding of Lessons: The coding of the eighteen-minute video-recorded
lessons was carried out by the three observers, with each using one of
the skill-coding instruments. For each lesson, totals of occurrence were
computed for each skill category, and corrections were made for any
deviations from the eighteen-minute standard lesson length.

Table 3 Correlations or Measures of Agreement Between Two Observers
on Use of Clarity of Explanation Coding Instrument

Category	r
Rule-e.g.-rule	7 agreements on zero, 1 agreement on one, 2 disagreements
Explaining Links	.60
Planned Repetition	.68
Use of A.V.A.	.78
Lack of Fluency	.74
Lack of Continuity	.69
Vagueness	.83
Inappropriate Vocabulary	6 agreements on zero, 1 agreement on one, 3 disagreements

Analysis of Data and Results

For each category of each skill, the treatment and subject-area means
were computed. Before computing a treatment by subject-areas
factorial analysis of variance, the scores from the modern languages,
science and mathematics groups were combined to produce a third level
of subject-area (Other), so as to produce adequate numbers within the
interaction-effect cells. These data were then subject to a 3 x 3
analysis of variance, the programme used being one adapted from
Veldman (1967, pp. 257-68), which allowed for unequal cell frequencies. The outcomes of the analysis of variance are shown in table 4.
As no interaction effects were shown to be significant, only the main-
effect means and the outcomes of the F-tests are indicated.

Discussion of Results

Variation: For none of the components of the skill of variation were
there found to be F-ratios significant at the .05 level for any of the
training treatment effects; nor was there any evidence of any significant
interaction effects among treatments and subject areas. However,
among subject-areas, there was significant differentiation on four of the
six components. The skill profiles of each subject-area group are shown
in figure 3 in terms of skill component scores standardised without
weighting on the component means for the whole sample. This indicates
that the combined group scores highest on all four of the significantly
differentiated criteria, with the history group tending to score higher
than the English group on three of the four components but almost
identically on the fourth.

Questioning: Significant treatment effects were found for two of the

Table 4 Main Effect Means and Outcomes of the Analyses of Variance on the Main Effects

	History	English	Other	p	Major	Intermediate	Minor	p
Variation								
1. Teacher Movement	4.42	1.92	5.48	.02	4.68	3.42	3.69	N.S.
2. Teacher Gesture	13.62	8.81	15.60	.01	11.68	12.23	13.96	N.S.
3. Change in Speech Pattern	13.46	11.69	13.76	N.S.	13.12	13.42	12.35	N.S.
4. Change of Sensory Focus	6.35	3.04	7.64	$< .001$	6.00	6.31	4.65	N.S.(.08)
5. Verbal Pupil Participation	18.88	21.15	19.08	N.S.	19.64	21.12	18.38	N.S.
6. Physical Pupil Participation	0.85	0.92	6.92	.0001	3.76	2.15	2.65	N.S.
Questioning								
1. Total No. of Questions	53.08	55.50	64.60	N.S.(.06)	64.08	56.81	51.80	N.S.(.06)
2. No. of Higher-Order Questions	2.96	6.00	2.80	.02	4.46	4.04	3.28	N.S.
3. No. of Middle-Order Questions	12.27	14.00	13.12	N.S.	16.77	12.00	10.52	.02
4. No. of Lower-Order Questions	37.85	35.50	48.52	.05	42.73	40.69	38.04	N.S.
5. No. of Follow-up Questions	5.69	6.62	5.80	N.S.	7.35	6.08	4.64	.02
6. No. of Non-Follow-up Questions	47.46	50.81	58.72	.05	56.73	50.65	49.24	N.S.
Clarity of Explanation								
1. Rule-e.g.-rule	0.08	0.31	0.24	N.C.	0.19	0.04	0.38	N.C.
2. Explaining Links	8.50	5.88	6.16	.04	7.31	6.20	7.04	N.S.
3. Planned Repetition	0.88	0.69	1.36	N.C.	1.58	0.72	0.62	N.C.
4. Use of A.V.A.	2.04	0.50	1.68	N.S.(.07)	1.88	0.60	1.69	N.S.
5. Lack of Fluency	11.96	8.62	6.16	.003	8.69	8.04	10.08	N.S.
6. Lack of Continuity	1.81	1.15	0.44	.008	0.62	1.48	1.35	N.S.(.10)
7. Vagueness	5.77	4.77	2.12	.002	4.77	4.20	3.77	N.S.
8. Inappropriate Vocabulary	0.38	0.27	0.64	N.C.	0.54	0.40	0.35	N.C.

N.C. = Not computed   N.S. = Not significant

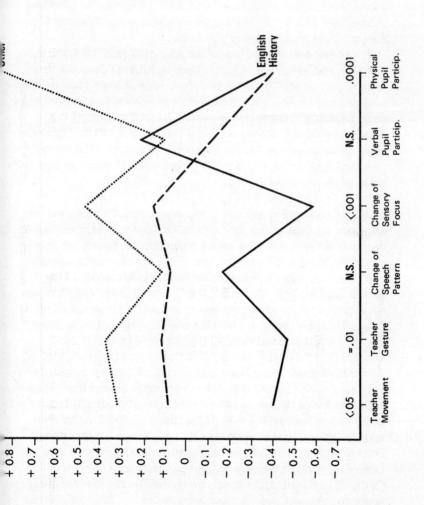

Figure 3 Standardised Scores on Each Category of Skill of Variation

questioning criteria – middle-order questions, and follow-up questions – where, in both cases, the trend of scores across treatments reflects the 'strength' of the treatments, with the major treatment group asking most of these kinds of questions, and the minor treatment group asking fewest. This pattern is also seen for Total Number of Questions, although the resultant F-ratio and its associated probability (p = .06) does not quite reach the acceptable level.

For subject-area effects, four of the six criteria reach statistical significance, and, as figure 4 indicates, these significant differentiations seem to arise through the combined group asking a larger total number of questions (p = .06), a larger number of non-follow-up questions and a larger number of Lower-Order questions than either the English or History groups; and for two of the positively-valued criteria, Higher-Order Questions and Follow-up Questions, a crossover effect occurs, with the English group asking more of these kinds of questions than either of the other two groups.

Clarity of explanation: Because of low frequencies, F-ratios were not computed for three of the eight criteria. Of those that were computed, no significant differentiation among treatments was found, but significant differentiation did occur on four of the five criteria for subject-area effects. As figure 5 indicates, the History group tended to use more Explaining Links than either the Combined or the English group, but they also tended to demonstrate most Lack of Fluency, Lack of Continuity and Vagueness, whilst the English group seemed to display more of these behaviours than did the Combined group.

All skills: Although the separate skill components are not intended to carry equal weighting and although any appropriate weighting system is unknown, it is of interest to compute the average standardised score for each group on each skill. For Variation, this was carried out by averaging the standardised scores on the six components; for Questioning, Total Number of Questions was excluded, reversed signs were used for Lower-Order and Non-Follow-Up and the means were computed; for Clarity of Explanation, the signs were reversed for the four negatively valued components, and the means were computed. Table 5 shows the results of these computations.

The mean standardised scores of table 5 indicate that for Variation, the Combined group does relatively well; the English group relatively badly. For Questioning, the order is reversed, with the English group doing relatively well, the Combined group doing relatively badly, and

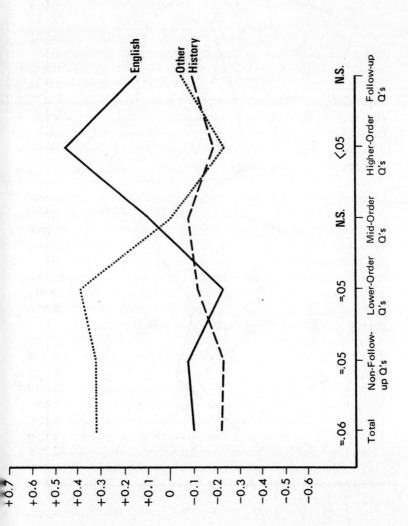

Figure 4 Standardised Scores on Each Category of the Skill of
Questioning

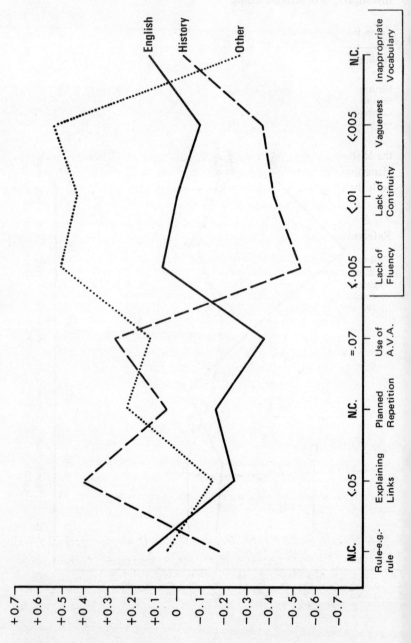

Figure 5 Standardised Scores on Each Category of the Skill of Clarity of Explanation

Table 5 Unweighted Mean Standardised 'skill' Scores

Subject-Area	Variation	Skill Questioning	Clarity of Explanation
History	– .01	– .01	– .12
English	– .31	+ .20	– .18
Combined	+ .33	– .21	+ .29

the History group again holding their median status. For Clarity of Explanation, the Combined group again performs relatively well, whilst both the History and English groups do somewhat badly.

References

Veldman, D.J. (1967). *Fortran Programming for the Behavioral Sciences*, Holt, Rinehart and Winston, New York.
Wagner, A.C. (1973). 'Changing Teaching Behaviour: a Comparison of Microteaching and Cognitive Discrimination Training', *Journal of Educational Psychology*, 64, pp. 299-305.

10 THE EFFECTS OF POSITIVE AND NEGATIVE MODELS ON STUDENT-TEACHERS' QUESTIONING BEHAVIOURS

Stan Gilmore

Introduction

The rationale for the use of videotaped models in microteaching derives from studies of imitative behaviour conducted by social psychologists. In a review of literature on the subject, Bandura and Walters (1963) concluded that behavioural modification was possible entirely through imitation and that modelling cues proved more effective than operant procedures, i.e. by reinforcement. At the same time, an important investigation by Bandura, Ross and Ross (1963) found that filmed models were as effective as live models in affecting behavioural change.

While the available evidence, reviewed by Young (1969), seems to provide some justification for the use of videotaped models in microteaching, there remain unresolved important issues regarding the use of such models. In particular, the relative effectiveness of positive and negative models seems unexplored in this country, and such evidence as there has been from elsewhere (e.g. Allen et al., 1967; Koran, 1968)* seems to provide contradictory answers.

The aim of this study was to compare the effects of positive and negative models on students' acquisition of a microteaching skill.

Method

(a) *Subjects*

The subjects in this study were thirty-eight students enrolled during the first semester in education at Stirling University. These subjects were assigned at random to one of three groups: two experimental and one control.

(b) *Model Tapes*

In all, six model tapes of average duration ten minutes were used. Four of these were selected from the records of a previous semester-group's practice of the skill of Broad Questions; two were made by the experi-

---

*For a fuller review of the relevant literature see Gilmore (1975).

154

menter. In selecting tapes, the criterion for 'positive' models was that
the number of broad questions should greatly exceed the number of
narrow questions, whilst the criterion for 'negative' models was that the
number of narrow questions should greatly exceed the number of
broad questions. A further constraint on choice of model tapes was that
both sexes should be represented as model teachers, as previous research
had suggested the importance of this factor. Thus, for the positive
model group, three model tapes were shown, one of a university tutor,
one of a female student and one of a male student, with the average
ratio of broad questions to narrow questions being 9:1. For the negative
model group, the lessons were taught by the same university tutor, by a
female student and by a male student, with the average ratio of broad
questions to narrow questions being 1:9.

(c) *Procedure*

Subjects in all three groups were given a definition of the skill to be
practised (Broad Questions) together with a description of the observational criteria to be used. This was the only treatment provided for
subjects in the control group (group C). In addition, students in the
first experimental group (E1) viewed the three 'positive' model tapes,
whilst students in the second experimental group (E2) viewed the three
'negative' model tapes.

All subjects then taught a microlesson of fifteen minutes to a micro-
class of five pupils, during which they were asked to practise the skill of
Broad Questions. All thirty-eight lessons were recorded on videotape,
with strict control being exercised so that lessons did not fall below or
exceed a fifteen-minute time limit.

(d) *Criterion Measures*

In its null form, the major hypothesis of this study was that there
would be no significant differences among the three experimental
groups on any of the indices used to assess the skill of Broad Questions.
There were eight such indices, derived from a coding of the videotaped
lessons using an extended FIAC observational system. The indices were:

1 instances of narrow questions (category 4N)
2 instances of broad questions (category 4B)
3 instances of pupil response behaviours (category 8)
4 instances of pupil initiation behaviours (category 9)
5 instances of questions based on pupils' ideas (category 3Q)
6 instances of questions to which no response was obtained

7 instances of questions when pupils were given an opportunity to formulate a response
8 instances of questions when pupils were not given an opportunity to formulate a response.

Of these eight criteria, the first four were of major importance in that the basis of the skill specification was that the use of broad questions should be increased, the use of narrow questions decreased, and that the likely outcome of this pattern would be an increase in pupil initiation and a decrease in pupil response.

Of the other four criteria, the frequency of use of two — questions based on pupils' ideas, and allowing opportunity for pupil response — were to be maximised, whilst two — frequency of questions obtaining no response, and frequency of questions allowing no opportunity for response — were to be minimised.

Analysis of Data and Results

A one-way analysis of variance on each of the eight criterion measures was carried out, and, where significant F-ratios were obtained, modified 't' tests were applied to the differences between groups. There is some difference of opinion as to how to make 't' tests following an F-test.

In this study, the procedure used was that suggested by Pilliner (1973) and described by Guilford and Fruchter (1973).

i.e. $t' = \dfrac{d}{\sigma d}$

where d = difference between sample means of groups 1 and 2

and $\sigma d = \sqrt{(MS)_w \left(\dfrac{1}{n_1} + \dfrac{1}{n_2} \right)}$

where $(MS)_w$ = within groups mean square

n_1 = number of subjects in group 1

n_2 = number of subjects in group 2

Table 1 shows the means and standard deviations for each group on each of the criterion measures, together with the F-ratios and associated probability levels derived from the analysis of variance. For those variables where a significant F was found, the significant outcomes of the t' test are also indicated.

Summary of Results

On all four major criteria of the microteaching skill — Broad and Narrow Questions, Pupil Response and Pupil Initiation — the positive model group outperforms the other two groups. Whilst the trend for the positive group to ask fewer narrow questions is not statistically significant, this tendency is clearly visible. The hypothesised correlate of fewer narrow questions is less pupil response, and here the positive group's superiority over the negative group is statistically significant. On the criteria of number of broad questions and frequency of pupil initiation, the positive group is shown to be clearly superior to both the negative group and to the control group.

On the four other more indirect criteria, only one set of significant differences is found with the positive group asking fewer questions based on pupil ideas than did either the negative group or the control group. One possible reason for this would seem to be the lesser overall number of questions asked by the positive group than by the other two groups. No significant differences were found on the other three criteria.

Discussion of Results

This study has provided fairly clear and consistent evidence that the positive model group has outperformed both the negative model group and the control group on their performance on the four basic criteria used to define the skill of Broad Questions. The positive group made more use of broad questions and produced more pupil initiation than did either the control group or the negative group, whilst at the same time tending to ask fewer narrow questions, and to produce significantly less pupil response than did the negative group.

It is unclear, however, how generalisable these results are, a major difficulty, in this and similar researches, being the transition from conceptual to operational definition of what constitutes positive and negative models. One contribution of this study was to make clear the operational definitions used in describing the positive and negative model conditions. Thus, whilst possibly utilitarian information is provided to the user of microteaching programmes, it is unclear as to how to give a general definition of what constitues a positive model and what a negative model. Thus, for example, would the results have been different if the ratio of broad to narrow questions had been reduced for the positive group and increased for the negative group, or if the nega-

Table 1 Means and Standard Deviations of each Group and Significant Differences among and between Groups

		E1	E2	C	F	p	t'
Incidence of Narrow Questions	M	25.15	35.1	30.1	2.68	N.S.	
	S.D.	(9.57)	(13.8)	(8.70)			
Incidence of Broad Questions	M	7.69	3.23	2.67	7.88	$< .01$	E1 $>$ E2 E1 $>$ C
	S.D.	(4.44)	(2.88)	(3.11)			
Incidence of Pupil Response	M	25.92	40.92	34.42	4.16	$< .05$	E1 $>$ E2
	S.D.	(10.03)	(17.05)	(11.67)			
Incidence of Pupil Initiation	M	4.77	1.85	2.33	5.16	$< .05$	E1 $>$ E2 E1 $>$ C
	S.D.	(2.24)	(2.34)	(2.84)			
Incidence of Questions based on Pupils' ideas	M	3.15	8.46	8.08	5.20	$< .05$	E1 $>$ E2 E1 $>$ C
	S.D.	(2.34)	(5.03)	(5.96)			
Incidence of Pupils' Nil Response	M	5.08	3.31	4.07	0.99	N.S.	
	S.D.	(2.96)	(2.81)	(3.70)			
Incidence of Pupils' 'Opportunity to Respond'	M	8.31	4.62	6.67	2.32	N.S.	
	S.D.	(5.25)	(3.40)	(4.27)			
Incidence of 'No Opportunity to Respond'	M	0.54	1.08	0.92	0.50	N.S.	
	S.D.	(0.97)	(1.44)	(1.73)			

tive models had been defined as ones which showed too many broad questions, or lots of inappropriate broad questions? Similarly, can the obtained results be attributed to the differential information provided by the model tapes, or the different quantities of information provided by them, rather than by their qualities of 'positiveness' and 'negativeness'? It would seem reasonable to hypothesise, for example, that the superior performance of the positive group was a consequence of the discrimination training provided by frequency of exposure to recognisably broad questions.

Answers to these questions must await further research, and preferably research which is guided by explicit hypotheses.

References

Allen, D. W. et al. (1967). A comparison of different modelling procedures in the acquisition of a teaching skill, paper presented at the AERA Conference, New York.

Bandura, A., Ross, D. and Ross, S.A. (1963). 'Imitation of film-mediated aggressive models', *Journal of Abnormal and Social Psychology*, 66, pp. 3-11.

Bandura, A. and Walters, R.H. (1963). *Social Learning and Personality Development*, Holt, Rinehart and Winston, London.

Gilmore, S. (1975). The Effects of Modelling on Student Teachers' Questioning Behaviours: a Study in the Microteaching Context, unpublished M.Ed thesis, University of Glasgow.

Guilford, J.P. and Fruchter, B. (1973). *Fundamental Statistics in Psychology and Education*, McGraw-Hill, London.

Koran, J.J. (1968). The relative effectiveness of imitation versus problem solving in the acquisition of a complex teaching skill, Doctoral dissertation, Stanford University.

Pilliner, A. (1973). Experiment in Educational Research, E341 Educational Studies: *Methods of Educational Enquiry, Block 5*, Open University, Bletchley, Bucks.

Young, D.B. (1969). 'Modification of Teacher Behavior using Audio, Videotaped Models in a Microteaching Sequence', *Educational Leadership*, 26, pp. 394-403.

11 AN ASSESSMENT OF MICROTEACHING IN THE CONTEXT OF THE GRADUATE TRAINING YEAR

David C. Butts

1. Introduction

Interest in microteaching developed at Jordanhill College of Education in the late 1960s and was increased by a number of exploratory trials of self-viewing as an aid to the discussion of students' practice teaching. In 1971, the history department expressed interest in a thoroughgoing experiment with their graduate students, to determine whether this technique could practicably and effectively be used to improve the quality of their training programme.

The principal aim of the enquiry was formulated as follows:

to test the hypothesis that,within the graduate teacher-training year, history students given training through microteaching in specific skills will, in their subsequent classroom teaching, achieve performance in those skills significantly superior to the performance of a matched group of students who have been given no microteaching training.

In addition, the research study set out to examine:

(i) the feasibility of identifying and analysing a set of skills appropriate to history teaching in secondary schools and of creating an appraisal instrument, based on these skills, which could be used reliably by lecturers visiting students on school teaching practice;

(ii) the extent of agreement between assessments of students made by lecturers using an appraisal instrument on school visits and assessments of the same students based on a detailed quantitative analysis of recorded classroom lessons;

(iii) possible effects (beneficial or adverse) of microteaching training on students' classroom performance as a whole;

(iv) the practical problems involved, for students and lecturers, in organising microteaching sessions within the graduate training year;

(v) the reactions of students to the experiment;

(vi)   the reactions of lecturers to the experiment.

The research was planned to extend over three sessions. In 1971-2, teaching skills would be identified and analysed; an appraisal instrument would be devised and tested for reliability; models of selected skills would be prepared and recorded; and pilot microteaching sessions would be held, to explore the organisational problems involved. The main experiment would be run in 1972-3. Session 1973-4 would be spent in analysis and interpretation of the results.

It was acknowledged from the start that this research study should have an operational character, even though this might involve some reduction in precision and the acceptance of certain uncontrollable variables. The department wished to discover whether microteaching in the graduate training year could be effective at a level which could be accommodated without making major changes in established training procedures; and whether the extra effort and organisation entailed on lecturers and students could be kept within reasonable and practicable bounds. Finally, in making an assessment of microteaching, the college was concerned with performance in the classroom, not in the laboratory.

2. Method and procedure: the preparatory year

The work of the preparatory year followed a logical sequence, beginning with the identification and analysis of skills, leading to the preparation and testing of an Appraisal Guide, the selection of skills of microteaching practice, the recording of skills models and the formulation of a programme for the main study in the following session. At the same time, pilot microteaching practices were held, in the college and in neighbouring schools, to study logistical problems, assess the students' ability to interpret the analysis of selected skills and give tutors a chance to learn the techniques of supervision. Progress in each of the main stages of the work is described below.

(a) *Identification and analysis of skills*

The history department lecturers were not prepared to make an immediate choice of skills for special study and practice without first attempting to make explicit the complete range of skills for history teaching from which these would be selected. Furthermore, they wanted to be able to relate performance on specific skills to teaching performance as a whole. For these reasons, it was decided to produce an appraisal instrument, broad enough to provide a reliable assessment of overall competence, but sufficiently detailed to give an indication of ability in each of the major skills.

The process of identifying and analysing skills proved difficult and time-consuming. A major problem was that of deciding upon the appropriate degree of breadth in terms of which skills should be defined, one aspect of this difficulty being that tutors felt it necessary for practical reasons to discuss skills in much broader terms than those commonly used in a microteaching context. This problem was resolved by identifying relatively broadly-defined skills of three types — basic, composite and specialist skills — and operationalising each of these skills in terms of a number of subskills defined in behavioural terms. Another factor which required considerable care was the need to take account of the distinctive discipline of history. The skills tentatively defined by the author on the basis of general theory and research often had to be redefined in the light of the historians' comments. After several exchanges of drafts, departmental meetings and attempts to use the skill definitions in practice, a final set of fourteen broad skills was established (cf. Butts, 1975, Appendix A).

(b) *Preparation and testing of Appraisal Guide*

This list of fourteen broad competences was embodied in an Appraisal Guide, students being rated in terms of teaching competence on a seven-point scale. Early experience of using the Guide produced a crop of problems, both conceptual and practical, which were examined in a series of staff meetings. Achieving inter-tutor reliability involved agreeing on a concept of 'average performance', but discrepancies in the assessment of videotaped student lessons revealed a number of different approaches to performance norms. Some tutors based their assessment on 'what could reasonably be expected from students at this stage of their training' and thus applied increasingly critical standards as the year progressed. Some tutors took 'average' to mean 'average performance based on my total experience of student lessons'. Some related their assessment to a generalised concept of 'an averagely effective lesson taught on this particular subject to pupils of this age and stage'. Some tutors, more than others, took account of pupil reaction as well as teacher performance. Some, but not all, made allowances for difficult classes and unfavourable school environments.

There were also varying approaches to the range of assessments given. Some tutors attempted to relate the points in the rating scale to absolute standards of performance. Thus, an 'A' was associated in their minds with a 'near perfect' lesson and was rarely, if ever, awarded.

Other tutors thought of the rating scale in percentile terms, although no general decision had been taken about the proportion of the population covered by each point on the scale, and accordingly tended to award a broader range of assessments. Problems of weighting affected the reliability of overall assessments. Tutors found it difficult to agree about which skills were 'most important'. For example, group assessments (and subsequent discussion) of videotaped lessons indicated that some tutors attached particular importance to ensuring pupil participation, while others put more emphasis on presentation skills. Thus, two tutors might agree in their ratings of these specific skills, but still differ widely in their overall assessment.

Morrison and McIntyre (1973) note that 'while one may be confident that a specified skill is of value in teaching, the decision as to whether or not it is *appropriate* to use that skill in the context of any particular lesson must generally be highly subjective'. The Jordanhill tutors attached great importance to appropriateness and making the most of opportunities in the use of a skill. It would be expected that the element of high inference thereby introduced into judgements of performance would tend towards unreliability, even when tutors were in general agreement about the kind of teaching behaviour which was desirable in a particular context. Analysis of student lesson ratings revealed, however, that such agreement did not always exist.

In observing student lessons, tutors saw themselves as filling a number of roles: diagnostician, counsellor, critic and assessor. Some tutors associated the use of the Appraisal Guide with assessment rather than diagnosis, and were consequently concerned about confidentiality. Had the student the right to see this detailed report? What would happen if he discovered that he had been given low ratings? Some effort was required to dispel this kind of anxiety, which may well have led some tutors to skew their ratings towards the upper end of the scale.

The most intractable problem for the majority of tutors was that of combining assessment of specific skills with judgement of the general quality of a student's teaching. To appreciate this quality, they felt that they needed to sit back from the lesson, to be aware of its overall rhythm and balance, to sense its cumulative impact upon the pupils. They accepted that the ability to combine a wide and narrow focus of observation would probably grow with training; but the time which they could spare for such training was limited, and meantime they were concerned lest, in concentrating upon the pulse tick of analysis, they should miss the heart beat of the lesson as a whole.

Four reliability trials were mounted in the course of the preparatory

year. The first two showed such wide variance among tutors in their
use of the Appraisal Guide that there was clearly no point in making a
full analysis until further training had been carried out. The two final
trials were mounted in June and September 1972, using a series of
videotaped student lessons.

In general, the results of the June and September trials indicated
that the problems revealed in practice sessions had not been fully resolved. Agreement on ranking students on general teaching performance was consistently high; but, while the overall level of reliability
for assessment of specific skills appeared reasonably satisfactory, the
wide variations in reliability both according to the criterion being
rated and according to the lessons being rated indicated that it would
be unwise to place much reliance on tutor ratings as the sole or even
the major basis for assessment in the course of the main experiment.

The failure of the history lecturers to achieve a consistently high
degree of reliability, after a year's experience of the Appraisal Guide
and the Skills Analysis on which it was based, supports the findings of
other researchers. Nevertheless, it must be emphasised that considerable
progress was made between the trials of November/February and those
of June/September, and that the training in the intervening period was
by no means intensive, not through any lack of good will on the part of
the tutors but because of existing heavy commitments.

(c) *Preparatory work on microteaching*

Microteaching sessions based on each of several skills were held each
term throughout the preparatory year, with the aims of studying practical problems and any difficulties experienced by students and of
giving supervisors experience in evaluating students' performance on
specific skills. These sessions were mounted both in the college and in
neighbouring schools. Neither arrangement presented any great practical
problems and the indications were that it would in future be
appropriate to use either system according to the particular function
for which microteaching was being used. For the purpose of the main
experiment it appeared preferable to organise sessions lasting several
days in the college. This involved the expense of transporting pupils
from the schools, but it allowed more time for setting up equipment
beforehand and was preferred by both tutors and students.

Experience at Jordanhill in the development of videotaped model
lessons paralleled that of the Far West Laboratory (cf. Borg et al.,
1970). The department, aware of students' critical reactions to any
hint of artificiality in teaching demonstrations, attached great impor-

tance to realism; but initial attempts by experienced lecturers to model the skills in the course of 'normal' classroom lessons proved on the whole to be unsatisfactory. Careful analysis of the tapes revealed that each aspect of the skill in question had been used, but the pattern of moves and sequences, of action and interaction, was so complex that even patient editing could not make the examples of the skill stand out clearly from their context. Second attempts were more carefully structured and taken at a slower pace, though scripting was never adopted.

3. Method and procedure: the main experiment

The selected skills were grouped under two headings as follows:

Asking questions
1 (a) Avoiding over-use of 'one-word answer' type questions
  (b) Avoiding over-use of 'yes/no' type questions
2 Varying the level and nature of questions, with particular attention to increasing the proportion of 'higher order' questions, demanding interpretation, judgement, etc.
Dealing with answers
3 (a) Giving pupils time for thought in formulating answers
  (b) Through prompting, encouraging adequately phrased and accurate responses
4 Making constructive use of initial answers by
  (a) probing, for extension, clarification and justification of response
  (b) redirecting initial answers for comment and discussion.

This selection from the skills listed in the analysis of Question Technique was aimed at encouraging students to use questioning not merely as a means of promoting recall and obtaining information but as a stimulus to thought and discussion at a higher cognitive level. The justification for adopting this approach to questioning, outlined, for example, by Gall et al. (1971, pp. 11-18), was accepted by the history department.

The experiment compared an experimental group of students, who were given microteaching experience in the second term of the year, with a matched control group. Pre-treatment comparisons were based on students' teaching in the first term, and post-treatment comparisons were based on their teaching in the third term. The design was complicated by the need to take account of a distinctive feature of the postgraduate programme: half of the students spent the first half of each term on school practice and the second half of the term in the college, while for the remainder of the students this pattern was reversed. From each of these two groups of students, twenty were randomly selected to take part in the experiment and these twenty students were then matched into pairs on the basis of their ability in the selected questioning skills as assessed by tutors on their first-term teaching practice visits.

Two types of criterion measures were used. Ratings of questioning skills and of overall lesson performance were made by tutors, using the Appraisal Guide, on the basis of the observations they made during their normal schedule of visits in the first term and then again in the third term. Secondly, sample lessons were audio-taped for each student in the first and third terms, and systematically analysed in terms of a Coding Instrument which was developed to provide reliable operational definitions of the specified questioning skills (cf. Butts, 1975).

The recordings of sample lessons had to be fitted into each half-term period while avoiding, as far as possible, any clash with the tutors' schedule of visits. There was thus time to record only one lesson by each student in each term.

The students were given guidance on format and asked to teach a 25-minute lesson, divided into

10 minutes of introduction and exposition
10 minutes of questioning and discussion
 5 minutes of summing up

and to submit a lesson plan indicating these three main divisions. Subsequently the ten minutes of questioning and discussion were identified and timed exactly from the recordings, and category analysis was applied only to this section of each lesson.

For experimental group students, microteaching practice replaced school practice for the third of their five weeks of teaching practice in the second term.

For both *Asking Questions* and *Dealing with answers* a programme of the type developed at Stanford University was followed:

analysis and modelling of selected skills
teaching of a short practice lesson
critique based on feedback of performance
replanning
reteaching the same lesson to a different group of pupils
critique based on feedback and discussion with supervisor.

One history tutor, selected from the microteaching team trained in the preparatory year, acted as supervisor throughout the sessions, and this tutor did not act as supervisor for any of the experimental or control group students on school practice. It was decided (on the evidence of student reaction to other reported experiments, e.g. Owens and Hatton, 1970; Turney, 1970; Young, 1970) to conduct the playbacks as group sessions. Students were given an Evaluation Form to complete for each playback, as a means of directing their attention to the various aspects of the skills being practised.

Evidence on reactions to the microteaching experiment was gathered through three questionnaires, for completion
    by the experimental group of students immediately after their microteaching sessions in term 2;
    by the same students immediately after their final teaching practice in term 3;
    by tutors at the end of the session.

4. Results of the main experiment

The symbols used throughout the tables in this section are defined as follows:
    HOQ — Higher Order question (involving analysis, synthesis, evaluation)
    MOQ — Middle Order question (involving description, explanation, application)
    LOQ — Lower Order question (involving recall of knowledge, unjustified opinions, random guesswork)
      P — Prompt (clue given by teacher to encourage response)
     XP — Prompt following a question which obtained no response
     Pr — Probe (follow-up question requiring pupil to clarify or justify initial response)
      R — Redirection (of initial response to other pupils, for comment and discussion)
      y — Question in a form which appeared to demand no more than a 'yes' or 'no' response
      x — Question which attracted no response
      n — Question where no opportunity was given to respond.

(a) *Measurements based on coding of recorded lessons*

Considering experimental and control treatments, and the groups on school practice in the first and second halves of each term, there were four groups, each of ten students, involved in the experiment. To assess 'gains' from the first to the third terms for each of these four groups, t-values for correlated measures were calculated; these are shown in table 1.

Table 1 Term 3 — term 1 t values for performance of experimental and control groups in selected skills

| | EXPERIMENTAL | | | | CONTROL | | | |
SKILLS	1st half term	Signi-ficance	2nd half term	Signi-ficance	1st half term	Signi-ficance	2nd half term	Sig-nifi-cance
		P		P		P		P
$\frac{HOQ}{Q}$	4.076	.005	1.643		0.321		-0.032	
$\frac{LOQ}{Q}$	-4.157	.005	-4.053	.005	0.425		-0.175	
$\frac{XP}{X}$	1.077		-0.278		0.809		-1.262	
$\frac{Pr}{Q}$	3.389	.005	0.991		1.145		3.346	.02
$\frac{y}{Q}$	1.669		0.080		-0.359		1.226	
$\frac{x}{Q}$	-2.066	.05	-0.254		1.786		1.146	
$\frac{HOX}{HOQ}$	-0.249		-0.682		—		—	
$\frac{n}{Q\ incl.n}$	-0.718		-0.468		1.645		2.235	

In connection with table 1, it should be noted that tests of significance are 1-tailed for the experimental group and 2-tailed for the control group.

In table 2, results are given of comparisons between experimental and control groups. Since students were matched, t-tests for correlated measures were again used. Results are given for the term 1 pre-measures and for the term 3 post-measures, and the groups on teaching practice in the different half-terms are again treated separately.

Examination of the *direction* of the differences between experimental and control groups shown in table 2 reveals that, whereas there is no general tendency for either to be 'superior' in term 1, fifteen of the sixteen differences in term 3 are in favour of the experimental group. While t-values have been presented in table 2 in order to facilitate communication of the results, the design of the experiment was such that two-way analysis of variance, with matched pairs nested

Table 2 Experimental-control t values for performance in selected
skills, term 1 and term 3

SKILLS	1st half term 1	Signi- ficance	2nd half Term 1	Signi- ficance	1st half Term 3	Signi- ficance	2nd half Term 3	Sig- nifi- cance
	EXPERIMENTAL CONTROL Term 1				EXPERIMENTAL CONTROL Term 3			
		P		P		P		P
$\frac{HOQ}{Q}$	1.653		−0.367		6.588	.0005	1.640	
$\frac{LOQ}{Q}$	−0.314		−0.027		−3.905	.005	−2.655	.02
$\frac{XP}{X}$	−0.443		0.444		0.113		1.308	
$\frac{Pr}{Q}$	1.090		2.134		2.372	.02	0.796	
$\frac{y}{Q}$	−1.102		−0.976		−0.454		−1.038	
$\frac{x}{Q}$	1.305		2.211		−1.410		0.456	
$\frac{HOX}{HOQ}$	−		1.363		−0.369		−0.075	
$\frac{n}{Q\,incl.\,n}$	−0.200		0.833		−1.846		−0.982	

In connection with table 2, it should be noted that the tests of significance are
2-tailed for term 1 and 1-tailed for term 3.

within half-terms, was appropriate. Such analysis confirms the results
set out in table 2: highly significant differences (p < .001) between
treatments were found for both Higher Order and Lower Order questions.

(b) *Measurements based on tutors' assessments*
The Appraisal Guide used by tutors on their visits to students in
schools provided both for broad assessments of overall teaching competence and for more detailed assessments of performance on each of
the selected questioning skills. t-tests were applied to examine the significance of any differences between experimental and control groups
which emerged from these tutor ratings. Results are set out in tables
3 and 4.

It should be noted that the seven skills rated by tutors are not iden-

Table 3 t-values derived from tutors' overall lesson rating of experimental and control groups term 1 and term 3

| | Experimental — Control | | | |
	Term 1	Sig.	Term 3	Sig.
		P		P
1st Half	0.437		0.930	
2nd Half	-1.259		-1.750	

N.B. All tests of significance were 2-tailed.

Table 4 t-values derived from tutors' term 3 ratings of performance on questioning skills

| SKILLS | Experimental — Control | | | |
	1st Half	Sig.	2nd Half	Sig.
		P		P
One-word answers	-0.700		-0.760	
Yes/no questions	-1.871	.05	-1.000	
Optimum use of HOQ	0.532		-0.667	
Allowing time for response	-0.817		-0.665	
Prompting	-0.158		-1.206	
Probing	-0.521		-1.306	
Redirecting	-0.853		-0.935	

N.B. All tests of significance were 1-tailed.

tical with the behaviours selected for quantitative measurement in the coding procedure, but are closely related to them.

Since the general pattern of tutor term 3 ratings ran counter to the pattern of evidence derived from the coding of term 3 lessons, tutors agreed that, working as pairs, they would make independent assessments of the term 3 lessons recorded for coding, so that levels of agreement, both between members of each tutor pair and between tutors and coder, could be examined, in terms of product-moment correlations for each criterion. The results revealed that such reliability in the use of the Appraisal Guide as had been achieved by the end of the preparatory year had been lost in the course of the following session; levels of inter-tutor agreement were very varied but generally low, so that it was inevitable that tutor-coder agreement was also very low.

(c) *Analysis of student and tutor reactions to microteaching*

In view of the small numbers of students and tutors involved in the project, no statistical procedures were applied to the questionnaire responses. Analysis indicated that, from the students' point of view,

   (i)   the actual experience of microteaching was acceptable, though there was some sense of artificiality about it;

  (ii)   peer grouping at the review stage was considered positively useful;

 (iii)   the presence of a tutor at the review stage was welcomed;

 (iv)   all students claimed to have made at least occasional attempts to apply the skills practised in microteaching during their subsequent teaching in schools, and most felt that they had achieved some measure of success, in spite of disciplinary problems and the need to cover a set amount of material;

  (v)   there was a strong preference for microteaching practice in the form of a complete cycle of activities;

 (vi)   the element of analytic rigour associated with the microteaching programme was appreciated.

From the lecturers' point of view, there was

   (i)   a cautious acceptance of the value of analysing specific skills, combined with an insistence on the importance of personality and intuitive approaches, as elements in effective teaching;

  (ii)   a division of opinion between those who welcomed the more objective approach to assessment demanded by the Appraisal Guide and those who questioned the validity of assessing effectiveness in terms of quantitative measures of the use of skills;

 (iii)   a belief that microteaching should continue to find some place in the graduate training course.

5. Interpretation and Comment

Table 1 shows the progress made, between terms 1 and 3, by experimental and control groups, on each of the categories under review. The first half-term experimental group achieved a highly significant shift towards a greater proportion of higher order questions, with a corresponding reduction in the proportion of lower order questions. The use of probing questions also increased significantly. It was encouraging that the shift in favour of higher order questioning was accompanied by a significant decrease in the proportion of questions obtaining no response; but disappointing that the proportion of questions demanding no more than a yes/no response increased, even though the avoidance of this type of question had been a specific element in the microteaching training. The use of prompting increased and the proportion of questions allowing no opportunity to respond was reduced, although these changes were not significant.

The second half-term experimental group achieved only one significant change in reducing the proportion of lower order questions. The figures for higher order questioning were affected by what was perhaps a freak performance by the weakest student in the group who in term 1 scored 54.5 per cent. The performance on probing was also disappointing — the four students rated highest increased their proportion of probes, but the remainder of the group did less well in term 3 than in term 1. It must be noted, however, that the term 1 performance of this group in probing was exceptionally high. Once again, the proportion of yes/no questions increased, though only marginally so, and the use of prompting decreased.

These figures must be viewed in contrast to the performances of the two control group sections. Apart from the improvement by the second half-term group in probing, there was no significant shift in behaviour; and, indeed, performance of the first half-term group deteriorated in four of the categories, while the second half-term group performance deteriorated in six of the categories.

Table 2 provides evidence on the main hypothesis which the experiment set out to test: that 'students given training through microteaching in specific skills will, in their subsequent classroom teaching, achieve performance in those skills significantly superior to the performance of a matched group who have been given no microteaching training'. The lack of any significant difference between experimental and control groups in term 1 is consistent with the high inference ratings by tutors, which were used as a basis for matching. In term 3, the first half-term experimental group was superior to the control group in all categories, with marked significance in terms of higher and lower order questioning and in probing. In the second half of the term, significant experimental group superiority was restricted to lower order questioning, though a measure of experimental superiority is shown in six of the other seven categories. Thus, in terms of significance for separate categories, the results fully support the main hypothesis in respect of lower order questioning; partially support it in respect of higher order questioning and probing; and do not support it in respect of prompting, avoidance of yes/no questions and reduction of questions allowing no opportunity for response.

A subsidiary aim of the study was to gather evidence of the effect of microteaching training on students' classroom performance as a whole, and it was to this end that the tutors' Appraisal Guide was designed to cover general teaching ability as well as specific questioning skills. Table 3 shows that no significant differences between experimental and control groups emerged, either in term 1 or in term 3, from the data provided by the Appraisal Guide on overall teaching competence. For each half term, the initial differences between groups increased slightly — in favour of the experimental group in the first half term and the control group in the second half term — but not significantly so. There is thus no indication that, in the tutors' judgement (which was made in ignorance of which students were in the experimental group and which in the control), microteaching had any significant effect, either beneficial or adverse, on teaching performance as a whole. This finding is of interest, in view of the impression formed by some tutors (reported below) that microteaching was distorting the balance of teaching behaviour as the year progressed.

Table 4 relates to the ratings by tutors of performance on specific questioning skills in term 3. Again, it must be stressed that these ratings were made in ignorance of which students had received micro-teaching training in the skills concerned. Only one difference achieves significance, but the recurrence of control group superiority — for six out of seven skills in the first half of the term and for all seven skills in the second half — is itself significant. These findings must be contrasted with the evidence from the coder's findings of superiority — all eight categories favouring the experimental group in the first half of the term and seven out of eight categories showing experimental group superiority in the second half term.

6. Conclusions

In the light of the evidence, it can be claimed that, at least on the basis of the coder's assessments, the experimental groups, on a post-micro-teaching classroom teaching occasion, made significantly greater use than did the control group of some but not all of the questioning skills in which they had been trained; and that their overall use of these skills was, in terms of probability, significantly superior to that of the con-trol groups. These findings hold good for both half-term sections, though the superiority is more clearly marked in the first half of the term, and the results provide a reasonable measure of support for the belief that some element of microteaching may usefully be incorporated into the pattern of the graduate teacher training year. The performance gains were achieved after only two days of microteaching, allowing for one complete cycle of training on each of the skills; half the minimal period considered by the Stanford University research workers to be essential for effective training. Under these circumstances it was perhaps not surprising that the students did better in acquiring and retaining the major skills of shifting emphasis to higher cognitive questioning and of probing questions — skills whose employment involved an element of conscious decision — than they did in avoiding yes/no questions and questions giving no opportunity for response: patterns of behaviour which may well have been strongly linked with habit or personality. Finally, in view of the limited and inconclusive amount of research evidence on transfer of microteaching performance gains to classroom practice, it is arguable that any study such as that at Jordanhill which provides at least some positive indication of transfer is worth following up. In particular, the fact that significant differences between experimental and control groups in classroom performance were found approximately three months after the training period provides more grounds for optimism than the evidence of Brusling and Stukat (1971), who found that positive effects of microteaching training had largely disappeared two months later when the students were observed in regular classrooms; and of Copeland and Doyle (1973), whose experimental group, seven weeks after they had completed an extensive period of microteaching, showed no significant superiority over a control group, on the basis of coded classroom lessons.

The second aim of the research study was to examine the feasibility of identifying and analysing a set of skills appropriate to history teaching in secondary schools, and of creating an appraisal instrument, based on these skills, which could be used reliably by lecturers. Like any well stocked rag-bag, the 'Analysis of Teaching Skills', produced in the first year of the project, had the merit of being comprehensive. In retrospect, the problem implicit in the analysis would appear to be that, under each broad heading, and as between the different headings, the specified units of behaviour varied constantly in level, so that the reader could retain no consistent concept of the nature and scope of a 'sub-skill'. These conceptual uncertainties in the Analysis of Skills may account in some measure for the difficulty experienced by some lecturers in achieving and maintaining reliability in their use of the Appraisal Guide. It may well be that the task of constantly changing perspective in their view of the lesson was more than they could cope with; and it is significant that the Appraisal Guide reliability trials revealed a much higher level of inter-rater agreement for assessments of broad teaching competences than for judgements of specific skills performance. However, in the tutors' own view, the main problem in achieving reliability with the Appraisal Guide lay not so much in defining skills as in agreeing upon the concept of average performance and in making allowance for 'appropriate use' and 'grasping of opportunities'. It must be admitted that the research project found no solution to the difficulty of devising a systematic technique of appraisal which would accommodate high inference assessment while achieving reliability at a departmental level. The task of identifying skills was a necessary first step in any process of reliable appraisal; but it must be concluded that, at the end of the day, the main value of developing such a comprehensive analysis and such a detailed appraisal instrument lay, first, in the opportunity for communal exploration of what had been to some extent private territory; and second, in the exposure of hitherto unacknowledged problems inherent in subjective judgements.

The third aim of the enquiry was to discover the extent of agreement between assessments of students made by tutors on school visits and assessments of the same students based on quantitative analysis of their recorded teaching. Because of the demonstrated unreliability of tutor assessments, it is not possible to infer that there were factors implicit in high inference judgements which pointed in a different direction from low inference measurements of performance. Moreover, an important question on which it had been hoped to gather evidence remains unsolved: the question of the link between increased use (fostered by microteaching training) of specific technical skills and teaching 'effectiveness'. The Jordanhill lecturers were convinced that the key to the effective use of skills lay partly in appropriateness — the right skill at the right moment — and partly in teaching style and personality. Their view is supported by the findings of Rosenshine and Furst (1971), that the presentation variables correlating most consistently with pupil achievement were identifiable through high inference ratings of performance. Conversely, some of the lecturers shared the doubts expressed by St John-Brooks and Spelman (1973) that, through the component skills approach of microteaching, 'highly visible but relatively trivial teaching skills have been emphasised at the expense of more subtle and individual techniques' and that 'the emphasis on individual skills may hamper student teachers in developing a full response to the highly complex patterns of behaviour which can be seen in the real classroom'. Evidence of term 3 classroom performance, based on demonstrably reliable high inference assessments,

would have provided a first step towards establishing a relationship,
positive or negative, between the kind of training offered by the microteaching programme and increased effectiveness. As it is, no conclusion
can be reached and there are no clues to follow up.

The final aim of this study was to examine the reaction of students
and lecturers to the experiment. These reactions have already been
commented on in some detail. In conclusion, it would seem worth
emphasising two points which have a bearing on any future development of these training techniques:

(a)   The students' reaction
       The recurring suggestion in responses to the final questionnaire
       that the pedagogical aims and approaches implicit in the struc-
       ture of the skills selected for microteaching were different
       from those to which pupils were accustomed or even from
       those to which students were expected to conform in teaching
       practice.

(b)   The lecturers' reaction
       While the questionnaire responses revealed views ranging
       from qualified enthusiasm to mild scepticism about an
       approach which seemed an additional and perhaps pointless
       complication of existing training procedures, the overall re-
       action would seem to illustrate the problems inherent in
       centre-periphery models of innovation. The drive in this
       instance came from the researcher associated with the
       principal and senior lecturers; and the impression which
       remains is that, although the department as a whole gave its
       intelligent and loyal support for the duration of the experi-
       ment, there was insufficient conviction about the value of
       microteaching to ensure its development once the thrust from
       the centre had been withdrawn.

References

Bellack, A.A. Kliebard, H.M., Hyman, R.T., Smith, F.L. Jr. (1966). *The Lang-
   uage of the Classroom,* Teachers College Press, Columbia University, New
   York.
Borg, W.R. Kelley, M.L., and Langer, P. (1970). *Minicourse 1: Effective Ques-
   tioning: Elementary Level,* Macmillan Educational Services Inc., California.
Borg, W.R., Kelley, M.L., Langer, P., and Gall, M. (1970). *The Minicourse: a
   Microteaching Approach to Teacher Education,* Macmillan Educational
   Services, Inc., Beverly Hills, California.
Brusling, C., and Stukat, K-G. (1972). Report on microteaching research at

Gothenburg School of Education, Educational Research in Sweden, 1971-2.

Butts, D.C. (1975). An Assessment of Microteaching in the Context of the Graduate Training Year, unpublished M.Sc thesis, University of Stirling.

Copeland, W.D., and Doyle, W. (1973). 'Laboratory skill training and student teacher classroom performance', *Journal of Experimental Education*, vol. 42, no. 1, pp. 16-21.

Gall, M.D. Dunning, B. and Weathersby, R. (1971). *Minicourse 9: Higher Cognitive Questioning* (Teachers' Handbook), Macmillan Educational Services Inc., California.

Morrison, A. and McIntyre, D. (1973). *Teachers and Teaching* (2nd edition), Penguin Education, Harmondsworth.

Orme, M.E.J. (1966). Effects of Modelling and Feedback Variables on the Acquisition of a Complex Teaching Strategy, unpublished doctoral dissertation, Stanford University, California.

Owens, L. and Hatton, N. (1970). ' "Telling it like it is" – microteaching in a teacher education programme', University of Sydney (mimeo).

Rosenshine, B. and Furst, N. (1971). 'Research on teacher performance criteria', in Smith, B.O. (ed.), *Research in Teacher Education: a Symposium*, Prentice-Hall Inc., Englewood Cliffs, N.J.

St John-Brooks, C., and Spelman, B. (1973). 'Microteaching', Trends in Education, no. 31, pp. 14-19.

Skailand, D. (1972). 'Minicourse 18: main field test report', Far West Laboratory for Educational Research and Development, Berkeley, California (mimeo).

Turney, C. (1970). 'Microteaching – a promising innovation in teacher education', *Australian Journal of Education*, 14 (2), pp. 125-41.

Young, D.A. (1970). 'Preliminary Report on the effectiveness of supervision on the acquisition of selected teaching behaviours in a microteaching series.' Paper presented at the annual meeting of AERA.

PART 5 STUDENTS' PERCEPTIONS OF THEIR MICROTEACHING PERFORMANCE

Microteaching was developed in response to a perceived practical need. It seemed clear that conventional procedures did not facilitate certain desirable kinds of learning, and the function of microteaching was to provide a context deliberately planned to foster such learning. For example, microteaching was planned so that students would concentrate their attention on one teaching skill at a time; and videotape feedback was provided in order that students' perceptions of their teaching might be more objective.

In retrospect, it is remarkable how little research there has been to assess the extent to which microteaching does lead to learning of the kinds it was designed to promote. There has been a substantial amount of research into microteaching, concerned with many different questions, but these questions have rarely been about the nature of student-teachers' learning; and this is as true of the research reported in earlier sections of this volume as it is of research elsewhere.

One reason for this neglect of 'obvious' questions about learning processes is that few of those concerned with microteaching appear to have been interested in the kind of theoretical rationale which might be offered for it. The initial formulation of microteaching at Stanford was certainly informed by more or less clear behaviour modification principles; but the great majority of users of, and researchers into, microteaching have shown an overwhelming interest in procedural rather than theoretical questions. In particular, there has been much greater interest in questions about manpower and, even more, about technological hardware than there has been in the ways in which students' thinking and behaviour change.

The four papers by MacLeod in this section are therefore particularly significant in that they provide evidence which can help us to develop a clearer understanding of students' psychological processes as they go through a microteaching programme. Like the work reported in part 3 on students' evaluation of observed teaching behaviour, this research starts from the assumption that the ways in which students construe teaching are of major significance in the development of their teaching behaviour. It is unlike the earlier work, however, in that it is directly concerned with students' cognitions of their own microteaching behaviour, and also in that it provides evidence of the validity of this initial assumption.

This research, then, provides extensive evidence of the kind which is necessary for the development of more articulate theoretical models of how students learn from microteaching. Secondly, it provides clear support for some of the beliefs which are taken for granted by many users of microteaching, and equally clearly calls other such beliefs into question. Finally, it exemplifies a type of research which, while rigorous in its design and its procedures, explores the meaning of students' microteaching behaviour not only in terms of the predetermined categories of the teacher trainers but also in terms of the students' own schemata.

12 THE ANALYSIS OF STUDENTS' PERCEPTIONS OF THEIR MICROTEACHING PERFORMANCE

Gordon MacLeod

Introduction

In this chapter, and the three subsequent ones, a series of interrelated investigations into students' perceptions of their microteaching performance will be reported. This first chapter will set the context for the research, and will describe the development of the data-collection procedures which were used in the three studies.

Context

The three studies reported here were carried out within an ongoing microteaching programme at the University of Stirling. Within this programme, students practised a series of microteaching skills based on an extended version of the Flanders' Interaction Analysis Category System (FIAC). During one semester, students were introduced to, and learned the FIAC categories and their extensions, and practised a total of seven microteaching lessons. Of these seven lessons, the first five were used in this investigation, and these consisted of an initial familiarisation lesson, of ten minutes' duration, and ten-minute teach and reteach lessons of the skills of Initiation/Response and Broad Questions. Following the initial lesson, and the teach lessons of both skills, students completed an open-ended questionnaire in which they were asked to report their perceptions of their performance. These written comments, together with the videotape records of performance, provided the raw data for the studies being reported here. Figure 1 shows in schematic form the pattern of the microteaching programme, the points at which data collection was carried out and the use made of the data in each of the three component studies.

Instrumentation

Common to all three studies were the measurement instruments used, and the fact that the coding of data was carried out by the experimenter alone. This next section will describe the two measurement systems used and report briefly on the studies of inter-observer agreement in their use.

181

Figure 1 Schematic view of the components of the three research studies

Occasion		Subjects' Tasks	Source of Retained Data	Use of Retained Data		
				Study		
				1	2	3
Initial Lesson:	Wk. 3	Teach Viewing of replay. Questionnaire completion	Questionnaire	*		
Skill 1: Initiation and Response	Wk. 5	Teach Viewing of replay. Questionnaire completion	Videotapes Questionnaires	*		* *
	Wk. 6	Reteach Viewing of replay.	Videotapes			*
Skill 2: Broad Questions	Wk. 7	Teach Four feedback conditions (Video/No video; FIAC/ No FIAC) Questionnaire completion	Videotapes Questionnaires	*	* *	
	Wk. 8	Reteach Viewing of replay	Videotapes		*	

(a) *Categorisation of Teaching Behaviour*

A very major advantage of operating within the ongoing microteaching programme was that an instrument for the analysis of teaching behaviour was available in the extended FIAC system which was being used in the course to familiarise students with analytic approaches to the study of teaching and as a means of operationalising the skills they were to practise in microteaching. Thus, for the students, the teaching tasks being asked of them were being specified in terms of fairly precise conceptual and operational definitions. For the research, this allowed the attainment of that rarity in teacher education — a set of quantifiable and agreed criteria for 'good' teaching. This is not to assert the general validity of these particular skills, but simply to note their value and measurability in a situation where they were agreed as criteria by those prescribing the course and apparently by those undertaking the course.

The extensions to the basic ten-category FIAC system which were required for this study were the division of the questioning category

into two — broad and narrow questions — and a similar modification of
part of the 'making use of pupils' ideas' category, first separating off
questions which made use of pupil ideas, and then subdividing that
category into broad and narrow questions. This procedure yielded a
thirteen-category research instrument which was used to code all
lessons, and which allowed the coding to be carried out without the
experimenter's knowing which lessons were teach, which were reteach,
which were skill one, which were skill two. The full instrument is shown
in figure 2.

Figure 2 The extended FIAC system

	Category	Key
	1	Accepts feeling
	2	Praises or encourages
	3	Accepts or uses ideas of pupils
Teacher	3N	Uses ideas of pupils in asking a narrow question
Talk	3B	Uses ideas of pupils in asking a broad question
	4N	Asks a narrow question
	4B	Asks a broad question
	5	Lecturing
	6	Giving directions
	7	Criticising or justifying authority
Pupil	8	Pupil talk — response
Talk	9	Pupil talk — initiation
	10	Silence or confusion

Before coding the experimental lessons, the experimenter and a co-
worker carried out a test of inter-observer agreement in their coding of
ten ten-minute microteaching lessons. Among the indices of agreement
which were computed were Scott's π coefficients (Flanders, 1965) both
for the basic ten-category system and for the extended system. The π
values were .91 against the usual but arbitrary recommended level of
.85 for the ten-category system and .87 for the thirteen-category
system. Three months later, on completion of the coding of the experimental lessons, the experimenter recoded the same ten ten-minute
lessons, and test-retest π coefficients were computed and found to be
.94 for the ten-category system and .81 for the thirteen-category system.

(b) *Assessment of Perceptions of Lessons*

(i) *Collection of Data* In developing a means for assessing students' perceptions of their microteaching lessons, certain criteria, both practical and methodological, had to be met. Among these were:

  (i)   that the outcomes should be quantifiable;
  (ii) that as little guidance as possible should be given to the respondents as to the nature of the responses which were appropriate, thus avoiding some of the difficulties of previous research (e.g. Webb, 1970);
  (iii) that the data-gathering procedure should not be so time-consuming as to disturb the ongoing microteaching programme;
  (iv) that the data-gathering procedure should be self-explanatory to the respondents and not require individual testing.

In that the first two of these constraints could be in opposition, it was decided that a pilot study be carried out involving two data-collection procedures, one of which offered easily quantifiable results but also provided guidance as to the kinds of response, the other of which offered little guidance as to response but implied complexity in the quantification process.

The first instrument was a lengthy, structured questionnaire in which respondents were asked to rate the degree of their 'awareness of' various features involved in their microteaching lessons. The sixty-three items in this questionnaire were either constructed by the experimenter or derived from other sources, especially Robertson (1957) and Wright, Nuthall and Lawrence (1969).

The second procedure was an open-ended questionnaire, derived from Millar (1972) and consisting of a short list of simple instructions together with blank pages ruled off horizontally in numbered sections. The instructions were:

  1. Please write down on the attached sheet your reactions (comments, evaluations, impressions, feelings, etc.) to your lesson.
  2. Please use a different numbered space for each comment you make, i.e. do not combine in one space points you feel can be differentiated.

3. See that each statement you make is clear and explicit.

Both questionnaires were administered twice to students undertaking a
semester-course of microteaching, first immediately after the videotape
replay of their first microteaching lesson, and then after the videotape
replay of their fifth microteaching lesson. On the first occasion, sixty-
eight randomly selected students completed the structured questionnaire, and sixty-six the open-ended questionnaire. On the second occasion, there was a strike within the university which meant that only
thirty-six could complete the open-ended questionnaire, whilst the
structured questionnaire was completed by seventy selected students.
The purpose in 'topping-up' the structured questionnaire group was to
ensure a minimally acceptable criterion for the planned factor analysis,
that there should be more respondents than questionnaire items.

The results from the structured questionnaire were subjected to a
fairly full analysis by means of an assessment of significant changes in
ratings from the first to the second occasion, and by factor analyses
with varying numbers of components being extracted. Overall, the
results were disappointing. Within the factor analysis, not only was
there difficulty in selecting a cut-off point for retaining components,
but also there were difficulties in interpreting some of those
components which were retained. However, this analysis did have positive features in that it seemed to show that two dimensions — 'awareness of' and 'evaluation of' — should be clearly separated, and it did
serve to identify some dimensions or broad categories for use in further
analysis (cf. MacLeod, 1976).

The open-ended questionnaire produced data of such richness and
diversity that no quick comparative analysis could be made at the
pilot-study stage. On the first occasion there was an average of 4.36
statements per respondent; on the second occasion the average was 3.72
per respondent.

In comparing the relative merits of the structured and open-ended
questionnaires, priority was given to the 'minimal guidance' criterion
over the 'quantification' criterion, and this, together with the difficulties of interpretation involved with the structured questionnaire, and
the apparent richness and complexity of information obtained by the
open-ended questionnaire, led to the adoption of the latter as the main
data-collection instrument. This decision implied the necessity of
developing a content-analysis system to allow quantification of the
results.

(ii) *Analysis of Data* In one of the best works on the methodology of
content analysis, Berelson (1954) suggests that

> Unless there is a sensible, or clear, or sound, or revealing, or unusual,
> or important notion underlying the analysis, it is not worth going
> through the rigor of the procedure, especially when it is so arduous
> and so costly of effort (p. 518).

The difficulties involved in content analysis serve to make it a relatively
infrequently used technique, not only because of its laboriousness but
also because, almost invariably, each investigator has to create his own
system. The first major methodological problem facing each investigator is the choice of an appropriate unit for the categorisation of his
materials. Both Berelson and Holsti (1968) list five possible units for
the categorisation of verbal content, ranging in breadth from the
single word to the complete text. Given that the desired aim of this
research was to focus primarily on what aspects are written about, and
how these aspects are evaluated, there seemed two possible coding
units — the theme or meaningful unit, and the statement, as defined
operationally in terms of its separate placement on an answer sheet. For
five reasons, the former was preferred:

1. Each statement could vary in length from one word to several
    sentences.
2. The use of the statement as a unit allowed only a gross coding
    of content and consequently seemed to lead to information
    loss.
3. The use of thematic units within statements would allow a re-
    constitution of the statement as a unit if required.
4. The use of thematic units within statements would allow analys
    analysis of perceived relationships among the themes.
5. The use of thematic units would produce a considerably
    greater number of response units, thereby more adequately
    meeting Berelson's condition that quantification or counting
    is justified only when there are sufficient numbers to allow
    it.

The choice of a thematic unit leads inevitably to difficulties of definition, for, unlike other units there are no physical markers to indicate
which are the units, where they begin or end. Given such definitions of
themes as 'a proposition about something' (Kerlinger, 1969, p. 549) or

'a single assertion about some subject' (Holsti, 1968, p. 647), the next step in the development of the coding system was to provide the categories of 'somethings' or 'subjects' about which propositions or assertions were being made. This involved a 'common-sense psychology' analysis, together with indications from the research literature and pilot study, of those aspects which might seem to constitute 'microteaching' for the self-viewer. The simple description which evolved was that a *person* is *teaching* a *lesson* to *pupils* in a structured and somewhat artificial *situation*. Consequently, it was hypothesised that these five aspects would be the most frequent foci of written comments about the *observed* microteaching performance, and further hypothesised that respondents would report both these observations and their *feelings* about, or *experiences* of, them.

Content-Analysis System: Stage I

The conceptual analysis outlined above provided the basis for the development of the first stage of the content-analysis system. The aim of the first stage was to identify the thematic units (or foci) and to categorise any structural links between and among foci. The division of the content-analysis system into two parts was principally so that a study of inter-observer agreement could determine whether units themselves could be reliably identified, as the aim of the second stage was to further categorise those units which had been identified.

The constituents of the first stage of the analysis system were a list of categories to be used in identifying the thematic units or foci, and a list of possible structural links between and among those foci which were identified.

(a) *Foci*

Six major categories for observed/observable aspects of microteaching performance were specified. These were:

	PERSONAL
	TEACHER/TEACHING BEHAVIOUR
RO FOCI	PUPILS/PUPIL BEHAVIOUR
	LESSON
	SITUATIONAL
	OTHER

The first five substantive categories were sub-divided in stage II of the analysis.

188 Investigations of Microteaching

A set of categories for reports of experienced/introspected states of mind, derived empirically through repeated analyses of the pilot study materials, was also provided:

	AFFECT: POSITIVE, NEGATIVE and OTHER
	NESCIENCE/KNOWLEDGE
RE FOCI	EASE/DIFFICULTY
	EXPECTATION
	DISCOVERY

None of these categories was later subdivided.

(b) *Structure*

Based largely on the system devised by Millar (1972), six types of structures or structural links, between, within or among the identified foci were specified:

CAUSE/CONSEQUENCE
ELABORATION (including exemplification, justification, substantiation, qualification)
ALTERNATIVE TO
'*re*' (as regards, concerning, about)
COMPARISON (including contrast).

Content-Analysis System: Stage II

The major aim of the second stage of the content-analysis system was to further differentiate among RO foci in terms of their content and to determine the evaluation (favourable, neutral or unfavourable) being assigned to each focus. Further goals were to determine whether respondents differentiated among pupils in their references to them, or differentiated temporally among different parts of the lesson. It was hypothesised that these two measures — dubbed pupil specificity and temporal specificity — would reflect a 'sophistication' in the comments being made. The final step of the stage II analysis was to reconstitute the statement as an additional analytic unit, by noting for each statement its primary or major focus and its evaluation.

(a) *Sub-Categorisation of RO FOCI*

The sub-categories of PERSONAL foci were:

VERBAL

                    NON-VERBAL
                    PERSONALITY/PERSONAL CHARACTERISTICS
                    APPEARANCE
                    OTHER

The selection of these sub-categories was influenced by the results of
the pilot-study factor analyses, by previous research (Webb, 1970) and
by the desire to provide criteria to assess the hypothesised effects of
the provision or non-provision of videotape feedback.
   The sub-categories of TEACHER/TEACHING BEHAVIOUR were:

PLAN IMPLEMENTATION
QUESTIONING
QUESTIONING – FIAC CONCEPTUAL
QUESTIONING – BROAD
QUESTIONING – NARROW
REACTING
RESPONSE-INITIATION – FIAC CONCEPTUAL
RESPONSE – FIAC 1, 2 and 3
INITIATION – FIAC 5, 6 and 7
PRESENTATION
CONTINUITY
INTERACTION
MOTIVATION
DISCIPLINE/CONTROL
PERSONAL
GENERAL EVALUATION
OTHER

   As can be seen, a large number of the sub-categories of TEACHER/
TEACHING BEHAVIOUR foci were designed to provide measures of
comments relating to skills or skill practice. This was also a criterion
influencing the sub-categories of PUPILS foci, for both skills to be
studied involved some part of the definition being in terms of pupil behaviour. The sub-categories for PUPILS foci were:

ATTITUDINAL/PERSONAL
KNOWLEDGE
LEARNING
RESPONDING (Coded as R, or RF if specific reference to FIAC)
INITIATING (Coded as I, or IF if specific reference to FIAC)

INVOLVEMENT/PARTICIPATION
STANDARD OF BEHAVIOUR
OTHER

The focus LESSON was intended to refer to what is being taught, and
its sub-categories were:

OBJECTIVES/AIMS
PREPARATION/PLANNING
CONCEPTUAL LEVEL
SUBJECT MATTER/TOPIC
ORGANISATION/STRUCTURE
OTHER

The focus SITUATIONAL was intended to refer to aspects of the situation or
context in which respondents found themselves. Its sub-categories were:

MICROTEACHING – GENERAL
MICROTEACHING – SPECIFIC
TIME
EQUIPMENT
PUPILS
ARTIFICIALITY
FEEDBACK CONDITION
OTHER

(b) *Evaluation of Foci*

All foci were coded for positive, negative or neutral evaluation, with the
basis for coding being either the writer's explicit assigning of a positive
or negative value to a focus, or being the implicit value implied by the
known desirable and undesirable characteristics of the constituents of
the comments.

Full details and explicit definitions of the categories of the system
are given in MacLeod (1976).

(iii) *Evaluation and Exemplification of Content-Analysis System* Two
major criteria were to be used in evaluating the content-analysis system
at the initial stage of the research. These were:

(a)   that the codings of statements should be able to be recon-
       stituted into fairly meaningful statements;

(b) that the system should be able to be used to produce similar
results by different coders.

The sample codings shown below exemplify the use of the eight major
criterion categories of the content-analysis system and show the kinds
of reconstructions which were possible from the codings.

Example 1 'My lesson was badly prepared so I kept on getting lost'

1. CATEGORISATION OF FOCI:	A.	RO/Lesson
	B.	RO/Teacher/Teaching Behaviour
2. STRUCTURE:	Focus B 'consequence of' focus A	
3. TEMPORAL SPECIFICITY:	No	
4. PUPIL SPECIFICITY:	No	
5. SUB-CATEGORISATION OF RO FOCI:	A.	RO/Lesson: Preparation/Planning
	B.	RO/Teacher/Teaching Behaviour: Continuity
6. FOCUS EVALUATION:	A.	Negative
	B.	Negative
7. PRIMARY FOCUS SELECTION	Focus A: Lesson	
8. PRIMARY FOCUS EVALUATION:	Negative	
RECONSTRUCTION:	Negative Preparation/Planning caused Negative Continuity in my Teaching Behaviour	

Example 2 'I expected the boys to be rowdy; in fact they were the ones producing the 9's, whilst the girls didn't respond at all'

1. CATEGORISATION OF FOCI:	A.	RE/Expectation
	B.	RO/Pupils
	C.	RO/Pupils
	D.	RO/Pupils
2. STRUCTURE:	Focus A 'as regards' focus B	
	Focus C 'contrast' focus D	
	Foci A/B 'contrast' foci C/D	
3. TEMPORAL SPECIFICITY:	No	
4. PUPIL SPECIFICITY:	Yes	
5. SUB-CATEGORISATION OF RO FOCI:	B.	RO/Pupils: Standard of Behaviour
	C.	RO/Pupils: Initiating (FIAC)
	D.	RO/Pupils: Responding
6. FOCUS EVALUATION:	A.	Other
	B.	Negative
	C.	Positive
	D.	Negative

7. PRIMARY FOCUS SELECTION: Focus C: Pupils

8. PRIMARY FOCUS EVALUATION: Positive

RECONSTRUCTION: My expectation for the pupils' standard
                                of behaviour contrasted with some
                                pupils producing FIAC initiation, some
                                not responding.

The study of inter-observer agreement in the use of the content analysis system which was carried out involved the experimenter and two co-workers in the independent coding of ninety-six statements drawn at random from the pilot study of the use of the open-ended questionnaire. Table 1 shows the levels of percentage agreement of the two 'external' coders with the experimenter on the eight criteria.

Table 1 Agreement with the experimenter of two external coders

1. Focus categorisation	78%	
2. Sub-categorisation of RO foci	79%	
3. Focus evaluation	88%	
4. Primary focus selection	97%	
5. Primary focus evaluation	84%	*
6. Structure	86%	
7. Temporal specificity	88%	
8. Pupil specificity	87%	

*Based on agreed units arising from
preliminary focus categorisation.

The substantial levels of agreement shown in table 1 seemed very satisfactory for a multi-category, thematic-unit content analysis system. Given both the complexity of the system and the minimal amount of training that it was practically possible to give to the coders, it was felt that these data did indicate a satisfactory operationalisation of the rules for coding, and demonstrated that the experimenter's use of the system was not an idiosyncratic one.

References

Berelson, B. (1954). Content Analysis, in Lindzey, G. (ed.), *Handbook of Social Psychology*, vol. I, Addison-Wesley, Cambridge, Mass.

Flanders, N.A. (1965). Teacher influence, pupil attitudes and achievement, Coop. Res. Monograph No. 12 (OE – 25040), U.S. Office of Education.

Holsti, O.R. (with the collaboration of Loomba, Joanne K. and North, R.C.)

(1968). Content Analysis, in Lindzey, G. and Aronson, E. (eds.), *The Handbook of Social Psychology*, vol. II (second edition), Addison-Wesley, Reading, Mass.

Kerlinger, F.N. (1969). *Foundations of Behavioral Research*, Rinehart and Winston, London.

MacLeod, G.R. (1976). Students' Perceptions of their Microteaching Performance, unpublished Ph.D thesis, University of Stirling.

Millar, C.J. (1972). A procedure for analysing evaluations of observed teaching and its application in measuring outcomes of professional education, unpublished M.Sc thesis, University of Stirling.

Robertson, J.D.C. (1957). 'An analysis of the views of supervisors on the attributes of student teachers', *British Journal of Educational Psychology*, 27, pp. 115-26.

Webb, Jeaninne, N. (1970). The Effects of Training in Analysis of Classroom Behaviour in the Self-Evaluation of Teaching Performance.Final Report, Alabama University, Alabama (ED059 963).

Wright, C.J., Nuthall, G.A. and Lawrence, P.J. (1969). 'A study of student-teachers' perceptions of observed lessons', *Educational Research Newsletter*, 2, 5-26, Department of Education, University of Canterbury.

13 A DESCRIPTIVE STUDY OF STUDENTS' PERCEPTIONS OF THEIR MICROTEACHING PERFORMANCE

Gordon MacLeod

Introduction

In the published literature on microteaching, it is commonly assumed that a 'cosmetic effect' occurs in which trainees focus on aspects of their appearance and voice as a result of self-viewing. This supposed cosmetic effect is treated in different ways by different writers. Brown (1975), for example, suggests that trainees should yield to the temptation to look at and listen to themselves at first self-viewing, whilst Claus (1968) suggests that to do so might prevent a 'rational' viewing of the videotaped lesson.

Surprisingly little evidence is available as to the extent of the cosmetic effect. Salomon and McDonald (1970) provide probably the most frequently cited finding that at first self-viewing almost six out of ten observations made by their subjects were categorised as 'physical appearance' whilst observations on 'teaching behaviour' approached only two out of ten. However, from the report of their study, it is by no means clear how justifiable this conclusion is, given the possible weaknesses in the execution of the research (MacLeod, 1976).

Similarly, the data provided by Webb (1970) and by Bedics and Webb (1971) on the outcomes of focused self-viewing (as in microteaching) may be deficient because of the experimenters' data-elicitation procedures which may have served to guide subjects to focus on aspects of themselves. However, their studies are of interest in suggesting both that the cosmetic effect may be less important at first self-viewing than is focus on teacher and pupil behaviour, and that it may diminish rapidly throughout a series of microteaching lessons.

In their review of the effects of self-confrontation, it is unfortunate that Fuller and Manning (1973) consider neither the deficiencies of these three studies, nor the difficulties of generalising from studies outside teacher education, for it is on the basis of their review that Travers (1975) concludes

Individuals who see themselves in live action on a screen ... typically become preoccupied with the appearance of their body and fail to

take note of the behaviour they see and the consequences of that
behaviour (p. 431).

In that a common aim of microteaching is to allow trainees to take note
of their behaviour and of its consequences, Travers' claim that this
typically does not occur is an important one. Yet, as has been argued
here, there is a paucity of data on this issue, with little substantial
evidence being available either to support or to refute such claims. It
was to provide such evidence that this study was carried out.

Subjects

The subjects in this study were those forty-nine from a semester-group
of sixty-five who had participated in the initial lesson and its questionnaire completion, had participated in the first skill practice (teach,
questionnaire completion, and reteach) and had participated in the
teach and questionnaire completion of the second skill practice (see
figure 1, chapter 12). This selection was carried out to ensure that all
subjects had undertaken at least equivalent microteaching practice.

Coding of Data

The points at which data were collected are shown in figure 1, chapter
12.

To prevent any possible experimenter bias arising from knowledge of
which lesson was being commented on, all of the subjects' responses
were copied from their questionnaires on to separate sheets and identified by number only. The content analysis of these comments was
then carried out. For each of the three testing occasions this yielded a
set of ninety-seven variables, consisting of all of the content analysis
categories and of measures derived directly from them.

Analysis of Data and Results

Tables 1 to 5 show the distribution of responses in terms of frequencies and percentages on each of the criterion variables on each of
the three occasions. Also indicated in these tables are the results of
treatments by subjects or single factor-repeated measures analyses of
variance (Lindquist, 1956, ch. 15; Winer, 1970, ch. 4) on thirty-three
selected variables. The selection of variables for these tests for trends
across the three occasions was based on two criteria — that on at least
one occasion (Initial Lesson, Skill One, or Skill Two), a category should
be mentioned by at least one third of the sample (N = 16), and on
another occasion must be mentioned by at least one quarter of the

sample (N = 12). These criteria were chosen for two purposes — so as to exclude variables whose overall frequency of occurrence was low on all three occasions, but so as to include those variables where the frequency of occurrence seemed sufficient to permit the analysis of variance, but where the frequency of occurrence on any one occasion was low. This latter procedure was adopted in so far as the purpose of the analysis was to test for trends across the three occasions, and where the logical initial or final status of any such trend might be near zero frequency of occurrence. Following these two criteria, the thirty-three variables were selected and subjected to analysis of variance.

It should be noted that although the analysis of variance can identify significant variations among the three occasions, the design of the study precludes the unambiguous attribution of any such significant differences to the effects of these three sequential occasions. A further limitation on the interpretation of the results is that the data for Skill Two are those arising from the 'pooling' of data from four differentially-treated sub-groups.

Table 1 shows the distribution of responses for Primary Focus Selection across the three test occasions, whilst tables 2, 3 and 4 show the analogous results for RO foci, RE foci and Negativity of Evaluation. The frequencies of occurrence of Specificity and of Links are shown in table 5.

Discussion of Results

Whilst it is not possible here to discuss all of these results, several findings seem of particular interest. One striking feature of the data is the lack of support they provide for a dominant and pervasive cosmetic effect. For example, when the primary focus of each statement is taken as the measure, as in table 1, Personal foci account for only 9 per cent of all primary foci at the Initial Lesson, this being less than half of the references to Pupil Behaviour at the same lesson, and only one fifth of the references to Teacher Behaviour. Equally striking is that on the second testing occasion, only 3 per cent, and on the third testing occasion, 0 per cent of all primary foci are categorised as Personal. These data do seem to suggest that the supposed emphasis on personal characteristics in microteaching is both less marked and less enduring than has been previously suggested.

The contrast, in terms of frequency of use, to Personal primary foci is primary focus on Teacher Behaviour. As table 1 shows, these foci constitute the highest, but not a significantly changing, proportion of all primary foci. The next most frequent category of primary foci is

Table 1 Frequency and percentage occurrence of PFS categories for Initial Lesson, Skills One and Two

Primary Focus on:	Occasion One; Initial Lesson		Occasion Two: Skill One		Occasion Three: Skill Two		
RO Foci	fr.	%	fr.	%	fr.	%	
Personal	22	9%	6	3%	0	0%	
Teacher	120	51%	104	47%	100	49%	NS
Pupils	50	21%	70	31%	76	37%	*
Lesson	23	10%	25	11%	17	8%	NS
Situation	11	5%	9	4%	1	0%	
Other	1	0%	1	0%	0	0%	
Total RO	227	96%	215	96%	194	96%	*
RE Foci							
Affec: Pos.	1	0%	1	0%	1	0%	
Affect: Neg.	1	0%	0	0%	1	0%	
Affect: Other	1	0%	0	0%	0	0%	
Ease	0	0%	1	0%	0	0%	
Difficulty	5	2%	4	2%	4	2%	
Expectation	1	0%	1	0%	2	1%	
Nescience	1	0%	1	0%	1	0%	
Total RE	10	4%	8	4%	9	4%	
Total PFS	237	100%	223	100%	203	100%	*

* = $p < .05$
** = $p < .01$
NS = Not Significant

Table 2 Frequency and percentage occurrence of RO foci for Initial Lesson, Skills One and Two

Focus on:	Initial		Skill One		Skill Two	
RO Personal	fr.	% of all foci	fr.	% of all foci	fr.	% of all foci
Verbal	15	4%	2	1%	0	0%
Non-verbal	7	2%	0	0%	0	0%
Pers. Chars.	8	2%	5	1%	0	0%
Appearance	3	1%	0	0%	0	0%
Other	0	0%	0	0%	0	0%
Total Personal	33	9%	7	2%	0	0%

Focus on:	Initial		Skill One		Skill Two		
RO Teacher/ Teaching Behaviour	fr.	% of all foci	fr.	% of all foci	fr.	% of all foci	
Plan Implement.	6	2%	13	4%	9	2%	
Questioning	20	5%	31	9%	20	5%	NS
Questioning (FIAC)	0	0%	0	0%	3	1%	
Questioning (Broad)	0	0%	1	0%	23	6%	
Questioning (Narrow)	0	0%	4	1%	11	3%	
Total Questioning	20	5%	36	10%	57	14%	**
Reacting	41	11%	9	3%	4	1%	**
Resp./Init. (FIAC)	0	0%	14	4%	5	1%	
Resp. (FIAC 1, 2, 3)	1	0%	11	3%	13	3%	
Tot. Resp./Init.	46	12%	38	11%	29	7%	NS
Presentation	3	1%	3	1%	0	0%	
Continuity	18	5%	6	2%	3	1%	
Interaction	6	2%	8	2%	7	2%	
Motivation	16	4%	6	2%	8	2%	
Discipline/Control	6	2%	2	1%	6	2%	
Personal	8	2%	3	1%	4	1%	
General Eval.	6	2%	6	2%	14	4%	
Other	34	9%	24	7%	23	6%	NS
Total Teacher	169	45%	145	41%	160	41%	NS
RO Pupils/Pupil Behaviours							
Attitud./Pers.	37	10%	34	10%	49	12%	NS
Knowledge	4	1%	5	1%	10	3%	
Learning	6	2%	3	1%	2	1%	
Responding	19	5%	19	5%	37	9%	*
Responding (FIAC)	0	0%	1	0%	6	2%	
Initiating	5	1%	11	3%	17	4%	
Initiating (FIAC)	0	0%	7	2%	7	2%	
Involv./Particip.	0	0%	6	2%	6	2%	
Standard of Behaviour	3	1%	5	1%	6	2%	
Other	9	2%	24	7%	20	5%	NS
Total Pupils	83	22%	115	32%	160	42%	**
RO Lesson							
Objectives/Aims	0	0%	2	1%	2	0%	
Prep./Planning	6	2%	2	1%	5	1%	
Conceptual Level	4	1%	3	1%	0	0%	
Subj. Matter	14	4%	35	10%	14	4%	**

Focus on:	Initial		Skill One		Skill Two		
	fr.	% of all foci	fr.	% of all foci	fr.	% of all foci	
Organis./Structure	7	2%	3	1%	3	1%	
Other	0	0%	0	0%	2	1%	
Total Lesson	31	9%	45	4%	25	7%	*
RO Situational							
MT/General	1	0%	1	0%	2	1%	
MT Specific	9	2%	7	2%	1	0%	
Time	7	2%	8	2%	5	1%	
Equipment	3	1%	3	1%	3	1%	
Artificiality	2	1%	0	0%	0	0%	
Pupils	1	0%	3	1%	1	0%	
Feedback Condition	0	0%	0	0%	2	1%	
Other	1	0%	0	0%	1	0%	
Total Situ.	24	6%	22	6%	15	4%	NS
RO Other	5	1%	2	1%	0	0%	
Total RO	345	92%	336	97%	360	94%	NS

* = p ⟨ .05
** = p ⟨ .01
NS = Not Significant

Table 3 Frequency and percentage occurrence of RE foci for Initial
Lesson Skills One and Two

Focus on:	Initial		Skill One		Skill Two		
	fr.	% of all foci	fr.	% of all foci	fr.	% of all foci	
RE							
Affect Pos.	3	1%	1	0%	7	2%	
Affect. Neg.	4	1%	1	0%	2	1%	
Affect. Other	5	1%	1	0%	0	0%	
Nescience	3	1%	1	0%	4	1%	
Knowledge	0	0%	0	0%	0	0%	
Ease	1	0%	2	1%	2	1%	
Difficulty	8	2%	5	1%	13	3%	
Expectation	4	1%	3	1%	3	1%	
Discovery	2	1%	0	0%	1	0%	
Total RE	30	8%	14	3%	32%	9%	NS
Total RO + RE	375	100%	350	100%	394	100%	NS

NS = Not Significant

Table 4 Proportions of foci which were negatively evaluated for Initial
Lesson, Skills One and Two

Category	Initial Lesson	Skill One	Skill Two
All primary foci (N = 49)	.78	.63	.59 **
'Teacher' primary foci (N = 34)	.92	.81	.68 *
'Pupils' primary foci (N = 19)	.43	.25	.31 NS
All foci (N = 49)	.71	.58	.51 **
'Teacher' foci (N = 34)	.81	.69	.53 **
'Pupils' foci (N = 30)	.47	.38	.39 NS

* = p $<$ .05
** = p $<$ .01
NS = Not Significant

Table 5 Frequency and percentage occurrence of Specificity, Links and
Effect of Viewing for Initial Lesson, Skills One and Two

Category	Initial Lesson		Skill One		Skill Two	
Specificity	fr.	%	fr.	%	fr.	%
Pupil Specificity	31	84%	23	68%	38	90% NS
Temporal Specificity	6	16%	11	32%	4	10%
Total Specificity	37	100%	34	100%	42	100% NS
Links						
Re	27	25%	31	30%	50	32% NS
Cause/Consequence	36	34%	39	37%	58	37% *
Elaboration	20	19%	20	19%	31	20% NS
Comparison	9	8%	7	7%	7	4%
Alternative	15	14%	8	8%	8	5%
Total Links	107	100%	105	101%	154	98%*

* = p $<$ .05
** = p $<$ .01
NS = Not Significant

Pupil Behaviour, a category whose use increases significantly across the
three occasions from 21 per cent of all primary foci, through 31 per
cent to 37 per cent. Primary focus on Lesson does not change significantly across the three occasions, and represents about one in ten statements. The frequency of occurrence of all other primary focus cate-

gories was low, with all RE foci combined constituting only 4 per cent of all primary foci. The total number of primary foci (or statements) decreased significantly across the three occasions, from an average of 4.84 statements per respondent on Occasion One to 4.84 statements per respondent on Occasion Three.

When all foci are used as criteria, as in tables 2 and 3, a pattern similar to that of table 1 emerges for use of the major categories of Personal, Teacher Behaviour and Pupil Behaviour. However, two differences also emerge. Firstly, use of Lesson foci varies significantly across the three occasions with this seeming to be due to the peak occurrence on the second occasion, and with this in turn being due to the large number of foci on Subject-Matter at this stage. One tentative explanation for this is that it was the first lesson taught by students following advice from curriculum specialists on their choice of subject-matter. The second 'anomalous' result of using foci as criteria is that there is no significant variation in the total number of foci used across the three occasions. Thus, while the number of statements has declined, the number of foci (which are the constituent elements of statements) has not. This suggests that respondents are perhaps making use of longer or more complex statements to convey approximately equivalent amounts of information on each occasion.

Within the major categories of foci, many other features are of interest, but only those categories which showed significant variation across the three occasions will be discussed here. Within the major category of Teacher Behaviour two sub-categories showed significant change – the number of references to any aspect of questioning behaviour increased significantly, while the number of references to teacher reacting behaviour decreased significantly. Both these results seem explicable in terms of the subjects' incorporation of FIAC criteria into their cognitive repertoires, for as table 2 shows, the increase in references to questioning seems due largely to the use of the skill categories of Broad Questions and Narrow Questions. Likewise, the decline in references to reacting behaviour can be attributed to subjects' shift towards describing reacting behaviour in terms of the FIAC system.

Within the major category of Pupil Behaviour the one significant variation was for references to pupil responding behaviour to increase, with the variation seemingly due to a peak occurrence on Occasion Three, the skill of Broad Questions. Within the Lesson category, the only significant variation was in terms of the previously noted peak occurrence of references to Subject-Matter on Occasion Two.

Table 4 shows the proportions of negative evaluations across the

three occasions on six criteria. As can be seen in the table, the number
of subjects involved for four of the six measures was less than forty-
nine. This was due to the removal from the three-occasion sample of
any subject who, on any *one* occasion, had a missing value for that
variable. Table 3 shows a fairly high proportion of overall negativity
both for primary foci and for all foci on occasion one, but this declines
significantly across the three occasions, although still showing a
majority of negative evaluations on occasion three. The major constituents of overall evaluation were evaluations of teacher behaviour and of
pupil behaviour. Evaluation of teacher behaviour is initially highly
negative but declines significantly, whilst evaluation of pupil behaviour
is much less negative, but does not change significantly across the three
occasions.

The data of table 5 show that differentiating among pupils, or
specifying a particular pupil or group of pupils, is much more common
than specifying a part of the lesson, but even Pupil Specificity tends to
occur only once in every fourteen statements. Of the structural links
examined, those coded as 'As Regards', Cause and Elaboration, account
for 85 per cent of all links across the three occasions, with causal links
being the most frequently occurring on all three occasions, and being
the one whose frequency of occurrence significantly increases.

Conclusions

The questions which gave rise to this study were on what do student-
teachers focus, when asked to report their perceptions of their microteaching performance, and in what ways, if any, do these perceptions
change across a series of microteaching lessons. One further factor
which gave impetus to the study was the emphasis in the literature on a
marked and persistent cosmetic effect arising as a consequence of self-
viewing in microteaching. For example, Fuller and Manning's (1973)
view was that

> unless some other focus, perhaps some powerful focus is provided,
> self-viewers seem to focus on themselves (p. 474).

It seems clear from the results presented here that some form of cosmetic effect does indeed occur, although its importance seems considerably less than Fuller and Manning suggest. However, it is also true that
in this study, 'focus' was provided in terms of instructions to, and
explicit goals for the subjects. Thus, while Fuller and Manning's general
conclusion cannot be dismissed, it would seem also to be only rarely

applicable to microteaching, where, in general, focus is present. Indeed, it is difficult to imagine how any focus-free situation can arise from self-viewing in teacher education, for, as Fuller herself has suggested

> focus may be provided by another person, by instructors, or even by goals implicit in the situation (p. 7),

and it is difficult to see how these conditions, especially the last, can be avoided.

What also seems clear from the results presented here is that the dominant features of subjects' perceptions of their performance are an important focus on teacher behaviour and a substantial and increasing focus on pupil behaviour. Indeed, if these two categories, together with focus on lesson, are taken together as examples of 'task-related' concerns, then these task-related concerns represent 75 per cent of all foci on occasion one, and 87 per cent and 88 per cent of all foci on occasions two and three. Thus, these three task-related categories account for the vast majority of comments made by the subjects on each of the three testing occasions. The results presented here also provide evidence of the incorporation of skill-related categories into subjects' perceptual repertoires, they show that subjects tend to be critical in evaluating what they perceive, with the major object of this negativity being their own behaviour, and they demonstrate that the most frequently occurring structural links between and among foci were of a causal-consequential nature and that the use of these links increased in frequency. For users of microteaching, whose aims are to allow trainees to focus critically upon their teaching behaviour, to focus upon the consequences of that behaviour in terms of pupil behaviour, to make use of the 'prescribed' skill categories, and to focus upon aspects of the lesson, these results are encouraging. Indeed, the data suggest a generalisation which is almost a direct reversal of the gloomy diagnosis offered by Travers (see pp. 194-5). On the basis of the results presented here, one could say of trainees in microteaching that

> Typically they become preoccupied with the behaviour they see and the consequences of that behaviour and fail to take note of the appearance of their body.

Like all simple generalisations, this probably serves to conceal some of the complexities of the data, but it does seem to provide a more faithful representation of the results of this study than would Travers' contrary view.

References

Bedics, R.A. and Webb, Jeaninne N. (1971). Measuring the Self-Evaluation of Teaching Behaviour through the Use of Videotape (EDO51 079).

Brown, G.A. (1975). *Microteaching: A Programme of Teaching Skills,* Methuen, London.

Claus, K.E. (1968). Effects of modelling and feedback treatments on the development of teachers' questioning skills, Technical Report No. 6, Stanford Centre for Research and Development in Teaching, Stanford University, California.

Fuller, F.F. (1973). Putting It All Together: an Attempt to Integrate Theory and Research about Self Confrontation in Teacher Education, Paper presented at the 1973 meeting of the American Educational Research Association, Research and Development Centre for Teacher Education, University of Texas at Austin.

Fuller, F.F. and Manning, B.A. (1973). 'Self-Confrontation Reviewed: a Conceptualisation for Video Playback in Teacher Education', *Review of Educational Research,* 43, 4, pp. 469-528.

Lindquist, E.F. (1956). *Design and Analysis of Experiments in Psychology and Education,* Houghton Mifflin, Boston.

MacLeod, G.R. (1976). Students' Perceptions of their Microteaching Performance, unpublished Ph.D thesis, University of Stirling.

Salomon, G. and McDonald, F.J. (1970). Pre- and post-test reactions to self-viewing one's teaching performance on videotape, R. and D. Memorandum No. 44, Stanford Centre for Research and Development in Teaching.

Travers, R.M.W. (1975). 'Empirically Based Teacher Education', *The Educational Forum,* 39, 4, pp. 417-33.

Webb, Jeaninne N. (1970). The Effects of Training in Analysis of Classroom Behavior in the Self-evaluation of Teaching Performance, Final Report, Alabama University (ED 059 963).

Winer, B.J. (1970). *Statistical Principles in Experimental Design,* McGraw-Hill, London.

14 THE EFFECTS OF VIDEOTAPE- AND SKILL-RELATED FEEDBACK ON STUDENTS' PERCEPTIONS OF THEIR MICROTEACHING PERFORMANCE

Gordon MacLeod

Introduction

In the previous chapter, a description was given of subjects' perceptions of their microteaching performance, and of how these perceptions changed across a series of microteaching lessons. In this chapter an experimental study of the effects on perceptions of video- and skill-related feedback will be reported.

Videotape feedback seems to have become almost a defining characteristic of microteaching. Despite the views of the early Stanford workers on microteaching that videotape is not a necessary part of the microteaching process (Allen and Ryan, 1969), or that it is not the essence of the concept of microteaching (McKnight, 1971), writers describing present practices of microteaching suggest that videotape has become almost an essential part of the process. Griffiths (1972) for example notes that 'it has been unusual to hear of the implementation of a microteaching programme without television involvement' (p. 16), whilst Foster, Heys and Harvey (1973) assert that the use of video feedback 'is now the dominant feature about which microteaching programmes are invariably organised' (p. 100).

Perhaps the reason for this is that the effectiveness of the provision of video feedback is well attested in reviews of the research literature despite the fact that the literature does not undeniably support this conclusion. Recent and careful reviews of the literature suggest that 'the contribution of mechanical feedback within microteaching is . . . more complex than some writers admit' (Griffiths, 1974, p. 18), and that 'Despite the predilection for videotapes, there is little clearcut evidence that it is necessary for improving all teaching skills' (Brown, 1975a, pp. 39-40).

The most ambitious study of the effects of videotape feedback on perceptions of performance was the experimental study carried out by Bierschenk (1972), which found no discernible effects of self-viewing as against no self-viewing, on 158 questionnaire items designed to assess individuals' ability to 'assimilate' and to 'digest' information. Having noted that the experimental condition had produced no effect, Bierschenk goes on to speculate that the reasons for this might be that the experimental conditions lasted too short a time, that self-confrontation requires systematic training in receiving and adapting first-hand information, and that the first experience of self-confrontation might produce 'feelings of surprise, fear, shock and/or the adoption of defensive attitudes' (p. 32). The one interpretation to which no consideration is given is that no effects of self-viewing were observed because no effects occur.

Bierschenk's view that systematic training is necessary for subjects to make use of videotape information is one which seems to have been implicit in microteaching practice from its earliest days, for most programmes have made use of operationalised skills, and have made provision for feedback of the skill-related information to trainees. Outside microteaching, interaction analysis feedback has been claimed to be an effective means of changing teacher performance (e.g. Hough, Lohman and Ober, 1969), whilst within microteaching, Brown (1975b) has also suggested that interaction analysis feedback is associated with changed performance but only marginally with changed perception, whilst training in the interaction analysis system was found to be associated with changes in perceptions of teaching, but only marginally with changes in performance. Brown's hypothesis that training in interaction analysis, like other forms of discrimination training, would be likely to change perceptions but not performance was confirmed. However, Wagner's (1973) work has shown that discrimination training does seem to be more effective than microteaching in producing performance change, whilst the models of microteaching being advanced by Bierschenk (1974) and at Stirling (MacLeod, 1976) both suggest that performance change presupposes perception change. Therefore, it was decided that this study should focus not only on the effects of videotape feedback, but also on the effects of interaction-analysis feedback on students' perceptions of their performance.

Design of the Study

The design of the study was a 2 x 2 factorial one with the main treatments being videotape feedback as against no videotape feedback and FIAC feedback as against no FIAC feedback. Subjects were assigned randomly to the four groups created by the combination of these treatments. Before their teach lesson (of the skill of Broad Questions — see figure 1, in chapter 12), subjects were informed of the experimental group they were in. All subjects then taught the teach lesson and re-

ceived the appropriate feedback treatment. For the group receiving
FIAC feedback, the coding of all lessons was carried out by the experimenter, and the information provided to the subjects was the relative
frequencies and proportions of broad and narrow questions and of the
kinds of pupil outcomes (FIAC 8's and 9's) which were occurring. The
positively valued criteria were use of broad questions and of FIAC 9's.

Following the feedback treatment, all subjects completed the basic
open-ended questionnaire and responded to four 'closed' questions. Of
these four, one asked for subjects' ratings, on a seven-point scale, of
how confident they were of improving their performance on the reteach
whilst the other three asked subjects to rate, again on a seven-point
scale, how satisfied they were with the number of broad questions they
had asked, how satisfied they were that their broad questions were producing pupil initiation, and how satisfied they were overall with their
practice of the skill of Broad Questions. As well as retaining the questionnaire, the videotape records of teach and reteach performance were
also retained to allow the assessment of the effects of the four experimental treatments on performance.

Subjects

The subjects retained for study at this stage of the research were those
forty-nine who had participated in the initial lesson and its questionnaire completion, and who had participated in teach, questionnaire
completion and reteach for the skill of Initiation and Response. This
selection was made to ensure that all subjects had participated in equivalent probable criterion-related treatments.

Analysis of Data and Results

Because of the large number of potential criterion variables, it was decided that the most parsimonious analysis could be achieved by retaining only those variables which were shown to be likely to be significantly differentiated by the analysis of variance. To this end, coded
vectors were created to represent each of the experimental treatments
and their interaction, and these were correlated with each of the
possible dependent variables. As the numbers in the groups were not
equal, these codings were not quite orthogonal, and it was therefore
decided to retain for further analysis all those variables which correlated at the conservative 15 per cent significance level with any of the
treatments. In all, there were eighteen such content analysis and questionnaire variables, and six performance variables, five of the latter
being derived from the observation of the teach performance which pre-

ceded the provision of the experimental treatments. All these twenty-four variables were subjected to a factorial analysis of variance, with the proportions of variance attributed to any one treatment being corrected for the correlation of that treatment with other treatments, thus allowing for the effects of unequal cell frequencies (Kerlinger and Pedhazur, 1973, p. 110). On eleven of the variables, F-ratios significant at or beyond the .05 level were found, and these significant outcomes are shown in table 1.

Summary of Results

The effect of the provision of FIAC feedback was to produce more use of Pupils/Pupil Behaviour as a primary focus, more use of Pupils/Attitudinal/Personal Characteristics as a focus, and less use of all the reacting categories of Teacher/Teaching Behaviour. Further, FIAC feedback was shown to interact significantly with two measures of the proportion of broad questions on the teach lesson which preceded the provision of FIAC feedback.

The effect of the provision of video feedback was to produce less use of Lesson foci and lower negativity in evaluating Teacher/Teaching Behaviour foci.

The significant interaction effects are less easy to interpret, although there is again evidence of interaction between the experimental treatments and the teach lesson on the amount of pupil initiation. Of the other three significant outcomes there seems to be a pattern indicating that groups receiving 'single' treatments (i.e. FIAC only, or video only) tend to one extreme of the set of responses, whilst those receiving 'both' or 'neither' feedback treatments tend to the other extreme. The 'both/neither' treatment groups tend to be more confident of improvement on reteach, less negative in evaluating Teacher Behaviour and to make less use of Other Links than do the 'single' feedback groups.

Discussion of Results

The most disturbing outcome of these results was the evidence of significant interaction between three of the measures of teach performance and the treatments. In terms of an analysis of co-variance model, the treatments are significantly correlated with the pretest measures, and the experimental groups which were created by random selection differed significantly before the treatments were administered. The causes of this are difficult to discern. Campbell and Stanley (1963) note that 'while simple . . . randomisation assures unbiased assignment of

Table 1 The significant (p ⟨ .05) effects of the experimental treatments on the dependent variables

A. Significant FIAC Effects

Dependent Variable	FIAC	No FIAC	p
Number of subjects making use of Pupils/Pupil Behaviour as a Primary Focus	88%	56%	⟨.05
Number of subjects making use of any reacting category of Teacher/Teaching Behaviour	21%	48%	=.05
Number of subjects making use of the Attitudinal/Personal Characteristics category of Pupils/Pupil Behaviour	83%	48%	⟨.05
Proportion of teach accounted for by broad questions	.13	.08	⟨.01
Proportion of teach questions accounted for by broad questions	.49	.32	⟨.01

B. Significant Video Effects

Dependent Variable	Video	No Video	
Number of subjects making use of any Lesson category	27%	57%	⟨.05
Mean proportion of negativity on Teacher/Teaching Behaviour foci	.43	.65	⟨.05

C. Significant Interaction Effects

Dependent Variable		Outcomes		p
		Video	No video	
Mean rating of confidence of improvement on reteach	FIAC	2.77	4.18	⟨.01
(low rating = high confidence)	No FIAC	3.54	3.00	
		Video	No video	
Number of subjects making use of Comparison and Alternativistic structural links	FIAC	23%	46%	⟨.05
	No FIAC	69%	25%	
		Video	No video	
Mean proportion of negativity on Teacher/Teaching Behaviour	FIAC	.48	.90	⟨.05
Primary Foci	No FIAC	.73	.64	
		Video	No video	
Proportion of teach accounted	FIAC	.23	.33	⟨.05
for by FIAC 9's	No FIAC	.40	.28	

experimental subjects to groups, it is a less than perfect way of assuring
the initial equivalence of groups, and this means that there will
occasionally be an apparently "significant" difference between the pretest scores.' However, they add 'It is none the less the only way of
doing so, and the essential way' (p. 185).

Apart from a failure of randomisation to ensure equivalence, there
seems one possible alternative explanation. This is that the knowledge
of which experimental treatment they were to receive, given to subjects immediately before their teach lesson, was sufficient to produce
the significant differences.

The significant main effect differences which did occur, with the
group assigned to FIAC having greater proportions of Broad Questions,
both as a proportion of all questions, and as a proportion of the entire
lesson, are consistent with such an explanation, but the significant
interaction effect on the proportion of pupil initiation, with the no
FIAC/Video group producing most pupil initiation and the FIAC/Video
group producing least, does not seem so consistent with the suggested
explanation that the FIAC group, through their knowledge of belonging
to that group, would produce more criterion-related behaviour.

Whatever the cause, what these significant differences do suggest is
that the identified effects of treatments on the planned dependent
variables must be treated with caution because of the non-equivalence
of the experimental groups in respect of teaching behaviour. The fact
of pretest-treatment correlation meant not only that a planned analysis
of co-variance on the reteach performance measures could not be
carried out (Lindquist, 1956; Evans and Anastasio, 1968), but also that
the simple effects of treatments on the reactions to the viewed lesson
might be of dubious validity.

The only experimental treatment not significantly related to any of
the measures of teach performance is video feedback and, therefore, its
significant outcomes are probably the most valid.

Despite the earlier 'caveats' as to the validity of the assessment of
FIAC effects, the significant outcomes would seem to remain of interest
although requiring to be treated with caution. The provision of FIAC
feedback seemed to lead to more frequent use of statements referring
primarily to pupil behaviour, to more frequent foci on pupils' attitudes
and personal characteristics, but to less frequent use of the teacher-
reacting categories. This latter finding suggests that the effect of the
systematic skill-related FIAC feedback was perhaps to reduce the
influence of the categories introduced by the previous skill of Initiation
and Response. The increased focus on pupil behaviour may perhaps be

due to the fact that part of the FIAC feedback consisted of information on pupil response and pupil initiation.

The significant interaction effects suggest that optimism, in terms of lower negativity and higher confidence of improvement, is maximised after receipt of both video and FIAC feedback, but minimised after receipt of only one of these. Likewise, the use of links coded as 'Other' seems maximised after either FIAC *or* video feedback, but minimised following both or neither of these.

Overall, the results of the Experimental Study have been disappointing because of the difficulties of interpretation caused by the non-equivalence of the randomly-selected groups. If the validity of the observed effects is assumed, which is most plausible for the video feedback treatment, then the paucity of significant outcomes does raise implications for users of microteaching. An argument previously advanced by MacLeod (1976) was that in a study such as this, few significant outcomes would emerge because subjects' perceptions of performance would be determined more by their existing cognitive and perceptual structures than by 'one-off' feedback treatments of short duration. In so far as the validity of this experiment is being assumed, the obtained results would support such conjecture. The results of this study, despite its imperfections, together with the results of Bierschenk's (1972) study, which found no effects on perceptions due to video feedback, and the results of Brown's (1975b) study, which found no effects on perceptions due to feedback from interaction analysis, do seem to suggest that the effects of both video- and skill-related feedback within microteaching programmes are perhaps less potent than has been assumed.

References

Allen, D.W. and Ryan, K.A. (1969). *Microteaching,* Addison-Wesley, Reading, Mass.

Bierschenk, B. (1972). Self-Confrontation via Closed-Circuit Television in Teacher Training: Results, Implications and Recommendations, University of Malmo, Sweden (mimeo).

Bierschenk, B. (1974). Perceptual, evaluative and behavioural changes through externally mediated self-confrontation, *Didakometry,* 41 School of Education, Malmo, Sweden.

Brown, G.A. (1975a). Microteaching: Research and Developments, in Chanan, G. and Delamont, S. (eds.), *Frontiers of Classroom Research,* NFER, Slough.

Brown G.A. (1975b). Case studies of teacher preparation, *British Journal of Teacher Education,* 1, 1, pp. 71-85.

Campbell, D.T. and Stanley, J.C. (1963). Experimental and Quasi-Experimental

Designs for Research on Teaching, in Gage, N.L. (ed.), *Handbook of Research on Teaching,* Rand McNally and Co., Chicago.

Evans, S.H. and Anastasio, E.J. (1968). Misuse of Analysis of Co-variance when Treatment Effect and Co-variate are Confounded, *Psychological Bulletin,* 69, pp. 225-34.

Foster, J.K. Heys, T.A. and Harvey, J.M. (1973). Microteaching: a Review and a Study of the Effect of Microteaching on Teaching Effectiveness as Measured by Pupil Achievement, *Forum of Education,* 33, 2, pp. 100-41.

Griffiths, R. (1972). Some Troublesome Aspects of Microteaching, Paper presented to the Annual Conference of the National Educational Closed Circuit Television Association, University of Stirling (mimeo).

Griffiths, R. (1974). The Contribution of Feedback to Microteaching Technique, in Trott, A.J. (ed.), *Microteaching Conference Papers,* APLET Occasional Publication No. 3, pp. 15-22.

Hough, J.B.,Lohman, E.E. and Ober, R. (1969). Shaping and predicting verbal teaching behaviour in a general methods course, *Journal of Teacher Education,* 20, pp. 213-24.

Kerlinger, F.N. and Pedhazur, E.J. (1973). *Multiple Regression in Behavioral Research,* Holt, Rinehart and Winston, New York.

Lindquist, E.F. (1956). *Design and Analysis of Experiments in Psychology and Education,* Houghton Mifflin, Boston.

McKnight, P.C. (1971). Microteaching in teacher training: a review of research, *Research in Education,* 6, pp. 24-38.

MacLeod, G.R. (1976). Students' Perceptions of their Microteaching Performance, unpublished Ph.D thesis, University of Stirling.

Wagner, A.C. (1973). Changing Teaching Behaviour: a Comparison of Microteaching and Cognitive Discrimination Training, *Journal of Educational Psychology,* 64, pp. 299-305.

15 RELATIONSHIPS BETWEEN TEACHER PERFORMANCE AND TEACHERS' PERCEPTIONS OF PERFORMANCE

Gordon MacLeod

Introduction

In recent years, increased attention has been paid to the role of cognitive variables in models of microteaching. One of the most interesting of such models is Bierschenk's (1974) use of Miller, Galanter and Pribram's (1960) TOTE paradigm. Bierschenk's view is that microteaching can be an effective medium for behaviour change, but that the behaviour modifications which occur

> presuppose a structural change in the individual's field of perception and his structures of values and beliefs (p. 14).

The assumption that behavioural change implies previous cognitive or perceptual change has also been implicit in discussion of the rationale for microteaching at Stirling University where the writer has argued that the importance of the skills approach, and of skill-related systematic feedback, is that it will tend to produce certain cognitive changes, involving trainees' incorporation or partial incorporation of the skill concept into their perceptual or cognitive repertoires. It is then argued that it is this cognitive repertoire which will largely determine what trainees 'perceive' of their performance, and it is these 'perceptions' which will largely determine subsequent performance and performance change.

The aim of the study reported in this chapter was to determine whether subjects' perceptions of their teaching performance could be shown to be related to 'objective' measures of that performance, and to measures of subsequent performance. In particular, the aim was to correlate subjects' content-analysed comments on their teach lesson of the skill of Initiation/Response with measures of their teach and reteach performance on that skill.

Design of the Study

The teach-reteach cycle of the skill of Initiation/Response was the second component of practical teaching undertaken by students during

213

their microteaching programme (see figure 1, chapter 12). The teach
lesson was, therefore, the second microteaching lesson undertaken by
students, following their first practice in the Initial Lesson.

The skill of Initiation/Response was defined for students in terms of
the basic ten-category FIAC system, with students being asked, in their
practice of the skill, to maximise their use of Teacher Response behaviours so as to maximise the amount of Pupil Initiation behaviours.
The pattern to be minimised was use of Teacher Initiation behaviours,
which, it was suggested, would lead in turn to a minimisation of Pupil
Response behaviours. The operational definitions of these categories of
teacher and pupil behaviour were:

Teacher Response	— FIAC categories 1, 2 and 3
Pupil Initiation	— FIAC category 9
Teacher Initiation	— FIAC categories 5, 6 and 7
Pupil Response	— FIAC category 8

As well as these 'valued' criterion categories, students were also asked
to take note of FIAC category 4 (Teacher Questions), which, it was
suggested, could be used 'along with' categories 1, 2 and 3.

Thus, explicit in the description of the skill of Initiation/Response
were three separable components — a set of categories for the analysis
of teacher-pupil interaction, a set of predictions about associations and
contrasts among these categories, and a set of values attached to these
categories. It was suggested that the use of Teacher Response behaviours would lead to Pupil Initiation behaviours — the positively
valued criteria — whereas Teacher Initiation would lead to Pupil
Response — the negatively valued criteria. These were the two major
suggested associations, whilst the two major contrasts were Teacher
Initiation with Teacher Response and Pupil Initiation with Pupil
Response. The fifth major descriptive category of the system, Teacher
Questions, was something of a 'neutral' category, both in terms of its
likely relationships with other categories, and in terms of its evaluation.

The instrument used to assess students' perceptions of their teach
lesson was the open-ended questionnaire, but added to it were seven
'closed' questions. Five of these questions asked for students' estimates
of the proportion of their lesson spent within each of the five criterion
categories; the other two questions asked for ratings, on a seven-point
scale, of how successful subjects had thought themselves in teaching the
Initiation/Response pattern, and of how confident subjects were of

being able to improve their performance on the reteach.

The teach-reteach cycle for the skill of Initiation and Response consisted of two ten-minute lessons, separated by a week, and taught to
groups of five eleven to twelve year-old pupils (see figure 1, chapter 12).
Both teach and reteach were video-recorded, and these tapes were retained for analysis.

On completion of their teach lessons, subjects were joined by a tutor
who outlined the purposes of the questionnaire and noted that he
could not comment upon the lesson until the questionnaire had been
completed. Subjects then viewed the replays of their teach lessons and
completed the questionnaire.

The completed questionnaire was returned to the tutor, who then
discussed with the subject how best he might improve his skill practice
on the reteach. One week later, the student retaught his lesson to a
different group of pupils and then, alone, viewed the videotape replay.

Subjects

Fifty-two subjects met the criteria for retention for study. These criteria were that the subjects should have participated in the Initial
Lesson and completion of its questionnaire, and should have participated in the teach of the skill of Initiation/Response and completion of
its questionnaire.

Measures Used in the Study

(a) *Teaching Performance Measures* The measures derived from the
codings of the teach and reteach lessons totalled fifteen. These fifteen
consisted of the five criterion categories from the teach, the five criterion categories from the reteach, and a set of five 'change' measures
obtained by deducting each teach measure from its associated reteach
measure. All measures were expressed as proportions of the entire set
of codings for each lesson.

(b) *Content Analysis Measures* Potentially, all categories of the content
analysis system could act as measures, but the expected low frequency
of occurrence of some meant that this was unlikely. As the planned
analysis was through correlation, a method of exclusion was devised so
as to include only those categories which seemed to meet the assumptions necessary for the computation of correlation coefficients. To this
end, all categories of the system which were mentioned by fewer than
30 per cent of the respondents were completely excluded, whilst only
those categories mentioned at least once by at least 70 per cent of the

respondents were allowed to remain as continuous measures. Those
categories mentioned by between 30 and 70 per cent of the respondents were dichotomised into 'mentioned' and 'not mentioned'.

(c) *'Questionnaire' Measures* A further set of thirteen measures was
derived from respondents' replies to the seven 'closed' questionnaire
items. Five of these were subjects' estimates of the proportion of their
teach lesson spent within each of the five criterion categories.

From the set of five estimates, six 'accuracy of estimation' measures
were derived. Accuracy was defined as the difference between the mid-
point of the estimated proportion of a particular category and the
'actual' proportion coded from the videotaped lesson. An estimate of
'overall accuracy' was obtained by summing these five separate scores.
Thus, low scores on the six accuracy scales indicate a high degree of
accuracy of estimation.

The final two measures were the ratings of overall success and of
confidence of improvement on the reteach.

Analysis of Data and Results

To test for relationships between the teach performance measures and
the set of forty-three content analysis and questionnaire variables,
correlation coefficients were computed, with the significant ($p < .05$)
outcomes being shown in table 1.

As table 1 shows, several of the content-analysed comments and the
questionnaire responses do correlate significantly with measures of
teach performance. However, a further correlation analysis showed that
teach performance also correlated significantly with reteach performance. A possible consequence of these two conditions was that the
simple correlation of reteach performance with the content analysis
and questionnaire variables might yield spurious results. Because of this
doubt, and because of the possibilities of systematic error in the use of
simple change scores (Lord, 1956; 1958), it was decided to carry out
partial correlation analyses, in which the predictor/reteach coefficients
were computed, partialling out the effects of those teach performance
measures which were significantly correlated with the reteach performance measures. This is the method for treating 'gain' scores in correlational analyses recommended by Cronbach and Furby (1970) and by
O'Conner (1972). Table 2 shows the significant ($p < .05$) outcomes of
the partial correlation analysis.

To gain some assessment of whether knowledge of subjects' responses allowed a more accurate prediction of reteach performance

Table 1 Significant (p < .05) correlation coefficients between teacher performance on teach and subsequent content-analysis and question-naire variables

	1 T1+2+3	2 T4	3 T5+6+7	4 T8	5 T9
No. of primary foci coded as Teacher/Teaching Behaviour		35*			
No. of primary foci coded as Pupils/Pupil Behaviour					32**
No. of RO foci			27*		
Total no. of foci			28*		
Use of foci coded as Teacher/Teaching Behaviour excluding those codes as Plan Implementation, Questioning and Other			30*		
Use of Pupils foci coded as Other	-30*				
Use of foci coded as Pupils but excluding those coded as Att./Pers. Char. and Other		-34*			31*
Use of Structure links coded as *re.*				31*	-29*
Total no. of structure links used				34**	
Use of Specificity		-27*			
Proportion of primary foci coded as negative		49***		33*	-56***
Proportion of primary foci on teacher behaviour coded as negative		32*			-39**
Proportion of primary foci on pupil behaviour coded as negative		36*			-34*
Proportion of all foci coded as negative		35**			-51***
Proportion of foci on teacher behaviour coded as negative					-33*
Proportion of foci on pupil behaviour coded as negative					-33*
Estimated proportion of T1+2+3	35**				
Estimated proportion of T4	33*	47***		32*	-41**
Estimated proportion of T5+6+7	-50***		72***		-38**
Estimated proportion of T8	38**		-35*	47***	
Estimated proportion of T9		-58***	-34*	-47***	77***
Accuracy of estimation on T1+2+3	69***		-41**	34*	
Accuracy of estimation on T5+6+7		28*			
Accuracy of estimation on T9			-34*		47***
Overall accuracy			-32*		

	1	2	3	4	5
	T1+2+3	T4	T5+6+7	T8	T9
Rated success		−50***			53***
Rated confidence			34*		−30*

* = p < .05
** = p < .01
*** = p < .001

Table 2 Significant (p < .05) partial correlation coefficients between teacher performance on reteach and preceding content-analysis and questionnaire variables

	RT1+2+3	RT4	RT5+6+7	RT8	RT9
Partialling out:	T1+2+3	T4, T8 T9	T1+2+3 T5+6+7	T4, T8 T9	T8,T9
No. of primary foci coded as Teacher/Teaching Behaviour	29*				
Use of Teacher/Teaching Behaviour foci coded as Questioning	35*	−33*	−40**		
Use of Teacher/Teaching Behaviour foci coded as Other			33*		
Use of Teacher/Eaching Behaviour foci within any Questioning category		−48**	−37*		33*
Use of Pupils foci coded as Attitud./Pers. Chars.				46**	−34*
Number of foci coded as Pupils/Pupil Behaviour	−29*				
Proportion of primary foci coded as negative	48*				
Proportion of primary foci on pupils coded as negative		−45*	−44*		
Proportion of all foci coded as negative	62**				
Proportion of foci on pupil behaviour coded as negative	48*				
Estimated proportion of T5+6+7	34*				
Estimated proportion of T8				−48**	
Accuracy of estimate of T5+6+7					32*
Accuracy of estimate of T8	−31*	34*			
Overall accuracy	−34*				
Rated success on teach					−33*
Rated confidence	41**				

* = p < .05
** = p < .01
*** = p < .001

than did knowledge of their teach performance alone, multiple correlation was used. To minimise the effects of the procedure's use of chance variations in the data, and to exclude uninterpretable suppressor variables, only those teach, content analysis and 'questionnaire' variables which were significantly correlated with any reteach performance measure were selected for use in the computation. Although the inclusion of other variables would probably have increased the size of the multiple correlation coefficients, it was felt that the procedure followed would prevent the obtaining of 'artificially' inflated results. The procedure adopted was:

1. Compute the multiple correlation coefficient between the selected teach performance measures and the reteach performance measure.
2. Add the selected content analysis measures to the set of predictors, compute the new multiple correlation coefficient and test whether it differs significantly from that obtained in 1 above.
3. Add the selected 'questionnaire' measures to the set of predictors, compute the new multiple correlation coefficient and test whether it differs significantly from that obtained in 1 above.

Given that only minimal variance was added by using more than one of the partially ipsative teach variables, these variables were used in the regression equation in conventional manner. Table 3 shows the outcomes of these analyses in terms of variance accounted for at each stage.

Table 3 Per Cent and Cumulative Per Cent of Reteach Variance Accounted for by Selected Sets of Independent Variables

Predictors	Teach	Teach + Content Analysis	Teach & Content Analysis + Questionnaire
Criterion			
RT1+2+3	34%	51%	54%
RT4	29%	—	35%
RT5+6+7	34%	66%**	66%*
RT8	30%	48%***	
RT9	31%	39%*	43%

* = p ⟨ .05   ** = p ⟨ .025   *** = p ⟨ .01

(Probability levels refer to significance of *increase* in variance accounted for, over that accounted for by teach variables.)

Discussion of Results: Teach

As noted in the introduction to this chapter, the definition of the skill of Initiation/Response provided to students consisted of three separable components — categories for the analysis of teaching behaviour, predictions about relationships among and between these categories, and values attached to the categories.

In examining students' use of the first of these components, the analytic categories, two sets of data from table 1 seem most relevant — those concerning accuracy of estimation, and those relating estimates of performance to measures of actual performance.

One feature of the accuracy scores which merits attention is that high scores on 'actual' teacher response and on pupil initiation tend to precede less accuracy in estimating the proportions of these performance measures. One plausible interpretation of this is that subjects tend to undervalue their own 'success' in that they underestimate the proportions of positively valued criteria when these are high.

Whilst the accuracy measures do provide this indication of systematic error in estimation, the most direct test of accuracy is by means of the correlations of estimated performance with actual performance. Here, all five estimate measures are significantly and often very highly correlated with the corresponding measures of actual performance (average $r = + .56$). This would seem to suggest that respondents are remarkably accurate in assessing their performance in terms of the 'provided' analytic categories.

To determine whether subjects appear also to have made use of the 'prescribed' values associated with the categories, the most appropriate data are the correlates of each performance measure with the six negativity of evaluation measures and with rated success. Here, several 'anomalous' results occur. For example, the 'prescribed' positive evaluation of Teacher Response and the 'prescribed' negative evaluations of Teacher Initiation are not seen. The one measure which subjects seem clearly to evaluate in the prescribed way is Pupil Initiation, which is highly positively evaluated. However, the one category which is highly negatively evaluated was the fairly neutral one of Teacher Questions, which is highly negatively correlated with rated success, and positively correlated with four of the six negativity measures. Thus subjects seem not to evaluate the categories in the prescribed way, but instead to see as positive and successful a lesson marked by high Pupil Initiation but low Teacher Questions.

In terms of how relationships among categories are perceived, the evidence from table 1 is less direct, but no less suggestive. As already noted, the major contrast seems to be between Pupil Initiation and Teacher Questions (as indicated by their correlations with the seven evaluation measures), whilst the correlations of estimates of performance with the non-corresponding measures of actual performance would seem to indicate few of the predicted associations or contrasts.

Overall, therefore, the data of table 1 seem to indicate that subjects have been able to perceive their performance in terms of the prescribed analytic categories, but there is also evidence to suggest that they have not made use of the prescribed values, nor viewed their performance in terms of the predicted relationships.

The next step in the analysis was to determine whether the predicted relationship did or did not occur. This was done by computing the intercorrelations of the five 'actual' performance measures. Despite the difficulties of interpretation caused by the partial ipsativity of these measures, it was clear from this analysis that the predictions as to interrelationships had not been fulfilled. As one example of this, the highest single correlation was one of – .72 between Teacher Questions and Pupil Initiation.

Given this result, it seemed possible that the 'anomalous' results concerning relationships could be explained in terms of subjects' accurate perceptions of the relationships which did actually occur. An indirect measure of how subjects did perceive the behavioural interrelationships was possible through the intercorrelations of subjects' estimates of performance and a comparison of this intercorrelation matrix with that arising from the 'actual' measures provided some assessment of subjects' accuracy in perceiving relationships. It was found that there were both similarities and dissimilarities between the two matrices. In general, the correlation coefficients of the 'estimates' matrix were lower than those of the 'actual' matrix, perhaps due to the systematic error in estimating suggested above. As with the 'actual' measures, the largest single coefficient of the 'estimates' was that of – .48 between Teacher Questions and Pupil Initiation, and, in general, the matrices were very similar on the correlations between pupil behaviour (especially Pupil Initiation) and teacher behaviour, but tending to be dissimilar on the intercorrelations of teacher behaviour.

What these results suggest is an interpretation of the obtained data in which Pupil Initiation – the positively evaluated pupil outcome – assumes a major role. An initial assumption might be that subjects saw the aim of the lesson as being to achieve Pupil Initiation. From the data, this assumption seems plausible. Pupil Initiation seems to be the criterion most salient to the subjects and much of the data seems explicable on the assumption of its saliency. Given this assumption, and given that the relationships between teacher behaviour and Pupil Initiation are perceived with a high level of accuracy, then the evaluations of teacher behaviour seem explicable on the basis of these perceived relationships.

Overall, therefore, subjects seem to show a high degree of rationality and skill in their perceptions of their performance. They seem able accurately to use the provided analytic categories; they show some inaccuracy in perceiving the interrelationships of teacher behaviours; they seem accurately to perceive the relationships between their own behaviour and the desired pupil outcomes, and their evaluations of their performance tend to be based on their (accurate) perceptions of these links between their own behaviour and the desired outcome of Pupil Initiation.

Discussion of Results: Reteach

From table 2 it can be seen that the two positively valued performance criteria — Teacher Response and Pupil Initiation — do seem to show a consistent pattern of partial correlates. It would seem that a successful reteach performance is one preceded by a focus on teacher behaviour, especially teacher questioning behaviour, and by the infrequent use of pupils' foci, especially those on pupils' attitudes and personal characteristics. Also associated with a high reteach proportion of teacher response is a high rating of confidence of improvement following the teach, whilst a rating of low success on the teach is associated with a high proportion of reteach pupil initiation.

Lack of success on the reteach — based on the negatively valued criteria of teacher initiation and pupil response — seems to be associated with infrequent use of the teacher-questioning categories but more frequent focus on the attitudes and personal characteristics of the pupils. There is also some indication that negativity tends to be a negative although non-significant correlate of teacher initiation, whilst four of the negativity measures tend also to correlate negatively with pupil response.

Thus, in terms of the four valued criteria of the skill specification, a fairly clear and consistent pattern emerges which suggests that to perform well on the reteach, subjects should, on viewing their teach lesson, focus primarily on teacher behaviour, especially teacher questioning, whilst avoiding focus on pupil behaviour, especially pupil attitudes and personal characteristics. Also correlated with 'success' on reteach is high negativity, whilst low negativity tends to be correlated with reteach 'failure'. The fifth criterion category, teacher questions, seems to be more frequent on reteach following the infrequent use of comments on questioning behaviour, and perhaps also following low negativity.

It is of interest to note that comments on teacher questioning play such a large part in these results, in that the amount of attention paid to questioning is positively correlated with 'success' on the reteach, negatively correlated with failure and negatively correlated with the proportion of questioning behaviour on the reteach. This suggests that questioning and perceptions of questioning behaviour do play a crucial part in performance modification, a part whose importance and centrality was already suggested by the discussion of subjects' perceptions of their teach performance.

Also noteworthy in these results is that support is provided for microteaching's implicit function of allowing trainees to focus critically on their own behaviour, thereby allowing purposive and directed change in that behaviour to occur. The results also demonstrate that the relationships between performance, perceptions of performance and performance change are by no means simple.

However, that these relationships deserve study is demonstrated by the data presented in table 3. Here, the additional percentage variance in reteach performance accounted for by the content-analysis and questionnaire variables is shown to be about 20 per cent for the four major prescribed criteria. This 20 per cent would seem a remarkably high figure given that these additional variables had been already selected because of their significant ($p < .05$) correlations with reteach performance measures. These results seem to give clear support to the hypothesis that students' cognitive and perceptual structures are an important determinant of their teaching performance.

References

Bierschenk, B. (1974). 'Perceptual, evaluative and behavioural changes through externally mediated self-confrontation', *Didakometry*, 41, School of Education, Malmo, Sweden.

Cronbach, L.J. and Furby, L. (1970). 'How should we measure "change" — or should we?' *Psychological Bulletin*, 74, pp 68-80.

Lord, F.M. (1956). 'The Measurement of Growth', *Educational and Psychological Measurement*, 16, pp. 421-37.

Lord, F.M. (1958). 'Further Problems in the Measurement of Growth', *Educational and Psychological Measurement*, 18, pp. 437-54.

Miller G.A., Galanter, E. and Pribram, K.H. (1970). *Plans and the Structure of Behavior*, Holt, Rinehart and Winston, New York.

O'Conner, E.F. (1972). 'Extending Classical Test Theory to the Measurement of Change', *Review of Educational Research*, 42, pp. 73-97.

PART 6 ASSESSMENTS OF MICROTEACHING BY SUBJECT-SPECIALIST TUTORS

The four papers in this section give the views of four members of the Stirling staff on the role of microteaching in their own areas of curriculum specialisation, namely science, English, modern languages and history. All four contributions are necessarily subjective and present individual views but common themes do emerge which seem of great importance for the future development of microteaching techniques.

One of these themes seems to centre on the extent of individual differences among students on entry to a microteaching programme, with some seeming highly competent in their exercise of teaching skills while others are not. These performance differences would seem large enough to serve as a basis for 'remedial' microteaching or for microteaching programmes tailored to the different needs of individuals. However, the most obvious but not yet available prerequisite for such programmes would be a battery of 'diagnostic' instruments to allow the matching of differential treatments with differential performances.

A second theme which emerges is the clearly perceived need for more account to be taken of differences in the practical requirements and ideologies of different subject-areas. One possibility of achieving this would be through the development of subject-specific skills or through the modification of already developed skills to take account of the distinctive requirements of different subject-areas.

A third and very important theme is a concern with the context of microteaching and in particular with either the links made between microteaching and school practice, or with modifications of microteaching which make more effective the transition to school practice.

A fourth perception which arises explicitly in three of the four papers is that microteaching is a 'behaviour modification' technique. This perception seems to take two forms — either that the skills practised in microteaching are derived from behavioural psychology, or that the rationale for the technique is derived from behaviour modification theory. We believe that this perception is a wrong one, but one which is fairly common, and thereby raises an issue for clarification.

There would seem to be two separable possible uses for behaviour modification theory in a programme of microteaching — firstly, to provide a rationale for particular skills, and secondly to provide a rationale for the learning of students undertaking a course of microteaching. In terms of skill-rationales, a behaviour modification model has been used at Stirling only for the skill of Reinforcement, and this skill has now been superseded by a skill of Reacting where behaviour modification theory is presented as one of three conceptual models underlying the skill. Other than this, the microteaching skills used at Stirling have been based on logico/linguistic analysis, on 'educational' models (e.g. Bloom, 1956), and on cognitive psychology, including theory and research on perception, attention and concept formation.

In terms of providing a rationale for microteaching technique, it is clear that the original Stanford programme was construed in terms of a practice reinforcement model derived from behaviour modification theory (McDonald, 1973). However, we suspect that few users of microteaching would justify microteaching techniques in this way, and that still fewer programmes could be seen as conforming to the kinds of principles of practice which behaviour modification theory would imply. In part 7 of this volume a tentative cognitive explanatory model for microteaching is offered which seems to fit more closely the practice of microteaching and of research on microteaching at Stirling than does any alternative model.

References

Bloom, B.S. (ed.) (1956). *Taxonomy of Educational Objectives, Handbook I: Cognitive Domain*, David McKay, New York.
McDonald, F.J. (1973). Behavior Modification in Teacher Education, in Thoresen, C.E. (ed.), *Behavior Modification in Education*, N.S.S.E. Yearbook, University of Chicago Press, Chicago.

16 MICROTEACHING: A PERSONAL REFLECTION ON INVOLVEMENT

J. Keri Davies

If this had been a sermon I might have chosen as my text:

> As so often in education discussion, one really wants to apply
> different correctives to different viewpoints. The self-satisfied
> traditionalist wants a dose of microteaching and interactional
> analysis. The facile innovator wants to take a more sympathetic
> and accurate look at established practice. The way forward lies
> in combining the strengths and purging the weaknesses of
> different techniques. (McFarland, 1973, p. 105.)

Perhaps what follows may appear more of a sermon than anything else
because it is not based on the careful analysis of empirically derived
data obtained through critically designed experiments. It is written in a
more personal, reflective, speculative manner which is necessarily subjective. There is no attempt to be explicitly critical of what has taken
place at Stirling in the microteaching activities — whether as part of
research and/or teaching programmes — and no catch-all prescriptions
are offered about the place of microteaching in teacher preparation
programmes or lines of research. My comments arise out of experience
through participating in microteaching activities of one sort or another
since 1970 in the Department of Education, University of Stirling, and
should be seen in that context. I have had experience of tutoring
students from a variety of subject areas on a number of microteaching
skills but my main concern has been with intending science teachers
and the skills relevant to them.

Before raising the issue of microteaching in a science-specific context I would like to comment on one or two aspects of microteaching
in a broader context. This may provide more realistic insights into the
discursive arena in which microteaching was and is conducted at
Stirling.

One of the key questions one might ask of any programme that has
pretensions of 'training' students is: How *effective* is the training? This
question can lead into a series of philosophical analyses and one is un-

likely to come up with clear, precise, and unequivocal answers. At one level it raises important issues of the kind: are intending teachers trained, instructed, taught or educated? Are the activities mutually exclusive? Should teacher preparation courses include all these activities, if so how and in what proportions? These questions and their like provide educational philosophers with employment. However, ever since the change of name from 'teacher training colleges' to 'colleges of education', the tendency has been to emphasise the broader educational intention of teacher preparation programmes rather than a narrowly conceived training function.

In the Stirling context education is offered as a subject in the undergraduate programme and has a dual function of providing content and activities that are academically *and* professionally acceptable. Therefore, when one considers microteaching with its overt emphasis on skills it should not be surprising that some tensions occur about the *training* function of microteaching in the context of an education course.

However, it is not too difficult to argue that in the role of the teacher there are elements of behaviour that can be recognised or identified as skills. The bases of these skills exist in common aspects of human social behaviour, for example asking questions, explaining something to another person, giving information, giving instructions. These skills take on a particularly critical function in the intentional act of teaching which is the bringing about of learning in another person. Therefore, it is not surprising that focal attention is given to skills such as: clarity of explanation, varying the stimulus, use of examples, questioning. It is not surprising also that the theoretical rationale for these skills is embedded more in the behavioural schools of psychology than in any other.

Having placed microteaching in this highly simplistic explanatory perspective it may help to highlight some of the tensions to which microteaching gives rise when put into practice. Microteaching — or at least a skills approach that incorporates a training element — is perceived by some staff and students as alien either *per se* or acceptable in some settings but not in the context of a teacher education programme. These perceptions of microteaching are usually justified by a personal view of life in general and education in particular, or commitment to a particular ideological view of education and/or psychology, or particular concept of teaching.

Science students, in the main, appear to accept their microteaching tasks. However, a number, particularly those who think in holistic terms about 'life' or 'teaching' or 'human relationships' comment on the artificiality of the experience but many modify their views of its role and function when these are fully explained. The explanation usually has increasing effectiveness the more experience the students have of microteaching! The main issue with which the students have to come to terms is that microteaching is for *their* benefit, it is not formally assessed, and it may not be too critical if the pupils do not appear to learn anything! After these initial reservations — and a little personal embarrassment at appearing on the televison screen — the majority of students settle down to concentrate more on micro-lesson planning, teaching, and the deliberate search for feedback on personal performance. Science students, in the main, appear to have fewer reservations about microteaching than some students in other subject areas. My impression is that students in some subject areas, for example, English, appear to retain their alienation or reservations about microteaching longer than others. The reasons for this might be worth exploring.

I raise these tensions surrounding microteaching, not so much because I want to develop them here but because I want to make it explicit that these issues did arise within the Stirling context. They were — and are — topics of frequent discussion at formal meetings and informal exchanges between staff, and between staff and students. There was — and is — no lack of sensitivity to these criticisms or uncertainties on the part of those involved from the research perspective. Certainly there is an apparent gap between the necessarily clinical, detached, neutral language and planning of an empirical experiment and the 'natural' affective involvement of human interaction in a teaching situation. However, through discussion, explanation, and voluntary participation the majority of staff participated in the Leverhulme experiments as well as the microteaching which was and is an integral part of the Stirling undergraduate programme.

To return to the issue of effectiveness: one of the main aspects of the effectiveness of microteaching is the proficiency by which students develop and use a skill. In the microteaching situation one observation that strikes me is the *level* at which students start. Some students with little or no formal preparation seem to have high personal ability in structuring and conducting a ten or fifteen or twenty minute sequence with five or so pupils to practise a particular skill, say, clarity of explanation. One wonders what use could be made of students with these 'apparent' natural talents — could they be used for model tape preparation to demonstrate to other students? Should comparative studies be attempted between students who might be crudely categorised as

'natural performers' and those who do not appear to have this ability?
Perhaps the effectiveness of microteaching could be examined on these
two groups? Or should we think in terms of different forms of microteaching 'treatments' for students with different apparent abilities?
This of course opens the question as to how these abilities could be
diagnosed in the first place.

The majority of students do require some help in choosing topics,
structuring and sequencing the lesson, and highlighting the particular
skill. It is my impression that in most cases of thorough student preparation (with or without tutor assistance) greater use of the skill
occurs in the lesson and more critical use is made of feedback information during and after the lesson by the student. In fact one of the most
useful roles a tutor can play with the diligent student in observing
video-feedback is to prevent the student from being too self-critical.

From whatever subject background the students come, I would
argue that they do need general and specific guidance and assistance in
preparing microteaching lessons and 'embedding' the specific skill to be
practised in that lesson. General in the sense that there is need for
explanation and information for the students about the role and function of microteaching skills, the rationale for them — based in psychological theory and in the professional practice of teaching — as well as
the role of microteaching in the context of the course being undertaken
by the student. More specifically the student does need support in
placing the particular skill in a functional framework of the teaching of
his or her own subject area: biology, chemistry, integrated science.
Therefore microteaching does provide an interface for a number of
course elements. In the Stirling context attempts have been made — and
are being continued — to provide an integrative teacher training programme in that the focal points of course organisation are the problems
of professional practice of teaching and learning which provide organising centres for theoretical input and student activities — microteaching
is an element in this.

Students can acquire skills effectively in the microteaching context.
In the preparation of intending science teachers the skills of variation,
clarity of explanation, use of examples, and questioning have been
encouraged because they suit many aspects of teacher-pupil interaction
expected in science teaching. However, this does raise the problem of
how generally one can introduce a skill, say variation, to a group of
students in different subject areas, and 'fit' the generalities to the perceived requirements of the subject, say biology. There is a clear need —
and I base this on student comment in seminar discussion as well as ob-

serving students during microteaching — for skills to be defined, exemplified and practised in a subject area context.

A skill so complex as 'questioning' can take on radically different operational meanings in biology, history and French. Because not only are the linguistic and logical elements of questions important but also the *contextual setting* of questions is crucial. Contextual in two senses: (i) within the subject area and the particular lesson and (ii) within the social context of the group where styles of questioning are as important as the structure of the questions themselves. However, I would not want to lose the tension of generality/specificity of skills because this does provide opportunities for discourse on the more general and generalisable aspects of teaching, the psychologising of subject matter, issues of theory and practice, etc.

Perhaps one of the most crucial and probing questions one can ask about microteaching effectiveness is: is there 'carry-over' by the student from the micro-situation which is in a controlled setting to the macro-situation of the school classroom and laboratory? Mechanical proficiency of one skill in microteaching is no guarantee of teacher effectiveness in the classroom. Microteaching is not only a training device, it is also a sensitising opportunity for the student — if only to sensitise him or her to the complexity of the teaching process and the vast range of skills that can be incorporated in the repertoire of teaching.

Any microteaching programme can deal only with a few skills. However, provided the appropriate theoretical framework for the skills is given in the context of a carefully constructed and sequenced course each skill can be 'removed' from the tapestry of holistic teaching, examined critically, exemplified, practised and 'replaced' in the tapestry.

The microteaching experience for the student in the context of a structured course can give the student time and opportunity to reflect upon the repertoire of teaching skills in use in the classroom and laboratory. Also it should point up the realisation that teaching skills themselves are only one set of components in the social and psychological interactions of teachers and pupils. Microteaching and the more traditional teaching practice in schools within a structured and sequenced education course does provide a basis for student analysis of situations and can be anticipatory of his or her role in such situations in the future.

Within the framework of pre-service courses microteaching can play a variety of roles. Apart from the skills noted above it can provide feedback situations for students practising the arts (skills?) of directive chairman/non-directive chairman, various aspects of discussion control, small group work, teaching towards specific objectives, etc. However, each activity should be carefully planned, practised and evaluated by the student — this in turn implies careful planning by tutors, preferably on a co-operative basis.

There are many aspects of science teaching in which microteaching could play a useful role in sensitising students: guided discovery, explaining complex ideas with a variety of audio-visual aids, small group discussion of experimental results to encourage attempts at generalisations by pupils, formalising familiar commonsense experiences in a framework of scientific knowledge, etc. Many of the subject-specific skills could be evolved from the skills noted earlier.

Personally I am sympathetic to the controlled and selective use of microteaching in the pre-service preparation of teachers, particularly in areas of work directly related to classroom practice. However, it is no substitute for the traditional in-school experience of students on teaching practice but linked with it it has distinct possibilities for teacher preparation. This brings one back to the McFarland quotation: 'The way forward lies in combining the strengths and purging the weaknesses of different techniques' (op. cit.).

Reference

McFarland, H.S.N. (1973). *Intelligent Teacing: Professional Skills for Student Teachers,* Routledge and Kegan Paul, London.

17 MICROTEACHING AND THE PROFESSIONAL EDUCATION OF TEACHERS OF ENGLISH

Stan Gilmore

It is often assumed that tutors and students in the humanities are less enthusiastic about microteaching compared with those in, say, science. If this is true then such lack of enthusiasm with concomitant reduction in motivation will affect the performance of humanities students in a skills-practice in a microteaching programme. This viewpoint has some support in the findings of one recent research study (MacLeod et al., 1977), relying solely on statistical data, which showed that humanities students had lower scores on criterion measures of certain specified teaching skills compared with those in other subject areas, such as modern languages, science, mathematics. One interpretation offered for the relatively poorer showing of the humanities students in the use of the skills is that the subject ideologies of English and history may be a related factor. Such an explanation, however, fails to take sufficiently into account the effects of the interaction between the subject ideology and the ideology of microteaching. It is probably truer to say that when the humanities student enters a microteaching programme, he enters a situation of *conflicting* educational ideologies with the result that his performance and the effectiveness of the programme are both vitiated. If in one particular training institution, where the research was under-taken, almost 60 per cent of the students who belong to the humanities group are in a state of conflict, to a greater or lesser degree, with the microteaching component of their training programme, then it is irresponsible not to examine the sources of the conflict in order to contain or resolve the conflict; it is likely that the intensity of the conflict is more marked among English students than any other group. This conflict, as far as English students are concerned, may be traced to two main sources as follows:

(1) the frame of reference which the student brings to elicit meaning from the context of microteaching;
(2) the concept of teaching skills as exemplified in microteaching.

Frame of Reference

When the English student participates in a microteaching programme he experiences a sense of alienation and dissonance similar to that described by the poet A.E. Housman:

> I, a stranger and afraid,
> In a world I never made.

The student is only too painfully aware of the mismatch between the frame of reference which he brings from his knowledge and experience of literary studies and that of the social science orientation of the microteaching programme. More specifically, the student perceives incongruencies between his ways of knowing the social reality of the English classroom and those of the microprogrammer over three broad aspects of microteaching:

(1) Disciplines and methods of microteaching and English teaching,
(2) The use of language in the protocol materials in the knowledge acquisition phase of the microteaching cycle,
(3) Conceptual model of microteaching.

The microprogrammer attempts to abstract and reflect classroom events by adhering to strict rules of evidence — with the steps leading from observation to generalisation. These generalisations are stated at a level of abstraction applicable to all subject areas and to a wide range of teaching situations. To translate scientific methods to microteaching, the programmer is bound and inhibited by his concern with evidence as one would expect. The English student often fails to understand this which is why he finds the microprogrammer's insistence on the use of operational definitions strange when he tends to define his interpretations of classroom events constitutively, that is by the use of words rather than by the description of observable behaviour. Many of the misconceptions which arise between the microprogrammer and the English students are due to the failure of both to appreciate the different, but equally valid, ways of construing classroom reality.

But it is in the microprogrammer's use of language to describe and prescribe teaching behaviour that the English student is made more immediately aware of the different worlds of thought occupied by the microprogrammer and that of the English student. The microprogrammer has recourse to a language vowed to poverty whenever he strips his language devoid of surplus meaning. He values the explicit statement above the implicit, oblique reference, the lucid expression over the ambiguous. The English student through his literary studies is sensitised to the richness and variety of language. He revels in distortion, unpredictable collocations, paradox, irony, in the many-layered levels and nuances of language. Methods used to elicit meanings from language by the social scientist and the humanist are neither identical nor conflicting but complementary, each is designed to produce different modes of knowing about classroom contexts for learning. The protocol materials produced by the microprogrammer to exemplify teaching skills testify to the failure on his part to take account of the English students' habitual use of language. To cite one example, among many, what is the English student to make of this question given as an example of a middle-order question:

What does the poet mean in this sentence?

Is the question designed to elicit information or to enable the pupil to generate the 'meaning potential' embedded in the text?

The student also finds incongruencies in his 'competence and growth' model of English teaching which guides the central task of the English teacher 'to foster the personal growth of pupils and to increase their capacity to use language for all those purposes which their lives make necessary' (Adams and Pearce, 1974), and that of the 'behaviour modification' model of microteaching.

Unlike the student of modern languages whose lesson strategies are mainly programmatic, or that of the science student who often employs heuristic procedures in his teaching, the English student's approach is often hermeneutic or interpretive. The English student cannot precisely determine pupil outcomes to the same extent as his peers operating in other subject areas because he perceives his role as that of providing 'enabling' conditions for the pupil to construe meanings from literary artefacts. The meanings which the pupil derives from these artefacts are in part determined by the individual dispositions and life experiences of the pupil over which the teacher has no control. Thus the behavioural modification approach of the microprogrammer is largely inadequate for many English classroom situations. The English student is reluctant to see 'teaching behaviour' alone as worthy of study — subjective emotion, attitude, and perception in relation to the full range of human experience are all within his domain. To the English student the study of 'texts' which are the symbolic transformation of human experience realised in linguistic form is the foundation of his teaching. Most current programmes in microteaching, regrettably, offer only marginal support to improve the English student's effectiveness in the treatment of texts in the classroom.

The Concept of Teaching Skills in Microteaching

Central to microteaching is the hypothesis that teaching can be described in terms of component skills. These skills can be identified, are relatively discrete, and are, therefore, capable of independent practice. The English student is highly critical of this hypothesis especially when the skills are defined in behavioural terms. The reasons for this attitude are usually given as follows:

(1) Microteaching does not take into account the socio-emotional features of the teaching encounter which figure largely in the concerns of the trainee teacher.

These concerns are confirmed by a sample of thirty-eight students who participated in structured interviews (Gilmore, 1975) designed to elicit their perceptions of their performance in microteaching. The percentage distribution of reported comments on most valued features of their performance which fell into the socio-emotional category was just under 70 per cent; on the least valued features the percentage was over 70 per cent. These responses are the converse of those task features which are generally highly valued in a microteaching programme. There can be little doubt that the primary concern of most trainee teachers in the initial phase of their teaching practice is managerial. A frequent remark made by students to their supervisors after microteaching is: 'How did I get on?'. What the student seeks is confirmation of his ability to 'manage' the group of pupils, rarely on the effectiveness of his teaching on the pupils' learning, or skill acquisition.

(2) Microteaching programmes do not give sufficient information for the English student to identify and select the most appropriate skills related to lesson content in the English classroom.

This was forcibly demonstrated by a student on teaching practice (again many more examples could be cited) who had selected a passage from Orwell's *1984* for interpretation which had been read by a fifth-form class. The social climate of the classroom was congenial, the pupils co-operative and the student skilful in her use of lower, middle and higher order questions. She also employed an array of follow-up probing, prompting, and redirecting questions in reaction to the pupils' responses. Yet the lesson was perceived as a failure by both student and supervisor on the basis of the quality of

the feedback provided by the pupils' responses. The failure of the
lesson was largely attributable to the inappropriateness of the
thematic content of the passage to the life experience of the pupils.
The array of skills practised in most current microteaching programmes generally fails to identify those skills and procedures
related to subject content. The English student, therefore, tends to
perceive a microteaching skills programme as too narrowly focused
on the media of teaching at the expense of the content of instruction — a case of *Hamlet* without the Prince of Denmark.

(3) The microskills are less relevant to the trainee English teacher
than the more global aspects of teaching, e.g. the selection and
sequencing of the content, lesson-planning, choice of optimal lesson
strategies in relation to content and the like.

   The notes made by a student while viewing a videotaped playback
of his microlesson designed to provide practice in the skill of the
'greater use of broad questions' reflect the conflicts of the student in
attempting to reconcile the competing demands of the microteaching programme and his intuitive understanding of teaching.

   ' . . . too much concerned with the subject in question than in
communicating with the children . . . therefore . . . not following up
statements made by boy on left which were more of a personal
nature . . . I talk too much . . . definitely narrow questions . . .
because I decided to go into the microteaching with a definite lesson
in mind and to keep things subject-centred . . . I don't feel that this
allows for the (lack of) control necessary over the direction of things
to enable the free development of broad questions . . . failed in obtaining the kids' enthusiasm about the need to save on recycled
paper . . . etc. . . . although it is possible they thought more about
these things than they usually would do . . . .'

It would be wrong to conclude that the pre-service English teacher finds
it difficult to justify microteaching as a relevant training procedure on
empirical, rational, or pragmatic grounds yet there is substance in his
criticisms to view microteaching as a flawed procedure for the training
of English teachers.

The misguided use of microteaching is probably related to an inadequate model of teacher training. In contrast to the older model *the
master teacher* approach to teacher training with its assumption that
the trainee is able to grasp the complexities of the ongoing classroom
events simply by observation, imitation, and practice in field settings,

the more recent *master the teaching model* approach, of which microteaching is often a component, with its emphasis on systematic observation and analysis of teaching behaviour is an improvement on the older
model in that it enables the trainee to conceptualise his teaching by
reference to the close texture of the pupil/teacher interaction in the
classroom. The newer model fails, however, to provide a co-ordinating
explanation for the broad and varied landscape of English teaching. This
can only be achieved by a model of English teaching which includes full
stress on the idea that in considering an English lesson, one must take
into account not only the lesson plan but also the actions in the classroom involved in implementing that plan. The lesson plan offers a
schematisation through which the content of the lesson comes to light,
but the actual learning by the pupils is an action of realisation
performed by the pupils. If this is so, then the lesson plan has two poles
which we might call the teaching and the learning; the teaching refers to
the lesson plan, which includes the selection and organisation of the
content and the methods, including the use of specified microskills,
created by the teacher, and the learning to that which is accomplished
by the pupil. From this polarity it follows that the lesson cannot be
completely identical with the lesson plan, or with the pupils' learning,
but in fact must lie halfway between the two. The lesson is more than
the lesson plan, for the lesson plan only takes on life when it is realised,
and furthermore the realisation is by no means independent of the
individual disposition of the pupils — though this in turn is affected by
different patterns of the lesson planning. The convergence of lesson
plan, teacher, and pupils brings the lesson into existence, and this convergence can never be precisely pinpointed but must always remain
virtual, as it is not to be identified either with the reality of the lesson
plan or with the individual dispositions of teacher and pupils.

In spite of the negative reactions of English tutors and students,
microteaching as a training procedure offers such a unique range of
positive advantages over many procedures that it should not be dis-
carded. The burden of the complaint of tutors and students is centred
on the restricted use of microteaching in the skill-acquisition phase. As
part of the ongoing review of teacher-training at Stirling a study has
been initiated in which microteaching forms part of a competency-
based programme in inferential comprehension reading skills for
English teachers which will be validated in school practice. Microteaching is a dynamic concept in teacher education and the broadening
of its scope and application will enrich and ensure its continued use, but
a necessary precondition for this is a continuous dialogue between those

teacher educators whose orientations lie towards the disciplines of the social sciences and those rooted in a humanist tradition.

References

Adams, A. and Pearce, J. (1974). *Every English Teacher,* Oxford Univ. Press, London.

Gilmore, S. (1975). The Effects of Modelling on Student Teachers' Questioning Behaviours: a Study in the Microteaching Context, unpublished M.Ed thesis, University of Glasgow.

MacLeod, G.,Griffiths, R. and McIntyre, D. (1977). The Effects of Differential Training and of Teaching Subject on Microteaching Skills Performance, Chapter 9 in this volume.

18 MICROTEACHING AND MODERN LANGUAGES

Richard Johnstone

This paper reviews such progress in the use of microteaching as has been made over the past four years, since the establishment of a concurrent programme of professional training for student-teachers of French, German and, more recently, Spanish.

The use of microteaching had been established at Stirling several years before the programme for student-teachers of modern languages was introduced; as it was then used, microteaching was intended as a deliberately simplified form of teaching in which a number of general teaching skills, rather than particular subject-teaching techniques, were practised. It was clearly necessary to evaluate the appropriateness of this established pattern for the training of modern language teachers, and where possible to adapt it to increase its usefulness. During these four years, the use of microteaching in the training of ML students has in fact changed considerably; it is now differentiated into three distinct models, each with a clear function, and it has become much more subject-based.

The established microteaching procedures, which were initially used for modern language students as for those in other subject areas, were similar to those developed at Stanford. A psychologist provided an analysis of a particular skill, e.g. variation, explanation, or higher-order questioning, which was then discussed by the ML students and myself. Each student then taught ten-minute teach and reteach lessons to five or six pupils from local secondary schools, concentrating on the given skill, and viewed videotape replays of the lessons, usually with a supervisor and guided by an observational schedule provided by the psychologist who had initially presented the skill-analysis. Most ML students attempted to teach modern language lessons.

Having viewed as many as possible of these microteaching lessons and discussed the replays of them with the individual students, I concluded, after roughly two years, that this use of microteaching had its strengths and its weaknesses:

Its weaknesses seemed to be:
1. Little could be known in advance about the pupils who would come from local schools for the microlessons. Were they learning a

ML at school? If so, which one? Which course were they following? How far had they got? By which approach were they taught? How good were they at this subject? The almost total lack of answers to these questions made planning difficult.

2. A ten to fifteen-minute lesson was too short. In school, it may take ten full periods before a lesson has been thoroughly presented, practised, explained, discussed, exploited and tested. Consequently, a microlesson could not possibly be the context in which a majority of *school* teaching skills could be practised. In particular it was impossible to practise any skills involved in enabling pupils to recombine newly learnt language with language learnt previously.

3. The skill of 'higher order questioning' (HOQ) proved intractable, for two reasons: (a) it presupposed in the pupils an existing foundation of ML knowledge and skills, and (b) in any case it is a skill that is not commonly practised in the initial stages of ML teaching in school where most questions are of a decidedly LOW order, e.g. 'Qu'est-ce que c'est?' 'Où est − ?' 'Que fait − ?' This does not suggest that HOQ ought to have no place in initial ML teaching in school, but it does suggest that so far I had not found the microteaching context in which this skill could be practised − with the exception of 'background' microlessons on life in the foreign country, in which the HOQ was in English.

4. The exclusive focus on one thing at a time − i.e. the particular skill being practised − provoked some highly dubious consequences. In one lesson a student scored high on *variation* − she used the blackboard, the projector, flashcards and a worksheet; she varied her voice and her gestures; she varied between choral and individual pupil response. Yet her lesson consisted of nothing but the regurgitation of the paradigm of the present tense of 'avoir', no attempt whatever being made at contextualisation. This convinced me that the notion of 'skills' on its own was misleading. There was a need to relate 'skills' to 'strategies'. For example, with an audio-lingual strategy the skill of explanation would not be important, but this would be a vital skill in a grammar-translation strategy.

5. One teach-reteach cycle per skill was perhaps enough for some students but not nearly enough for others for whom fifty such cycles per skill might have been more appropriate.

Its strengths seemed to be:

1. Television is an excellent feedback device. The video-replay has proved most useful in helping tutor and students to relive the lesson in a way that would not be possible if they were relying solely on memory.

2. It provides a practical element in the course, making the students plan, teach and evaluate lessons with real children. There is no doubt whatever that the students place high value on this kind of experience.

3. It forces students to discipline themselves in their planning. 'Exactly what can I achieve in a ten to fifteen- minute one-off encounter with six unknown twelve-year-olds?' is a useful question to ask, even though the range of teaching skills that can be practised will be limited.

4. It provides a context for the discussion of certain crucial ML-teaching questions, e.g.

   (a)   How am I to teach meaning? By English? By mime? By visuals? By paraphrasing?

   (b)   Should I teach a single-skill lesson (e.g. one based on listening comprehension) or a multi-skill lesson (e.g. listening, speaking, reading, writing)? If the latter, in what order should these skills be introduced in the microlesson? If I emphasise an oral approach, what will be the function of reading and writing? Microteaching does not, of course, provide a final answer to these questions, but it does provide a context in which they can meaningfully be discussed.

   (c)   If I aim to teach a small point of grammar, will this be on an inductive or a deductive basis?

5. It allows students to view and to discuss each other's lessons. This does not normally happen in school where it is perfectly possible for a teacher in his entire career never to see another teacher teaching. There is surely something wrong here. Microteaching, once the barrier of shyness has been broken, which in my experience does not take long, can be immensely useful in enabling students to learn from their peers who have been teaching the same kind of lesson as themselves. They probably learn more from this than from the demonstration microlessons provided by my colleagues and myself.

Such then were what seemed to me to be the strengths and the weaknesses of microteaching during the first two years or so in which it was
used with ML students at Stirling. Over the past two years certain
developments have taken place which have led to the extension and, I
believe, the improvement of microteaching with the ML students. The
two main advances have been (i) the linking of microteaching with
other elements in the training course, thereby creating a context in
which microteaching is used no longer on its own but rather as a means
of exemplifying or practising what is being discussed in this wider context; and (ii) using three different models of microteaching, in
semesters 4, 5 and 7/9, each with a clear function.

Semester 4: Microteaching Model 1

We provide two courses which work in harness — 'Lesson Planning' and
'Microteaching'. These courses are 'taught' jointly by a ML tutor and a
psychologist. In the *'Lesson Planning'* course the focus is on the
planning of individual lessons. Topics for discussion are: the value or
otherwise of performance objectives; the teaching of meaning; the
stages of presentation, practice, exploitation; the uses and abuses of
(a) English and (b) visuals in ML lessons; analysis of the 'four skills';
inductive and deductive approaches; audio-lingual, audio-visual, direct
and grammar-translation lessons; individual differences among
children along the concrete-abstract dimension; types of ML learning,
e.g. stimulus-response, verbal chaining, multiple discrimination, concept
learning, principle learning; the importance of contextualisation.

The main aim of *'Microteaching'* in semester 4 is still to practise
teaching skills: these are now 'variation' 'questioning' and 'reacting'.
The conditions are exactly the same as described previously, with at the
end of the semester an additional longer lesson in which each student
aims to practise all three micro-skills together.

Some of the initial weaknesses of microteaching still persist, especially the shortness of the lesson, but I believe that the students
benefit more from this kind of microteaching now than they used to,
mainly because 'Lesson Planning' courses give them considerable help
in planning their lessons, just as their practical experience of microteaching makes the theoretical discussion of the 'Lesson Planning'
topics more meaningful to the students.

Semester 5: Microteaching Model 2

There are basically two courses which we link together. 'Lesson
Planning' of Semester 4 gives way to 'Teaching Strategies'. In other

words, we now look at the ways in which individual lessons hang together within the framework of a two-week unit of work, and the ways
in which units of work hang together within a school term or year. This
involves the analysis of ML course materials that are currently used in
schools. Topics for discussion are: the course-writer's aims for a unit of
work and for a term or year; selection, grading and revision of language
items; the balance of the 'four skills'; the teaching of life in the foreign
country; the range of equipment and materials that are (a) necessary
and (b) optional when using the course; the suitability of the course
materials for the target population, e.g. a mixed-ability class; the usa-
bility of these materials in team-teaching, class-teaching, group-work
and individualisation; techniques of assessing pupils' performance when
learning from these course materials.

   'Microteaching Model 2' runs in parallel with 'Teaching Strategies'.
The conditions differ greatly from Model 1. Students now work in
teams of two or three. They teach the same class of fifteen final-year
primary school pupils one lesson per week for eight weeks, each lesson
lasting twenty-five to fifty minutes. Each lesson is video-recorded and
the team of students discuss the replay with a ML tutor.
   The aim of this second model of microteaching is to give students
practice in planning, implementing and evaluating an eight-week unit of
work. To do this, they must put into operation much of what is being
discussed in the 'Teaching Strategies' course. They must select, grade,
teach, revise and test their own language items. They must make
lessons hang together. They must devise roles for each member of the
team, e.g. the 'animateur', the preparer of materials, the 'assistante',
etc. They have to learn to adapt their initial plans in accordance with
their developing relationship with the pupils they are meeting every
week. They must learn to respond to individual differences.
   This kind of microteaching is much nearer 'the real thing' than is
Model 1 particularly as it gives students the chance to set up situations
in which pupils will recombine new with previously learnt language. I
have not tried to evaluate it in any systematic way, but my strong impression is that it does provide a context in which many aspects of ML
teaching can most usefully be discussed and practised. The students
themselves tend to become deeply involved and indeed excited by this
prolonged contact with fifteen schoolchildren.

Semester 7/9: Microteaching Model 3
In this final semester the ML methodology course consists largely of

work at O-grade and above. *Microteaching Model 3* has been devised with the aim of giving students practice in this area. This involves, for the first time, peer-group microteaching, since it is not possible for the students to practise with O-grade pupils from school. Each student teaches at least one fifteen-minute lesson pitched roughly at O-grade standard. The lesson is video-recorded then discussed. Initially, the students were suspicious of this model, but they soon entered into the spirit of things and their view at the end was that it had been of some value. In particular, the post-mortem discussion was extremely useful: 'Why did you tell the story over yourself, rather than use the tape-recorder?' 'Would it not have been better to give us the key new vocabulary *before* we heard the story?' 'I thought your questions were badly graded.' 'I.'d have preferred to see the text sooner.'

Model 3 allows the students to practise certain aspects of their teaching which they cannot practise in Models 1 or 2, e.g.

(a)   Teaching a fairly complex point of grammar.

(b)   Narrating a story of some complexity in the ML.

(c)   Asking a range of questions, involving various tenses.

(d)   Paraphrasing in the ML, e.g. a student says something in the ML which a 'pupil' does not understand, so the student has to keep on reformulating this until the penny drops.

(e)   Sophisticated textual analysis, e.g. of a poem.

Conclusion

Now that microteaching has been differentiated into three models, each with a clear purpose, and each being linked to other aspects of work done in each semester course, I believe that it has a useful part to play in the professional training of our ML students. After four years experience I have formed the following conclusions:

1. Microteaching is more useful in providing a meaningful context in which aspects of ML teaching may be analysed and discussed than in developing a particularly high level of performance in any pedagogical skills. Really to develop a skill — say, variation — would demand a great deal of practice both out of and in school — far more than we can possibly provide.

2. Microteaching is a 'different' but not essentially a 'simplified' form of teaching. It is wrong to say: 'Concentrate on this one skill and don't worry about anything else'. Far better to say: 'In the conditions under which you are going to teach (Models 1, 2 or 3) what

are the relevant questions to ask yourself?' These vary depending on the model, and there is never any shortage of them.

3. Not all students need the same 'treatment'. If their strengths and weaknesses could be detected early enough, then it might be possible to use microteaching in a 'remedial' sense.

4. A closer link with (a) teaching practice in school and (b) post-training teaching must be established. I have already taken some tentative steps in this direction, in two ways: (i) I audio-record some of the lessons taught by students when on teaching practice in school. They subsequently write out a full transcription of the lesson. All sorts of questions can be discussed on this basis; (ii) I am compiling a 'library' of video-recordings of qualified teachers teaching in school. Their performance is then analysed, preferably both by the teacher and myself, and the analysis plus the video-recording become available to students in their professional training programme. This serves to exemplify in a 'real-life' context the skills that students will be practising in microteaching.

5. The notions of 'skill' and 'strategy' require considerable further analysis. I still do not know what a 'skill' really is. Are ML skills different from general teaching skills? I have equal difficulty with 'strategies'. 'Audio-lingual', 'audio-visual', 'grammar-translation' are three of the most common ML strategies as described in methodological textbooks. Yet, observation of many lessons taught in school has convinced me that these are in fact *not* the strategies that are actually used by teachers. So the notions of 'skill' and 'strategy' as used in ML teaching in school are still highly problematical, as is the relationship between the two.

19 MICROTEACHING AND THE PREPARATION OF HISTORY TEACHERS: SOME REFLECTIONS

John M. Lloyd

. . . Bell noticed the children learning to write by tracing with their fingers in a sand-tray. This appeared to him to be an ideal method of teaching and he resolved to introduce it into the asylum . . . Bell selected John Frisken, a boy about eight years of age, and commanded him to take the class. Under Bell's instructions, Frisken taught the lowest class successfully and was made the permanent teacher. (S.J. Curtis, *History of Education in Great Britain,* University Tutorial Press, 6th edn., London, 1965, p. 206.)

The reader will possibly forgive the historian a glance backward in time. Bell and Lancaster's monitorial system, which contained elements to be found in the concept of microteaching, was a response to the inefficiency of teachers in particular circumstances at the beginning of the nineteenth century. The establishment of the Education Department in the new University of Stirling in the late 1960s came at a time when, after a decade in which the education of teachers had been considerably broadened and liberalised, some misgivings were being expressed by educationists in various countries about the efficacy of teacher education courses. Significantly, but not surprisingly in retrospect, microteaching became a constituent part of the education programme of all undergraduates taking concurrent courses in various subject disciplines and educational studies, with the latter fulfilling a dual purpose in contributing to both their academic and professional development. Now that several cohorts of qualified teachers have graduated it is, perhaps, an appropriate time to review briefly the nature, role and effectiveness of microteaching in a teacher education programme.

The few reflections which follow are, necessarily. of a personal and very subjective nature; they are not based upon empirical data derived from any systematic study of the impact and effectiveness of microteaching on the attitudes and classroom performance of students and teachers over the short or long term. My comments are the outcome of my experience in participating in microteaching programmes over the last five years, during which time I have tutored numerous students in several subject disciplines although my major concern and responsibility lies with prospective history teachers. I have also been in the advantageous position of seeing and meeting students in other situations, including – perhaps crucially in this regard – the school classroom. The following views are inevitably coloured by my qualified support for 'skills-based' microteaching as a valuable addition to the array of techniques and approaches available to those professionally involved in the pre-service preparation of teachers. This implies my acceptance of the highly debatable assumption that complex pieces of human behaviour can be critically analysed into discrete 'skills', exemplified, practised and successfully 'put back together'.

Inevitably, the question is asked: how effective is microteaching in the pre-service context? Any serious attempt to answer this question should be prefaced by philosophical analysis of the concept of 'effectiveness', but what is usually implied in the more casual enquiry is how successful are the techniques of microteaching in equipping the student for, at the very least, his early career in the secondary classroom? Are we, in other words, as successful with our students in our present social and economic context as Andrew Bell was with John Frisken in his? Without any empirical data at hand with which to assess the durability of the effects – for good or ill – of a skills-based approach to teacher preparation, I would venture that Stirling graduates, after a short period in the classroom, are, *in the main,* indistinguishable from their peers. They are, in fact, no better and certainly no worse than their colleagues from Scottish colleges of education who have completed end-on postgraduate courses. This is a fairly safe prediction and is not a pessimistic reflection upon the efficacy of microteaching, or concurrent courses at Stirling. It is more an acknowledgement of the intense pressure exerted on probationary teachers to conform to existing, and often dubious, practice followed unthinkingly in history departments in many secondary schools. Chameleon-like, many students soon reflect the characteristic methods and attitudes of older, wiser, and frequently sadder departmental colleagues. Only a few, the very resilient – perhaps the most foolhardy – cling tenaciously to skills, techniques and approaches experimented with, often with great success, in the microteaching studio.

Are the accommodations made to patterns of instruction experienced in the impressionable probationary years permanent? What are the sifting processes at work in this period and what sort of compromises, if any, are eventually made, when confidence has been gained, between these patterns and the more adventurous strategies frequently encouraged in teacher education courses? These are factors worthy of consideration in pondering over this question.

The issue of effectiveness can be seen in a different, but equally vital, perspective. It is important that students become sensitised to the problems of the school, the classroom and the complexity of the learning-teacher process; many prospective history teachers perceive their role initially as a rather intellectually undemanding one in terms of teaching strategies. The molecular approach of a skills-based microteaching programme has helped to overcome the traditional, blinding preoccupation of the history undergraduate with 'knowing that . . . ' as the sole requisite for entering a classroom, sometimes to such an extent, perhaps, that the skill to be practised has become predominant and content merely a vehicle. For some it has been a relatively painless process; for others, who tend to view life in holistic terms, it has caused considerable heart-searching and, very occasionally, emotional crisis, although this has been more apparent among English rather than history students for reasons which are open to speculation. The majority of history students regard the microteaching experiences as providing, at the very least, some information on the personal and crucial motivational question as to whether they will be able to stand in front of a class and teach. They tend to accept the skills approach, perhaps, it might be argued, because of the lack of an alternative, plan their lessons and seek earnestly after the feedback on performance that the television screen and the tutor, in combination, can supply.

A skills-based approach to microteaching has allowed, also, the formulation of a new juxtaposition of the so-called 'practical' component in teacher preparation with the 'theoretical'. What theoretical underpinnings the various skills possess derive principally from psychology and some educational psychologists regard this as an opportunity to bring more focus and 'relevance' to their work, while others are dismayed at the alleged misuse of the discipline in the pursuit of an eclectic sanctification of unvalidated teaching skills. This tension is unlikely to be easily resolved, but this pragmatism has helped to provide an intellectual meeting-place for educational psychologists and subject tutors. Their co-operation in planning and teaching 'integrated' courses at Stirling, sometimes on a team basis, has broken down the compartmentalism of traditional teacher education programmes which assumed, rather ingenuously, that the students would make the desired intellectual linkages and translate these somehow into virtuous classroom practice.

Yet the 'generalist' approach, whereby teaching skills and procedures are regarded as universal in application, may well be challenged by future attempts to make microteaching a more effective technique. The assumption that component technical skills can be defined which have general applicability over a wide range of subjects must, inevitably, be questioned. The effectiveness of microteaching, and of associated courses, might be increased by a consideration of the development of the component skills of teaching which are defined in such a manner as to relate more closely to appropriate educational objectives in a particular area of subject content. It has been observed in the practical experience gained at Stirling, for example, that the ways in which so-called 'higher-order' questions are used in, say, the teaching of history and mathematics, may differ so widely as to necessitate distinctive formulations of the relevant skill behaviours within subject areas.

Additionally, as well as looking for generalised teaching skills, it might be rewarding to consider whether there are 'supplementary' skills, or refinements of the generalised skills used by history teachers. The practical and theoretical difficulties encountered in David Butts' project at Jordanhill (reported in paper 11) suggests that delineation, let alone validation, of such skills would be a complex problem. Nevertheless, experience and intuition lead one to suspect that a number of areas of history teaching would merit sustained investigation: the handling of source materials and discussion, the use of narrative and analogy are a few which spring immediately to mind. If we could identify and, perhaps, validate 'supplementary' or 'refined' skills within such areas, it might provide a means of injecting greater 'vigour' into traditional 'methods' courses and effect ever closer co-operation between subject tutor and educational psychologist. Yet a balance would have to be struck here for the assumption that teaching skills are of a generalised nature has facilitated discussion of broad educational issues and it would be a pity to become so immersed in subject considerations as to lose these wider perspectives.

For all our careful fostering of an armoury of relevant skills, there remain the associated difficulties of effectively orchestrating the skills-related behaviour, nurturing that sense of 'appropriateness' which allows the habitual selection of a skill to suit a particular context, and the transfer of such competencies from the micro-environment of the studio to the macro-situation of the classroom in a school. As Griffiths has pointed out, and experience at Stirling substantiated, there is a great need to develop a practice programme which moves gradually from a specific form of microteaching to classroom teaching. Thus, while the initial experience of a history student would be with small groups of children for short periods concentrating on specific skills, subsequent experience might be directed towards creating a more effective 'bridge' to the classroom. Not only can the length of the lesson and the size of the group be increased but the teaching skills practised could be rigorously, but less narrowly, defined; the focus could be upon not one particular skill, but a group of skills. Such a graded increase would not only allow the combined practice of skills experienced previously but would permit the placing of more emphasis on skills such as lesson structuring, decision-making and classroom management which would become increasingly more relevant as school-based work approached. Although the Education Department at Stirling has been slowly feeling its way in this direction over the past three years, these bridging experiences require far more attention with closer specification and definition of such experiences in a more carefully graded progression than prevails at present.

Graded practice implies a closer relationship between microteaching and teaching practice and a healthier relationship between school teachers and teacher educators. School practice could be seen partly as an opportunity for students to synthesise component skills into more general teaching strategies. Such co-operation could reduce the rigid compartmentalising of micro- and classroom teaching experience in the minds of students, hinted at earlier.

In a more ideal world, too, one could envisage an important role for microteaching, with or without visual feedback, in the in-service education of history teachers. It could help them to learn how to use new curricula and how to evaluate curricula and teaching performance. Perhaps the most signal contribution that microteaching programmes at Stirling have made is in the promotion of more flexible attitudes and greater professional awareness in students which, surviving the vicissitudes of the probationary period, may allow part of a new generation of teachers not to dismiss such possible innovations without due consideration. The masters and ushers at Madras Military Male Orphan Asylum rejected Bell's 'ideal method of teaching'; instead he turned to John Frisken.

PART 7 TOWARDS A MODEL FOR MICROTEACHING

Gordon MacLeod and Donald McIntyre

Introduction

Despite literally hundreds of investigations into microteaching and its various components, only little that is conclusive or reliable can be said about its value or effectiveness. In this paper two reasons for this are advanced — the inappropriateness of some comparative studies of microteaching, and the precipitous rush to pragmatic experimentation. From a review of some microteaching research at Stirling University, several data-based generalisations are drawn, and used as a basis for inferring characteristics of a general explanatory model for microteaching. The final section explores some of the implications of this explanatory model for a rationale for microteaching.

Research on Microteaching

A minority of studies on microteaching have attempted to assess the comparative effectiveness of the technique in relation to conventional procedures. However, such comparisons seem misguided, in that the issue is not primarily one which can be resolved on the basis of empirical evidence. The move to microteaching is not simply one of finding more effective means to attain the same goals, but rather a shift towards a different conception of what professional teaching might involve and *therefore* of new ways of preparing people for teaching. The 'problems' which microteaching was designed to overcome were at least as much ideological as technological.

Perhaps for this reason, the majority of research on microteaching has been concerned with comparisons among different versions of microteaching with the aim of finding the most effective combination of components to optimise students' use of the skills being practised. As a procedure involving a number of possible components, each of which can be included or excluded and, if included, can be used in several different forms, microteaching is a very convenient target for experimental research. But although much of this research has been technically highly competent, there is not a great deal which one can conclude from it. For example, concluding his review of the feedback phase of microteaching — the aspect which has probably received most attention — Griffiths (1974) writes:

It can be seen that though the feedback phase of microteaching has received considerable research attention there are still very few consistent results. There certainly is evidence that mechanical recordings, tutors, peers and pupils can provide feedback which produces changes in teaching behaviour. Equally, there are studies which demonstrate that such feedback can be ineffective. Currently we can only guess the conditions under which each source of feedback may or may not be valuable. As always we need more research (pp. 20-21).

Whilst it is true that somewhat more positive conclusions can be reached with regard to some other aspects of microteaching, in general the outcomes of this considerable body of experimental research have been unenlightening.

Our diagnosis as to why this should be so is that we researchers on microteaching have fallen into the same trap as did researchers in other fields, such as classroom teaching and programmed instruction, in that we have been premature in our concentration on the use of experimentation. Experimental research designs have a double attraction — they are intellectually respectable, and they offer the enticing prospect of quick and firm solutions to practical issues. But we should know by now that such experiments on limited numbers of programmatic variables are but a waste of time. Experimental research is of crucial importance in testing hypotheses derived from coherent theories; but in the absence of such theories and hypotheses, experiments are almost certain to leave one as ignorant on their completion, whether one knows it or not, as one was when one started. In the long run, it is a far more economical research strategy to use looser and more exploratory designs in the hope that from their results we shall have the insight to be able to begin the development of theoretical ideas.

In this diagnosis, we have suggested that the underlying problem has been that we have lacked any theoretical understanding of the kind of learning with which we are concerned in microteaching, or therefore of the factors which might influence this learning. However, this suggestion requires immediate qualification. As originally developed at Stanford, microteaching practices were supported by an explicit theoretical rationale, that of behaviour modification. McDonald (1973), one of the originators of microteaching, has justifiably complained that this theoretical rationale has been generally ignored, both by researchers and practitioners. He makes his position clear by suggesting that beyond research of a simple practical kind,

there is very little else about microteaching as a methodological
device that is worth studying. What is worth investigating is the
applications of behavioral modification principles that can be made
when microteaching is used (p. 73).

In so far as McDonald identifies the general problem as the lack of an
explicit theoretical rationale for microteaching, we concur. In that he
suggests that this rationale should be derived from behaviour modification theory we are less willing to concur. However, it should be noted
that for McDonald, behaviour modification principles are taken to include principles derived from Bandura's (1971) social learning theory,
which itself allows ample use of quasi-cognitive constructs. Thus,
critiques of such a rationale for microteaching must be rather less
simplistic in their caricatures of behaviour modification theory than
those previously offered (e.g. by St John-Brooks and Spelman, 1973).
  Given the possible extension of behaviour modification principles
offered by modelling theory, this may well be one appropriate and
fruitful perspective from which to view microteaching. None the less,
the concepts of behaviour modification theory which have so far been
elaborated appear to us to offer little help either in the discussion of
many issues which users of microteaching have come to see as important or in interpreting much of the evidence which researchers have
gathered.

Evidence Towards an Alternative Theory

In attempting to bring forward evidence as to how we might begin to
develop an alternative theory which could inform our practice in, and
research on, microteaching, we will focus on recent work carried out at
Stirling. This is not to suggest that we have solved the problems of
research on microteaching, for the first three studies we mention
exemplify well the kind of unproductive and premature experimentation discussed above.
  The first of these investigations was a study, based on a considerable
amount of pilot work, of the effects of different styles of supervision
at the feedback phase of microteaching (Griffiths, MacLeod and
McIntyre, 1977). Two main variables and the interaction between
them were studied. The variables were:

(1)   the directness with which the supervisor attempted to influ-
      ence the students, direct supervision being where the super-
      visor took the initiative in analysing and commenting upon the

lesson, and indirect supervision being where the supervisor encouraged the student to analyse and evaluate the lesson himself, with the supervisor's comments being limited to reactions to what the student said.

(2)   whether the supervisor focused his attention on the strengths of the lesson, attempting to make reinforcing comments on skill-appropriate behaviour, or on the weaknesses of the lesson attempting to suggest or to lead the student to suggest alternative courses of action in order to use the skill more, or to use it more effectively.

Combining these two variables, there were thus four treatments. The skill being practised was the use of examples, and the main criterion measures were based on systematic observation of the subsequent reteach of the lessons to other groups of pupils. Further criteria were based on student responses to a questionnaire completed after their lesson critiques. This questionnaire consisted of two sections — one to assess students' evaluations of the help they had received, and one to monitor their perceptions of the supervisor's strategy. From the results of the latter section it was clear that the four treatments had been validly implemented.

The results from systematic observation of the reteach sessions showed that, with one minor exception, there were no significant differences among the four groups on any of the criterion measures. However, responses, derived from the questionnaire, to questions asking for evaluations of the help received from supervisors and asking for suggestions as to how the critiques could have been more helpful, did produce significant differentiation among the groups. In all cases, subjects tended to want what they had not been given: if the supervision was direct, they wanted more opportunity to discuss their *own* perceptions, but if the supervision was indirect, they wanted to know more about how the *supervisor* had perceived the lesson; if the supervision had concentrated on their strengths, they wanted to have advice on how they could *improve* their use of the skill, but if the supervision had concentrated on suggesting alternatives, they wanted to be told what they were *doing well* already.

At first sight these findings seemed unsurprising and perhaps not worth reporting. However, the implications of these results seemed of importance: the teaching behaviour data seemed to lend no support to any of the theories of instruction or learning which underlay our experi-

ment; but in the questionnaire data, the students were reporting themselves as wanting, and being able to use, several different kinds of skill-
relevant information. They were asserting, whether rightly or not, that
the kind of learning involved in microteaching is of a highly complex
kind of information-processing. Similar results were found by McIntyre
(1977), in an experiment in which students planned and later analysed
their microteaching lessons in various groupings; in that study too,
interesting data came from questionnaires, with students reporting, on
the one hand, that they found their peers' comments and suggestions
very valuable but, on the other hand, that these could not replace the
judgements of an experienced supervisor. Again, they were asserting the
relevance to their learning, and their capacity to make use, of different
kinds of skill-relevant information.

The third experimental study (MacLeod, Griffiths and McIntyre,
1977) is one which exemplifies some of the complex relationships we
tend to find in examining the effects of microteaching. It involved a
comparison of three treatments: one of these consisted simply of the
explicit definition and brief justification of the skills; the second involved in addition the modelling of the skill with cued videotapes,
microteaching practice of the skill, videotape and supervisor feedback,
and reteaching of the skill; the third involved in addition discrimination
training, or practice in identifying the use of the skill, before students
themselves practised using the skill. Three skills were involved: Variation, Higher Cognitive Questioning, and Clarity of Explanation. Criteria were based on students' teaching behaviour in an eighteen-minute
lesson in the microteaching context in which they were asked to use all
three skills. Significance tests were carried out on fourteen criterion
measures derived from systematic observation of the criterion lesson.
On twelve of these measures, the microteaching + discrimination
training treatment had higher mean scores than the non-microteaching
group, but differences between groups were significant for only two of
these twelve measures. These two significant differences were on two
of the three criteria for the skill of Higher Cognitive Questioning.
Students were also grouped according to their subject specialisms, but
because the numbers were relatively small in some subject areas, they
were categorised as English, history or 'other' students, the 'other'
group including modern languages, science and mathematics specialists.
On ten of the fourteen measures, there were significant differences
according to subject specialism, with the 'other' group having the highest
mean score in seven of these ten cases.

Three features of these results demand attention. First, although

258   Investigations of Microteaching

there is a clear trend for microteaching with discrimination training to
lead to superior performance of the skills, this trend is in general over-
whelmed by the extent of the individual differences among students.

Second, the effect of discrimination training and microteaching is
very much greater for one of the skills than for the other two.

Third, differences due to treatment are generally small compared
with differences according to subject specialism. One might interpret
this in terms of the different demands and opportunities involved in
teaching different subjects, although it should also be noted that
different subject specialists in the Stirling department vary in their
enthusiasm for microteaching. However, these two explanations may
perhaps be usefully blurred by suggesting that the results indicate that
students' use of the skills appears to be closely related to subject ideologies.

In summary, the results of the experiment suggest that any discussion of the effects of microteaching and of students' acquisition of
teaching skills should give considerable attention to individual differences among students, to the nature of the particular skills being practised, and to differences among subject ideologies.

The next series of investigations to be considered are those by
MacLeod (1976) of students' written reactions to their own microteaching lessons, usually after receiving videotape feedback on their
lessons. These investigations were conducted in the context of a
semester-course in which students studied and learned to use Flanders'
Interaction Analysis categories and practised skills defined in terms of
this system. Four general questions were asked:

(1)   What kinds of comments do students make and how do their
       comments tend to change with increasing experience of
       microteaching?

(2)   How are variations among students in the comments they
       make related to variations among the lessons they have taught?

(3)   How are variations among students in the comments they
       make related to variations among the retaught lessons which
       they subsequently teach?

(4)   What effect does videotape feedback and/or feedback of FIAC
       codings of their lessons have on the comments students make?

It is not possible here to give a detailed account of the findings, so only the main trends of the evidence are summarised.

Students reveal a high degree of *task-orientation*. The number of comments they make about their own personal characteristics is initially small and quickly decreases. Most of their comments are about their own teaching behaviour, but a large and steadily increasing proportion of comments are about pupils' behaviour. A steadily increasing proportion of comments, also, are made in terms of Flanders' concepts and categories. Their estimates of the proportions of their lessons in each of Flanders' categories tend to be accurate.

Students' self-evaluations reveal a high degree of *rationality*. That is, they do not so much evaluate their behaviour in the terms which have been prescribed, but rather they evaluate their *lessons* primarily in terms of the pupil behaviour prescribed as desirable, and evaluate their own behaviour in terms of their generally accurate perceptions of how it was related to this pupil behaviour. (The relationships between teacher and pupil behaviour were, as it happened, systematically different from those predicted by Flanders.) Although students tend to evaluate their lessons negatively (but decreasingly so with time), their negative judgements tend to be related to accurate perceptions of behaviour they perceive as undesirable.

Variations among students' teaching on the four major skill-related criteria in their 'teach' lessons tend to account for some 30 per cent of the variation among them in their teaching of 'reteach' lessons. But *an additional 20 per cent* or so of the variance in the reteaches — a remarkably high proportion — can be accounted for by variations in the comments they make after their teach lesson. Predictors of successful use of the skill in the reteach include a tendency to focus comments on their own behaviour, negative evaluation of their behaviour, confidence in their ability to improve and apparently — though this is an inference, not a direct finding — a tendency to attribute weaknesses in the lesson to themselves rather than to the pupils or other factors.

In summary, four ways have been noted in which the pattern of students' comments shows a significant trend as their experience of microteaching increases: an increased focus on pupils, and (in this particular context) an increased use of Flanders' constructs; and a decrease in negativity and in attention to their own personal characteristics. With the exception of this last one, these and other changes are gradual, and the patterns of comments on successive occasions give an overall impression of a high degree of stability, though not inflexibility.

Finally, very few differences appeared between the comments on their lessons made by students who had no feedback on them and the comments made by those who had either videotape feedback or FIAC feedback or both.

Implications for an Explanatory Model of Microteaching

From the various strands of evidence outlined above, one may infer some of the characteristics of a general model of what is happening in microteaching, as follows:

(1)   Before entering microteaching programmes, each student has distinctive, complex conceptual schemata relating to teaching, these schemata having strong evaluative associations.

(2)   Individual differences in these conceptual schemata are large, but large areas of commonality may also obtain, through the embedding of the schemata within (*inter alia*) a network of schemata representing specific subject ideologies.

(3)   These conceptual schemata show a high degree of stability, but can change gradually through the assimilation of new constructs and principles, acquired through instruction and experience.

(4)   Students' conceptual schemata to a large extent control their teaching behaviour, and changes in behaviour result from changes in schemata.

(5)   New concepts and ways of perceiving teaching are acquired largely as a result of instruction, but new principles and ways of evaluating teaching are acquired not only from instruction but also from students' perceptions of what actually occurs in their microteaching lessons; and where these two influences conflict, it is the latter which predominates.

(6)   Since the constructs in terms of which students will perceive their lessons are largely determined before they teach the lessons, the kinds of mechanical or descriptive feedback with which they are provided will have only little influence on the nature of their perceptions or therefore on their subsequent teaching behaviour.

(7)   Since students' explanations of the effects of teaching be-
        haviours, and consequently their evaluations of it, are influ-
        enced by what happens in their lessons, the interpretations and
        judgements of others on lessons they have taught, and the
        alternatives they offer, are potentially influential factors in
        students' learning.

The first four of these inferences suggest a cognitive interpretation of
microteaching, and it is about the value and validity of this general kind
of interpretation that we are most confident. The latter three inferences, concerned as they are with the effects of different phases or
components of microteaching are more tentative, although we think
the evidence is sufficiently strong for these too to be points of depar-
ture for further research.

Conclusions

These characteristics of an explanatory model for microteaching are
inferred from the evidence presented earlier. Their value and validity
must be tested by research, with that research being guided by hypotheses derived from these principles. At the same time, this putative
model can be considered in terms of its implications for a rationale for
microteaching as a teacher education technique. In considering such a
rationale we shall take as our starting-point, one of the end-points of a
teacher education programme – the classroom.

One striking feature of classrooms is the sheer complexity, quantity
and rapidity of classroom interaction. As many as 1,000 interpersonal
exchanges each day have been observed, and the multiplicity of decisions which have to be made, and the volume of information relevant
to each decision are such that for the teacher logical consideration and
decision-making would seem impossible.

Yet, as teachers commonly assert, every situation with which they
have to deal is unique: every class, every pupil, every different unit of
content, every incident, and indeed every teacher is unique. Therefore,
in each of these unique situations, the teacher must use his professional
judgement in order to decide upon a course of action or unique solution. This seems to represent an ideal to which many teachers attempt
to approximate, but this ideal is unreachable if our analysis of classroom complexity is correct and if each teacher decision has to be considered fully in the light of all relevant information.

Yet most teachers cope, and many are deemed excellent. We
suggest that this coping is achieved through teachers' use, in their class-

room thinking, of a small number of very broad and crude cognitive structures, which allow for the processing of unique incidents as exemplars of more general categories. This allows much decision-making and information-processing to be automatic or habitual. We see this sophisticated cognitive strategy as being directly analogous to the 'conceptual simplicity' identified by Jackson (1968) in teacher talk, which, he suggests, may be related to 'the ability to tolerate the enormous amount of ambiguity, unpredictability, and occasion chaos created each hour by 25 or 30 not-so-willing learners' (p. 149).

The role we suggest for these cognitive structures or schemata is to allow ways of escape 'from the complete sway of immediate circumstances' and to provide ways of matching 'infinite diversity by increasing delicacy of response' (Bartlett, 1932, p. 301).

When classroom life is construed in this way, then our explanatory model for microteaching can be seen to be consonant with a prescriptive model for microteaching which emphasises students' cognitions. Microteaching can be seen as a means of producing changes in one's cognitive activities while teaching, changes in the ways one construes the courses of action open to one and the effects of one's actions, with its prescribed role being to provide for the development and induction of functional and adaptive cognitive structures. Thus, for example, the value of a skills approach to microteaching would depend on the extent to which the disparate and discrete events of the classroom came to be perceived as exemplars of a more general skill concept, rather than as unrelated events each requiring an entirely new decision.

This explanatory/prescriptive model would seem to have three major attractions, and to imply two major tasks. It seems likely that short-term behavioural changes — the conventional criteria — are likely to be matched by similar and enduring changes in classroom teaching behaviour only if they reflect changes in cognitive structures. Likewise, the incorporation of the *theory-based* concepts into the *practically necessary* conceptually 'simple' cognitive structures used by teachers in classrooms would automatically contribute to the bridging of the traditional gap between theory and practice, and, in consequence, would lead to a more satisfactory assessment of 'relevance' by the participants.

The major tasks which the model implies are firstly the testing of the characteristics of the model itself, and secondly the development of teaching skills which, in their definitions, reflect the conceptual simplicity which appears to be an almost necessary characteristic of teachers' classroom decision-making. Although there are probably good

reasons why student-teachers should acquire a sophisticated understanding of classroom interaction and of the effects of teachers' behaviour upon pupils' learning, unless this sophisticated understanding
can be reduced to straightforward principles in terms of easily
operationalisable constructs, student teachers are not likely to make
practical use of their understanding. To formulate principles of this
kind, which are also compatible with an awareness of the complexity of
classroom processes would seem to be one of the most intellectually
challenging tasks faced by the teacher educator.

Acknowledgement

The ideas presented in this paper owe much to our collaboration with
Roy Griffiths, now of the Department of Education, University of
Manchester.

References

Bandura, A. (1971). *Social Learning Theory*, General Learning Press, New York.
Bartlett, F.C. (1932). *Remembering*, Cambridge University Press, Cambridge.
Griffiths, R. (1974). The Contribution of Feedback to Microteaching Techique,
  in Trott, A.J. (ed.), *Microteaching Conference Papers*, APLET Occasional
  Publications No. 3, pp. 15-22.
Griffiths, R.,MacLeod, G.R. and McIntyre, D.I. (1977). Effects of supervisory
  strategies in microteaching on students' attitudes and skill acquisition,
  Chapter 8 in this volume.
Jackson, P.W. (1968). *Life in Classrooms*, Holt, Rinehart and Winston, New York.
McDonald, F.J. (1973). Behavior Modification in Teacher Education, in
  Thoresen, C.E. (ed.), *Behavior Modification in Education*, NSSE Yearbook,
  University of Chicago Press, Chicago.
McIntyre, D.I. (1977). Microteaching Practice, Collaboration with Peers and
  Supervisory Feedback as Determinants of the Effects of Microteaching,
  Chapter 7 in this volume.
MacLeod, G.R. (1976). Students' Perceptions of their Microteaching Perfor-
  mance, unpublished Ph.D thesis, University of Stirling.
MacLeod, G.R.,Griffiths, R. and McIntyre, D.I. (1977). The Effects of Differ-
  ential Training and of Teaching Subject on Microteaching Skills Performance,
  Chapter 9 in this volume.
St John-Brooks, C. and Spelman, B. (1973). Microteaching, *Trends in Education*,
  31, pp. 14-19.

CONTRIBUTORS

Donald McIntyre is Senior Lecturer in Education at the University of Stirling. He is currently co-directing a research project on innovations in science teaching, and his other interests are teachers and teaching, research methodology, and relationships between professional responsibilities and public control over education. He is co-author, with Arnold Morrison of *Teachers and Teaching, Schools and Socialization,* and is co-editor of *The Social Psychology of Teaching.*

Gordon MacLeod is a Senior Research Fellow at the University of Stirling, and co-director of a research project into the strategies and skills appropriate to the teaching of modern languages in the initial years of secondary education. Other research interests are microteaching, classroom studies, and adult psychology. Published work is in microteaching, and in the education of the deaf in Scotland.

Roy Griffiths now lectures in Education at the University of Manchester. He joined the Stirling Education Department in 1971 to conduct research on microteaching, and from 1972 until 1976 he was on the lecturing staff at Stirling. He is especially interested in analytic approaches to teacher education, including microteaching. He has published several reviews of microteaching research in various journals.

David Butts is Principal Lecturer in Audio-visual Media at Jordanhill College of Education, Glasgow. He conducted his research into the use of microteaching at Jordanhill while taking a master's degree at the University of Stirling. He has since been responsible for introducing microteaching and related procedures into Jordanhill courses on a wider scale.

Keri Davies is Senior Lecturer in Education at Stirling University and director of the M.Ed. degree programme. He is a contributor to a variety of curriculum projects at secondary and tertiary levels, his main interests being science education, curriculum development and the professional development of teachers.

Jack Duthie is a Professor of Education at Stirling University. He is the author of The Primary School Survey, and his chief interests are the individualisation of instruction, educational resources and cognition. He is presently involved in the development of teacher-education programmes in Maharashtra, India, commissioned by the British Council.

Stan Gilmore lectures in Education at Stirling, with his teaching responsibilities being English/Drama in the secondary curriculum. His interests are in microteaching, performance-based teacher education, and in the language development of pupils in the 11 to 15 age-group.

John Lloyd lectures in Education in the University of Stirling. He is particularly concerned with the preparation of teachers of history, and also lectures in comparative education. His research interests are in urban education and in the impact of the first and second world wars on British education.

Dick Johnstone is a lecturer in Education at Stirling, concerned particularly with the preparation of teachers of modern languages. He is Convener of a Working Party developing new French curriculum materials for use in the first two years of secondary school, and is co-director of a research project into the strategies and skills appropriate to the teaching of modern languages.

Philip McKnight, after completing his doctoral degree on microteaching at Stanford University, joined the staff of the University of Stirling for a year as Leverhulme Visiting Research Fellow. He is now Associate Professor of Education at the University of Kansas.

Clive Millar is Professor of Teaching Science at the University of Fort Hare. He spent a year with the research group at Stirling while on sabbatical leave from his previous post as Senior Lecturer in the University of Capetown. His interests include teacher education, curriculum theory, and African literature.

Donald White is Senior Lecturer in Education at the University of Rhodesia. He spent a year with the research group at Stirling when on sabbatical leave from his previous post as Principal of Bulawayo College of Education. His interests include teacher education, educational administration and science education.

AUTHOR INDEX

Acheson, K. 118, 130.
Adams, A. 235, 239
Adams, T.H. 49, 56
Allen, D.W. 10, 19, 71, 76, 118, 130, 132, 141, 154, 159, 205, 211
Anastasio, E.J. 210, 212
Aronson, E. 193
Aubertine, H.E. 71, 76

Bandura, A. 154, 159, 255, 263
Barnes, D. 50, 56
Bartlett, F.C. 262, 263
Bedics, R.A. 194, 204
Bellack, A.A. 47, 56, 60, 69, 83, 93, 176
Berelson, B. 186, 192
Bierschenk, B. 205, 206, 211, 213, 223
Black, J. 43
Bloom, B.S. 47, 56
Borg, W.R. 118, 130, 164, 176
Britten, J. 56
Brown, G.A. 71, 76, 194, 204, 205, 206, 211
Brustling, C. 174, 176
Butts, D.C. 17, 116, 160, 162, 166, 177, 250

Campbell, D.T. 104, 114, 208, 211
Cattell, R.B. 74, 76
Cicirelli 79, 80, 83, 86, 98
Claus, K.E. 118, 130, 194, 204
Cochran, W.G. 136, 141
Cope, E. 57, 69
Copeland 174, 177
Cronbach, L.J. 216, 223
Curtis, S.J. 247

Davies, J.K. 227
Doyle, W. 174, 177
Dunning, B. 177
Duthie, J.H. 16, 21, 23

Evans, S.H. 210, 212

Flanders, N.A. 181, 183, 192, 258, 259
Fortune, J.C. 71, 76
Foster, J.K. 205, 212
Fruchter, B. 156, 159
Fuller, F.F. 194, 202, 203, 204
Furby, L. 216, 223
Furst, N. 175, 177

Galanter, E. 213, 223

Gall, M. 71, 76, 130, 165, 176, 177
Gilmore, S. 116, 154, 159, 233, 236, 239
Griffiths, R. 71, 131, 141, 142, 205, 212, 239, 250, 253, 255, 257, 263
Guilford, J.P. 156, 159

Harvey, J.M. 205, 212
Harvey, O.J. 98
Hatton, N. 167, 177
Heys, T.A. 205, 212
Hoffmeister, J.K. 98
Holsti, O.R. 186, 187, 192
Hough, J.B. 206, 212
Hyman, R.T. 56, 176

Jackson, P.W. 262, 263
Johnstone, R. 240

Kallenbach, W.W. 71, 76
Kelley, M.L. 130, 176
Kerlinger, F.N. 186, 193, 212
Klieband, H.M. 56, 176
Koran, J.J. 154, 159
Krathwohl, D.R. 98

Langer, P. 130, 176
Lawrence, P.J. 79, 82, 99, 101, 114, 184, 193
Lindquist, E.F. 195, 204, 210, 212
Lindzey, G. 193
Lloyd, J.M. 247
Lohman, E.E. 206, 212
Loomba, J.K. 192
Lord, F.M. 216, 223

Manning, B.A. 194, 202, 204
McDonald, F.J. 118, 130, 132, 141, 194, 204, 226, 254, 255, 263
McFarland, H.S.N. 227, 232
McIntyre, D.I. 9, 16, 17, 19, 21, 23, 35, 36, 57, 60, 71, 79, 117, 131, 133, 142, 163, 177, 239, 253, 255, 257, 263
McKnight, P. 16, 27, 32, 36, 60, 118, 130, 133, 205, 212
McLeod, G.R. 17, 71, 131, 142, 179, 181, 185, 190, 193, 194, 204, 205, 206, 211, 212, 213, 233, 239, 253, 255, 257, 258, 263
Meux, M. 88, 98
Millar, C.J. 17, 79, 86, 91, 98, 100, 184, 188, 193

SUBJECT INDEX

accuracy of self-perceptions 216, 220, 259
advantages of microteaching 11, 238, 242-3
appraisal guides 71, 161-4
appropriateness of teacher behaviour 60, 62, 93, 236-7, 241, 250
artificiality 21, 164-5, 229
assessment in microteaching 16-17, 33-4, 36-56, 133, 139, 144-7
assessment in school practice 16-17, 34-5, 57-70, 71-4

behaviour modification 179, 225-6, 235, 254-5

clarity of explanation 50-3, 71-6, 100, 119, 124, 143, 146-8, 150, 152-3, 257
closure 24, 63
collaboration with teaching staff, 13, 229
complexity of teaching 9, 261
conceptual simplicity 262
confidence of improvement 207, 208, 209, 216, 259
content analysis 82-95, 186-92
content of lessons 26-7, 230, 237, 238, 245
cosmetic effect 194, 196, 202
curriculum development 12-14
curriculum seminars 29-30

discrimination training 142, 206, 257-8

economic factors 31-2
effectiveness of microteaching 11-12, 160-77, 227-8, 229-31, 248-50, 253
English, student-teachers of 143, 147-53, 229, 233-9, 249
evaluations of microteaching by tutors 18, 171, 175-6, 225-57
evaluations of observed teaching 17, 77-114, 122-3, 125, 126
experimental designs 64-9, 100-14, 115-77, 253-5
explaining 51-3, 61-2, 66, 84, 101
explanatory model of microteaching 260-1
exposition 24

factor analysis 74-6, 185

Flanders Interaction Analysis Category System 142, 155, 181, 182-4, 207, 209-11, 258
foci of evaluations of teaching 82-6, 100, 101-3, 105-10, 113
foci of students' self-perceptions 187-90, 196-204, 217-8, 222-3, 259
functions of educational research 18-19

graduate training year 160-77
group microteaching 117-30, 167, 242

high-inference judgements 62
history, student-teachers of 143, 147-53, 160-77, 247-51

ideologies 98, 225, 228, 233, 253, 258
individual differences 225, 241, 246, 258
information-processing 256-7, 261-2
interaction analysis feedback 206, 208-11
interval between lessons 24-5

Jordanhill College of Education, 17, 160

language of microteaching 234-5
length of lessons 24, 241, 243
lesson preparation 55, 63-4, 66, 68, 84, 190, 198, 230, 242, 243
lesson sampling 63-4
logic of evaluation 88-91
low-inference judgements 59, 60

mathematics, student-teachers of 143
modern languages, student-teachers of 143, 235, 240-6
modelling of skills 17, 29-30, 116, 119, 154-9, 144, 164-5
motivating 66, 68, 83, 85

observation schedules 29-30, 36-56, 58-70

partial correlations 216-8
peers 17, 28, 117-30
personal characteristics 66, 68, 84, 85, 101, 187, 188-9, 196, 197, 202-4